CHALLENGING
EMPIRE

CHALLENGING EMPIRE

HOW PEOPLE, GOVERNMENTS, AND THE UN DEFY US POWER

BY PHYLLIS BENNIS

FOREWORD BY DANNY GLOVER

OLIVE
BRANCH
PRESS

An imprint of Interlink Publishing Group, Inc.
www.interlinkbooks.com

For the dead of Iraq and New Orleans
who paid the price for empire

First published in 2006 by

OLIVE BRANCH PRESS
An imprint of Interlink Publishing Group, Inc.
46 Crosby Street, Northampton, Massachusetts 01060
www.interlinkbooks.com

Library of Congress Cataloging-in-Publication Data
Bennis, Phyllis, 1951–
Challenging empire : how people, governments, and the UN defy U.S. power /
by Phyllis Bennis.—1st American ed.
p. cm.
Includes bibliographical references and index.
ISBN 1-56656-607-X (pbk. : alk. paper)
1. United States—Foreign relations—2001– 2. Iraq War, 2003—Protest
movements. 3. United States—Foreign public opinion. 4. United Nations.
I. Title.
JZ1490.B46 2005
327.73—dc22
2005022702

Printed and bound in Canada

10 9 8 7 6 5 4 3 2 1

To request our complete 40-page full-color catalog, please call us toll free at
1-800-238-LINK, visit our website at **www.interlinkbooks.com** or write to
Interlink Publishing
46 Crosby Street, Northampton, MA 01060
e-mail: info@interlinkbooks.com

CONTENTS

FOREWORD

I have come to seek out anything Phyllis Bennis writes and says and I urge you to do the same. I need her coherent understanding to help me as I travel and speak publicly about the present nightmare called US foreign policy. The reasons for my trust in and reliance upon Bennis's analysis lie in her unerring clarity; her responsible, informed, profoundly intelligent offering of historical context and political reality as it pertains to US policy in the Middle East; the barometer she gives of the international climate and official powers in relation to the peoples of the world; her insistence on the fusion of policy interpretation with the conditions of real human beings and their (our) needs. She refuses to separate factual, analytic documentation from the truth that can be derived only from listening to and seeing people whose lives are affected by government policies and actions, the legacies of movements for change. She understands that history comes out of the struggles of real people, their families, their needs, their agonies, their hopes. I believe, echoing Che Guevara's statements, that the true revolution is guided by love.

In this book Bennis lays out an historic context for the war in Iraq and the Bush Administration's quest for empire. At the same time she offers a framework for looking at the US and global movement against the war and for peace and justice. She helps us remember what I've learned so poignantly in my travels throughout Africa and the diaspora, and from the history of Africans in America, that change is a process passed, fought for, and earned through generations, not a quick fix. She puts the historic, extraordinary "The World Says No To War" demonstrations throughout the globe, on February 15, 2003, in their appropriate place—as the beginning of a new movement, the continuation of an historic movement, a promise. Not as the failure to prevent a war. This is critical to our ability, as thinking, caring, conscious, and committed people, to move forward with energy and possibility.

This new movement for peace, for justice, against empire, is global. It is not defined by a series of actions, but a conscious worldwide, growing consensus, vision, recognition of complexity, international in identity, scope, and understanding, multi-foliate in strategy, still emerging. This development, described by Bennis, shows maturity, long term promise, and depth, distinguishable in this way from past peace and justice movements.

This book gives us the framework, if we pay attention, for our work in this period to understand that the current US administration is defined by war and empire, beginning with Afghanistan and Iraq, but certainly not limited to those countries. She builds on the statement made in a *New York Times* article on February 7, 2003, after millions took to the streets internationally to say no to war, declaring that there were now two superpowers in the world—the US and the people of the world galvanized to prevent a war. This second superpower has grown exponentially, historically through momentous events and movements throughout time, including confronting slavery, colonialism, foreign dominations, neo-colonialisms, military dictatorships, strengthening the battle of ideas that is in some sense a battle of the human soul. Bennis proposes that the second superpower in fact is, can be, must be comprised of three elements: 1) the people's movements for peace and justice, 2) governments throughout the world opposed to US empire building, and 3) a strengthened and supported United Nations. Following this proposal will help us map out and create a true alternative and counterbalance to US empire.

Many people dismiss the importance and still existing possibilities of the United Nations, focusing only on its inability to prevent the Iraq war. But Bennis reminds us of the eight months of triumph when the UN did join the vast numbers of people around the world and the many governments in opposing the drive to war. She challenges us to reclaim the UN. As a UN

Goodwill Ambassador I've repeatedly been moved, surprised, and uplifted by the stunning impact of the UN's work around the world, the impact on the lives of people struggling for their very survival, often otherwise abandoned. I believe the UN could be an extraordinary force if it could more fully address the realities of all economic classes of people, dealing with issues of water, urgent problems faced by women and girls worldwide, as a start. The UN would need to engage in deeper ideological dialogue to more fully address the devastating class divide internationally and thereby be of even greater service. But I believe we must work toward that capacity.

The United Nations needs to take the lead in building new kinds of relationships between cultures and countries, movements and communities, based on humane and rational commitments and definitions. At this time in world history, the United Nations still offers the only real structure for this kind of work. While supporting national integrities and sovereignties, the United Nations must explore and embrace a new integration globally in civil society, in the public arena, rearranging the constraining definitions that now restrict diplomatic and potentially imaginative development.

Bennis shows the ways in which the distortion, lawlessness, deceit, and destruction expressed by current US foreign policy make the domestic disasters possible—the hacking away of basic rights, drastic cutbacks in social services, and so forth. Further, she makes it clear that our particular brand of racism is a major component in all of it.

Bennis challenges the US peace movement to understand that to connect with the majority of this country, the "mainstream," to build a truly meaningful, representative movement that can create real change, means to engage, work with, listen to communities of color, who are at the heart of US struggles for justice, peace, survival. The "mainstream," she insists, is not an ever-undefined white, middle-class mass out there in this America. The book also underscores the ways in which the new peace movements have developed, grown from the past, grasping integrally, in leadership and action, the truth that peace cannot be achieved absent justice. Racism, at the core of our policies, must be addressed in our movements, if we are to achieve meaningful change.

Finally, and of critical and urgent significance, this book places the illegal, horrific Israeli occupation of Palestinian lands, and US support for it, at the centerpiece of US policy in the region. Bennis makes it clear that it is not possible, nor acceptable, to dance around this reality any longer. She calls for a logical, rational, and moral opposition to the dual occupations of Palestinian lands and of Iraq.

We need more information all the time, backup, tools, analysis presented coherently, to help us with the next conversation. We know this is not a short-term struggle, the struggle of our souls, to honor the best in us, in this human history. We understand where we need to go we have not yet been. We know in our veins, in all our consciousness, and the unconscious rivers of our own histories and voices and stories, that the very notion of peace, claiming democracy, inventing the language and programs to achieve these mandates, involves generations. We also know we must move, put ourselves, our wisdom, imagination, hearts, in the way of the danger in our midst, strengthened by those on whose shoulders we stand and by those around us courageously making new paths each day.

This book helps us in our job.

—Danny Glover

ACKNOWLEDGMENTS

Documenting the crises and catastrophes wrought by empires and would-be empires somehow seems an easier task than chronicling the adversaries, the challengers, the "other side" of those powers. My task was helped immeasurably by being situated inside and working closely with key centers of the rising US and global movements, which gave me the clear vantage point, ready sources, and crucial collaborations that made this book possible.

While all mistakes, misjudgments, and unanswered questions remain my own responsibility, many others provided the wide range of support that brought this project to fruition. Marc Raskin, despite his not-quite-as-funny-as-he-thinks jokes and his preposterous beliefs in things like democracy and liberalism, remains my intellectual touchstone, mentor, and extraordinary friend. Kathy Engel continues to inspire me with new ways of seeing the world, and proves with her words and her art that poet-activists are also passionate analysts and fiery organizers.

My political home at the Institute for Policy Studies provides a wider range of new ideas turning into action than I can ever keep up with. Discussions with John Cavanagh, Sarah Anderson, Emira Woods, and the rest of the IPS family keep me grounded between flights. And across the pond Fiona Dove and my other friends, comrades, and co-conspirators at the Transnational Institute keep me focused on a global vision central to all of our work.

In Washington, ongoing crises—from the global disasters of Iraq and Palestine and US efforts to destroy the UN, to the raw racism laid bare by the death and destruction of Hurricane

Katrina, to far more everyday personal nightmares including months of being grounded by chemotherapy—were made bearable, sometimes productive, and on occasion even fun by my loyal peeps who give me a new definition of family. Geoff Hartman, Jeanne Butterfield, Barbara Neuwirth, Bruce Dunne, Joe Kakesh, Justine Hranicky, and Al Frye were all there at crucial moments with jokes, lemon tarts, West Virginia weekends, and dogs. From farther afield, my scattered sisterhood of Nancy Parson, Judy Bennis, Ellen Kaiser, Rachelle Kivanoski, and Linda Bennis provided support in person and by phone. Andreas Zumach kept me focused and sane.

A host of activists, movement leaders and agitator/ journalists motivated me with inspiration and illumination of new ideas and strategic approaches. Leslie Cagan, Hany Khalil, the rest of the UFPJ leadership, Laura Flanders, Amy Goodman, Khaled Mansour, David Wildman, Nadia Hijab, Chris Toensing, Denis Halliday, Peter Lems, Andrew Rubin, and the steering committee of the US Campaign to End Israeli Occupation all provided more than they know. The International Coordinating Network on Palestine, as well as Wolfgang Grieger and the rest of the staff of the UN's Division for Palestinian Rights, helped ground much of my work on Palestine. Michel Moushabeck, Pam Thompson, Juliana Spear, Hilary Plum, Kerry Jackson, Brenda Eaton, and Moira Megargee worked to get this book out far faster than seemed reasonable to expect. Danny Glover's powerful introduction reflects his extraordinary capacity to inspire, to reach beyond, and to link our struggles, our work, and our victories to those who have gone before.

And activists and organizers from around the world—from the rainbow-flagged peace marchers flooding the streets of Rome, to the anti-war and Palestine conference planners of Jakarta and Malaysia, to the governmental and civil society collaborators who quietly plotted behind-the-scenes strategizing at the UN—continue to inspire and inform my work.

The idea for this book grew out of the extraordinary experiences of the first years of the 21st century, when the government of the United States under George W. Bush moved to escalate from a kind of traditional, somewhat prudent imperialism into an extremist push toward power, resources, and the consolidation of empire. As the unilateralist and military goals and methods of that undertaking became clear around the world, a global movement against empire began to rise.

In countries around the world, global justice and peace activists who had long recognized the danger that untrammeled and strategically unchallenged US power held for the peoples of the world, took to the streets in unprecedented numbers and with renewed fervor. In capitals around the world, governments first murmured and then some dared to speak up to express their countries' and their peoples' fear of what they saw as the Texas cowboy. And at the United Nations came the first official diplomatic challenges to US unilateralism and disdain for international law, resulting in Washington losing its seat in key UN agencies.

So when US war in Iraq loomed, and people thronged their capitals in the monumental protests of February 15, 2003, and the *New York Times* declared the birth of the "second superpower," it was clear that people in the streets were not all that made up that second superpower. The people were the center, the strength and the power, the steadfastness at the core of the global resistance. But the people's movements were powerful enough that they forced governments—however opportunistic their other reasons—to stand defiant of the US war. And finally, with enough governments standing up to say no, the United Nations itself was pulled, however reluctantly, into anti-war resistance. It was the intersections between these three components that would create a new kind of resistance, a new kind of internationalism—powered by people, implemented by governments, and legitimized by the United Nations and its Charter—that would ultimately go head to head with the empire.

But it wasn't as easy as that. Everyone agreed that the people and the social movements were the core. Most people also agreed that it was governments who had to be the objects of that global pressure, and that the key demand was for governments themselves to say no to US demands. But many people doubted that the UN could ever play a role, however secondary or even tertiary, in the international challenge to empire. The doubts were not surprising. Too often the UN had been seized by US power, used and abused as an instrument of legitimation, as a multilateral fig leaf to hide a whole range of unilateral sins. Many believed it could never be different. But the UN proved them wrong.

And for eight and a half months, together with the people's movements and a host of disparate and unevenly reliable governments, the UN and its leadership and staff and myriad agencies stood defiant of war, resistant to empire, and unyielding to pressure. The moment was brief, but it held enormous promise as a model of what could be built again, some day, embodying the covenant of the UN Charter to

> save succeeding generations from the scourge of war... to reaffirm faith in fundamental human rights, in the dignity and worth of the human person, in the equal rights of men and women and of nations large and small, and to establish conditions under which justice and respect for the obligations arising from treaties and other sources of international law can be maintained, and to promote social progress and better standards of life in larger freedom.

In this examination of the three parts of the internationalist challenge to empire, many things have been left out. Most grievously, perhaps, given its key role in the building of the worldwide anti-war mobilizations, the global justice or anti-corporate globalization movement gets short shrift. The reason is simple—I was simply far less familiar with the players and the trajectories of that movement, with its own history and dynamics in the US and internationally, before it came to join the traditional peace and anti-war sectors of the movement during the rise of the Bush empire. My own work was centered far more in the peace and anti-empire sectors of the movements, again both in the US and around the world, and the emphasis of this book reflects that greater familiarity. I have had over the last several years the enormous privilege of traveling across the globe to meet with new and longstanding activists and to participate in seminal events of the growing global peace and anti-empire movement, and I have tried to reflect some of that movement's breadth and vigor and excitement in this analysis.

Some may criticize this investigation for even discussing the Iraq war and resistance to it in the context of "empire" without putting the economic realities of that imperial drive—the privatizations, the lifting of protective legislation, the corporate war profiteering, the concentration of economic power—as well as the consequences of those features of unchecked globalization and the movements challenging them, at its center. The book might well have gained greater analytical rigor as a result of such an emphasis, and again its insufficient discussion certainly echoes in part my own uneven understandings of the different components of our movement. But equally, the extraordinary rise and richness of the global movement against war reflects one of the key particularities of the Bush brand of empire: while shaped around a neoliberal economic framework as ruthless— perhaps more so—as any that came before it, this early 21st-century empire is driven as well by a much greater centrality on the political/strategic and especially military components of empire.

So it is on the opposition to those elements of empire— military, diplomatic, political—that this book focuses. The wars in Iraq and Afghanistan still rage and the world's peoples still stand defiant of those wars, even when most governments' and the United Nations' resistance have for the moment largely collapsed under the relentless US pressure. Yet the tripartite internationalism that challenged the beginning of the Iraq war is still an important model, though it will require a great deal of work to reclaim and recapture that moment. This book aims to help that process.

I

INTRODUCTION

As the South Pacific's summer sun rose early in the morning of February 15, 2003, tens of thousands of people began gathering in New Zealand and Australia to protest the looming US war against Iraq. A few hours later, following the sun, hundreds of thousands more took to the streets of Manila, Jakarta, New Delhi, across the South Asian peninsula and up into snowy central Asia, throughout Africa south to Durban and Johannesburg, gathering in tiny towns and moving north and west across the Middle East to throng the chilly capitals of Europe. The protests jumped across the Atlantic to dozens of Latin American towns and more than 400 cities throughout the wintry United States. Everywhere from Fiji, where the day before, anti-war campaigners had a Valentine's Day protest aimed at representatives of the US, British, and Australian governments,[1] to Antarctica, with its demonstrations at the McMurdo base and at the Amundsen-Scott Station at the South Pole, people rose up in protest to the looming US war, offering visions of a more peaceful world. As Paolo Calisse reported from Antarctica, here "no wars have ever happened and... all countries recognize that the only way to survive is through collaboration."[2]

In New York, peace campaigners outside the headquarters of the United Nations on New York City's East River passed the half-million mark, despite police efforts to divert tens of thousands more trying to reach the rally site. There, on a huge stage overlooking the enormous, shivering crowd braving a bitter wind on the coldest day of the year, a parade of activists, politicians, cultural workers, and artists repeated the call that had rocketed around the world on that singular day: "The World Says No to War."

The demonstrations were largest in countries whose governments were, against massive popular opposition, supporting Bush's moves toward war. In Rome, estimates of up to two million people thronged the streets to protest Silvio Berlusconi's agreement to send troops to Iraq. In London one million people protested Tony Blair's backing of George Bush's war. And in Spain, where the pro-war Aznar government was still in power, massive protests took place throughout the country; in Barcelona alone 1.3 million demonstrators filled the streets. Bulgarians protested their government's siding with the US war in the Security Council with banners reading "Send Weapons Inspectors to US."[3]

By the time the first events began in New York, demonstrators had taken over the streets in more than 660 other cities around the world.[4] According to the 2004 Guinness Book of Records, it was the largest mass protest in history. More than twelve million people had come out to say no to Bush's militarism, no to unilateralism and empire, no to war.

It was an extraordinary weekend. In New York, the global events of February 15 actually began the day before. On that Friday morning the mainstream US press had finally realized something historic was underway, with that day's Security Council meeting and the next day's planned demonstrations. CNN assigned a reporter and crew to cover the "peace beat," and they spent the day in the office of United for Peace and Justice (UFPJ), whose headquarters was in the offices of 1199, the largest New York trade union. Every hour they did live interviews and shots from the chaos of the office. We heard later that top officials from the US Mission to the UN complained to CNN. But the reports continued.

I was in the UFPJ office, crouched on the floor next to a little portable radio, taking notes on the Security Council meeting. Secretary of State Colin Powell had urged foreign ministers to attend the meeting, rather than simply UN ambassadors, to hear the ostensibly "final" reports of Hans Blix and Mohamed el-Baradei, the two UN arms inspectors for Iraq. Many had anticipated that their reports would somehow legitimize Bush's claims regarding weapons of mass destruction, that they would be at least ambivalent enough to justify war. But they were not. Both of them were careful, nuanced, and—as we now know—thoroughly accurate in their account of the reduced state of Iraq's weapons programs.

Following their reports, the French foreign minister Dominique de Villepin, responded with an extraordinary call, that "the United Nations must remain an instrument of peace, and not a tool for war." There was no television in the UFPJ office, but when I heard the applause erupt after his speech, I knew what the Council chamber must look like. It was unprecedented—a huge rolling ovation among the diplomats themselves, in that usually staid and formal chamber.

Early Saturday morning, groups of people with signs were already heading toward the rally site. By 9 AM the ecumenical church service led by South African Archbishop Desmond Tutu and a couple dozen religious figures representing a host of different religions was underway at a church just a few blocks from the UN. After the service, a small group of us walked with Bishop Tutu (and a pre-arranged police escort) the four or five blocks through the police-controlled empty streets to the United Nations. The singer, activist, and actor Harry Belafonte and his wife Julie and I were going with the Bishop to meet with UN Secretary-General Kofi Annan. Every UN security guard (in fact every NYPD officer too—almost all of whom were black) was deferential, eager to make eye contact or have a brief word with Tutu—and then they all seemed to do a double-take when they recognized Belafonte.

The meeting with Annan was brief. Bishop Tutu introduced the meeting, saying

> we are here on behalf of the people marching today in 665 cities around the world. And we're here to tell you that those people marching in those cities all around the world, we claim the United Nations as our own, we claim it as part of our global mobilization for peace.

It was an extraordinary moment, marking the new link that had emerged between the United Nations and the rising international peace movement. It was also about the last thing Annan wanted to hear at that moment. His friends, UN supporters, putting the pressure on him to do exactly what

Washington was pressuring him not to do. Bishop Tutu talked about the importance of the UN in trying to prevent war. Belafonte talked about the scope of anti-war sentiment around the world; his wife talked about the devastation of war for mothers and grandmothers; and I talked about the global anti-war movement's commitment to defending the UN's role as an instrument of peace and defiant of war. The secretary-general was very cautious. He told us he hoped that the diplomats who were returning to their capitals after the Friday meeting would be able to find a compromise that would make it possible to avert war. (Two hours later he gave an interview to Abu Dhabi television saying—for the first time—that if force were to be used, a second UN resolution would be required. It was, at that moment, a significant shift.)

Belafonte was wearing one of the blue "The World Says No to War" buttons on his overcoat, and as we were pulling on more layers of clothes before heading back out into the cold, Annan leaned over and asked him what it was. I pulled another one out of my pocket and gave it to the secretary-general.

The crowd already filled First Avenue as far as the eye could see—which was about as far as the 59th Street Bridge—and we were hearing already about people filling the streets up into the East 70s or even further. It was the first time I had ever seen a crowd that so completely resembled New York City and this country. It was as multiracial and multiethnic and multigenerational as could be, with longtime activists and first-time demonstrators, fur-clad wealthy liberals, contingents of hospital janitors and community organizers—it was a snapshot of the real America commentators like to rhapsodize about.

The press had finally got it, and all of them were there. I did a bunch of interviews, everyone from al-Jazeera to the *New York Times* magazine to the terrific coalition of independent media groups that brought *Democracy Now!*, Pacifica Radio, Free Speech TV, and others together for a collaborative effort that provided the only live real-time broadcast of the entire rally. There was an incredible feeling of power, that for the first time in a long time we were really on the edge of a sea change. It was a very emotional time—I found myself weeping every other moment. It seemed other people were feeling that way too—there were a lot of tears backstage in the warm-up tent.

Belafonte called out to the rising US movement against war and empire, reminding us that our movement could change the world, and that the world was counting on us to do so. "The world has sat with tremendous anxiety, in great fear that we did not exist," he said.

> But America is a vast and diverse country, and we are part of the greater truth that makes our nation. We stand for peace, for the truth of what is at the heart of the American people. We WILL make a difference—that is the message that we send out to the world today.

Following Belafonte came his close friend and longtime colleague, the activist-actor Danny Glover. He spoke of earlier heroes, of Sojourner Truth, and Harriet Tubman and the great Paul Robeson. And then he shouted "we stand here today because our right to dissent, and our right to participate in a real democracy has been hijacked by those who call for war. We stand at this threshold of history, and we say to them 'Not In Our Name'!" The enormous crowd, shivering in the bitter cold, took up the cry, and "Not in our name! Not in our name! Not in our name!" echoed through the New York streets.

All the speakers had been told we had to reduce the already ridiculous two-minute time limit we had been given originally to just 90 seconds. I'm not sure how many complied, but the program certainly moved pretty fast. Ninety seconds—what can you possibly say? They even had a guy with giant signs crouched 30 or 40 feet in front of the stage—30 seconds after you started your speech he held up "ONE MINUTE" then "30 SECONDS" and then "END!"

A little while later, someone backstage got a call (what did we do before cell phones?) about an Associated Press story that had just broken, dateline UN. They wrote down the two-line story, scrawling it on the back of a leaflet. There was a huddled discussion, should we go public, should we wait. But pretty quickly we realized that this was big news the crowd should know. After a minute's discussion, Leslie Cagan said, "Phyllis, you're our UN person, you've got to do it." And she pushed me back on stage.

I added only one sentence of my own, looking out at this huge mass of people that had now grown to monumental, historic proportions. "If anyone here thinks that our protests today don't matter," I said, "listen to this." And then I read the AP piece:

Rattled by an outpouring of international anti-war sentiment, the United States and Britain began reworking a draft resolution Saturday to authorize force against Saddam Hussein. Diplomats, speaking on condition of anonymity, said the final product may be a softer text that does not explicitly call for war.

People roared. Reading that report, at that moment, at that place, to that crowd, was one of the greatest privileges I will ever have. A half million people had come together, for the same cause, making a difference.

The program, logistics, press, security, all the myriad things that make a gathering of so many even possible, let alone triumphant, in the face of police and governmental intransigence, were done brilliantly. The organizing—in only six weeks!—was astonishingly successful, and it was truly global in a whole new way.

Even the *New York Times* acknowledged the change in the international balance of forces. There are once again "two superpowers in the world," the *Times* reported on their front page. "The United States, and global public opinion."[5] This definition captured not only the dynamism of the day's events, but the understanding that the core of the new challenge to Washington's unilateral war was centered in the streets, in the massive demonstrations that brought millions out in countries around the world to protest. While the journalists may not have fully grasped exactly what was underway, it was clear that the *Times* recognized that something, somehow, was different.

Street demonstrations had happened before and would happen again. International activists in many countries had planned simultaneous protests before. The hard work of building a movement would continue whether or not the specific demands of a particular demonstration were won. What was different this time was the power that emerged from linking the three major components of what would soon together become the second superpower: the global peoples' movement reinforced by its unified call to stop Washington's war; the assortment of governments around the world who recognized that the US drive toward empire was not in their interests and responded (whatever their other motivations) to their populations' anti-war mobilizations by rejecting Washington's demands; and the United Nations itself, which for that historical moment stood defiant of US pressure and thus played the role its Charter mandates. Massive mobilizations of people forced governmental decisions that enabled UN defiance—and this ultimately empowered and strengthened the world's civil society.

The world's sole superpower had met its match.

Empire on the Rise

In January 2004, Vice President Dick Cheney struck an aggressive, not-quite-defensive tone at the World Economic Forum in Davos, Switzerland, telling the gathered glitterati that "if we were a true empire, we would currently preside over a much greater piece of the earth's surface than we do. That's not the way we operate."

From the narrowest vantage point, that was true. Presiding directly over territory, as in Afghanistan and Iraq from 2002 and 2003, was never Washington's only choice of how to dominate other countries and control strategic resources. Cheney asserted what even the *New York Times* called an "unapologetic defense of the administration's threat to use military force." But however old-fashioned the current US global crusade for dominion, relative to other modern efforts toward control of strategic lands and resources, the Bush administration drive toward empire necessarily must take into account the changed realities of the early 21st century.

Of course the drive toward power and empire is not itself a new phenomenon. The rise of a single global superpower is not unprecedented—after all, the empires of Rome, the Mongols, the Byzantines, the Ottomans, the British all had their day in the sun and controlled huge swathes of territory, treasure, and people. The claims of empire—exemption from international law, enforced loyalty of the vassal states, exclusive rights to the perquisites of power—remain constant today.

This Bush administration, with its militarized unilateralism, was from its 2001 unelected ascension to office bent on establishing a global force more powerful, with greater military reach, deeper cultural influence, bigger economic clout, and a greater political, strategic, and diplomatic capacity than any empire that has ever existed in history.

Certainly the war in Iraq was about oil. It was certainly about expanding the US military presence throughout the region; it was about creating a "weapon of mass distraction" to sway the US elections in November 2004, and it was about undermining the United Nations and international law. But most of all the war was about power. And that is why the cavalier unilateralism that shaped the run-up to the war reflected such extraordinary hubris. It was the arrogance of absolute authority, the arrogance of those who claimed that because the US had the power of domination, it somehow held the right to dominate. It reflected the commitment to the view that because the US military and nuclear arsenals dwarf all others in the world combined, that using those deadly instruments was somehow okay. Because it would be Americans wielding that overweening might, use of the power was somehow inherently, congenitally right.

Certainly the September 11, 2001, terror attacks on Washington and New York facilitated the White House's capture of false legitimacy and US public acquiescence to the newly defined exigencies of empire. But Washington's drive for consolidation of a US empire traces its roots not only to the expansionist dreams of the neo-conservative and militaristic cabal that form the operational center of George W. Bush's White House, but to ancient and not-so-ancient history itself.

What was new, relative to those earlier empires, was the staggering level of globalized power that Washington has concentrated in the new imperial center. It was not for nothing that French intellectuals at the beginning of the 21st century had begun describing the US as a "hyper-power." The rising US empire had achieved military reach beyond the dream of any Roman legionnaire, extending indeed into space and across the very skies. It had seized access to treasure exceeding even the most predatory of King Leopold's colonial thieves. Diplomatic control tighter than that of the entire coterie of Queen Victoria's striped-pants emissaries. And cultural influence far surpassing the imagination of the most visionary Athenian philosophers.

But what was also different was that the vast reach of this

newest empire was still not sufficient to withstand the challenges of the 21st century. The US was able to invade Iraq and capture Saddam Hussein, but its military occupation and ruthless privatization plans faced a rising military resistance, as well as a huge crisis of legitimacy that showed up in the widespread demands for US troops to go home. The US empire was willing to go to war virtually alone in the face of unprecedented UN opposition, with its narrow coalition of the coerced providing a false veneer of international credibility, but even years after the invasion Washington's war-shredded alliances still proved difficult to mend. The US continued its uncritical economic, military, and diplomatic support for Israel's occupation of Palestine, but the occupation's escalating brutality posed a serious challenge to US efforts to impose regional stability and "democracy" across the Middle East. The US continued to exert significant domination over the trajectory of corporate globalization, but even the most intense US efforts to reshape global trade rules could not prevent the Brazil-led Group of 20 from yanking the 2003 Cancún summit of the World Trade Organization out from under Washington's thumb.

And the fact that the "second superpower" challenging the US includes its own citizens represents a key distinction between the US empire and those of its ancient predecessors. Perhaps remembering that earlier empires were brought down from outside, with fire and blood and great violence, citizens of the US played and continue to play a key part in building a global movement. Joining their counterparts in international civil society, a host of governments across the globe, and the United Nations itself, US activists crafted campaigns aimed at bringing down this latest empire from within its own borders. Their tools would not be weapons of war, but rather the instruments of non-violence and democracy.[6]

As a result, the White House's efforts to consolidate an empire, an age of Pax Americana remain so far incomplete.

1991 Gulf War Sets the State for Post-Cold War Hyper-power

In January 1991, on the eve of what would be the first US war against Iraq, the great Pakistani scholar Eqbal Ahmad addressed a New York teach-in broadcast live on a nationwide radio hookup.

On that remarkable night, people gathered to listen in living rooms, union halls, campus dormitories, and church basements across the United States, seizing a moment's respite from the round-the-clock campaign that was trying, however fruitlessly, to prevent what was already understood to be an inevitable war.

Eqbal spoke of the history of war, describing how for 300 years before that time Europe and the United States had fought wars in and for and over their colonies, and how they had devastated lands and peoples. "The seventeenth, eighteenth, and nineteenth centuries witnessed the genocidal destruction of grand civilizations," he said.

> The great Mayas, the Incas, Aztecs, and the Indian nations of North America; the conquest and subjugation of the rest of humanity. Eventually, even India was colonized; so was China, all of Africa, and ultimately the Middle East. These were the centuries that witnessed the transformation, forced and bloody, of land and labor into commodities in the capitalist sense of the word. Slavery was but one manifestation of this reality; the conversion of common land into individual estates, the wholesale dispossession of nations and peoples were the other manifestations.

Whole populations were slaughtered, he said, whole civilizations were destroyed. Yet few in the colonial countries spoke of those wars.

Eventually, Eqbal reminded us, "the wars of greed and expansion came home to roost. The colonial have-nots of the West took on the haves. Europeans fought a war among themselves, called it a World War, and gave it a number—One." And then some years later they fought each other again, and they called it World War II. Yet still they did not talk about the earlier colonial wars that had wiped out populations around the world. And Eqbal looked at those sitting, rapt, in the audience in New York and spoke to all of those listening around the country, and said, "the history of our time is studded with unrecorded holocausts."[7]

When Washington launched its 1991 war against Iraq a few days later, when US bombers lit the sky of Baghdad's night, it was clear that that war would not go unrecorded. CNN was there as the war began, broadcasting the bombing around the world.

In fact, despite Washington's success at coercing the United

Nations into endorsing its war, the Security Council itself and the UN Secretary-General had to learn from CNN that the war had actually started. The Council was in session that night—not on the crisis in Iraq, but on the question of Palestine. A reporter came downstairs to the Security Council chamber where a group of journalists waited. He came running, shouting: "There's something happening in the sky over Baghdad; we don't know what it is, but there is something. It's on CNN." So the Council's ambassadors and UN staff, and the secretary-general himself first learned from a UN security guard who happened to overhear the journalists' tumult that Washington had taken the world to war.

The 1991 war and the years of sanctions that followed did nothing to eliminate the government repression that had characterized Iraq for twenty years, repression that had been not only tolerated but succored, armed, financed, and supported by the United States. But the war would lead to the destruction of much of Iraq's—and civilization's—ancient past, would undermine its modern present, and would threaten the health and very lives of its future.

Following what was called a "success" in destroying Iraq in a record short time, the use of US military power increased throughout the 1990s. Invasions were often presented in the human-rights-friendly language of "humanitarian intervention." The deployment of US troops and US bombers in Haiti, in Somalia, in Bosnia, in Kosovo, as well as the ruthless decisions to ignore growing crises deemed less than strategically important, such as the 1994 Rwandan genocide, only served to increase the militarization of US foreign policy and undermine the potential for non-military solutions.

Those years, with Bill Clinton's claims of "assertive multilateralism" masking the reality of a growing unilateralist trajectory, set the stage for George W. Bush's ascension to power in 2001. Even before the attacks of September 11 that year, the new Bush administration was already moving toward absolute abandonment of international law, rejection of multilateral institutions and instruments, and the emergence of a consciously asserted law of empire.

When the second Bush administration took over in Washington, the Clinton-era trajectory of unilateral militarism disguised as "humanitarian intervention" escalated. All the major players in Bush's foreign policy and international security teams agreed that with the Cold War consigned to history, and the US now an unrivaled global power, it was time to assert the legitimacy, as well as the capacity, of the US to declare itself leader of the world. The time for unchallenged American dominion had come.

But within that broad political agreement a serious strategic split emerged over just how that US domination could best be maintained. The debate began right at the beginning of the new presidency, during the early 2001 Senate confirmation hearings for Bush's cabinet nominees. The debate was most sharply visible between Secretary of State Colin Powell, on the one hand, and the Pentagon chiefs, Secretary of Defense Donald Rumsfeld and his deputy Paul Wolfowitz, on the other. The civilian leadership of the Pentagon included both old-fashioned Cold War-style nationalist militarists like Rumsfeld, who had told Bush even before the administration came to power that he believed US military power was needed "to help discipline the world."[8] Then there were the neo-conservative ideologues— Wolfowitz and others—filled with visionary ideas of over-throwing tyrants and installing American-style "democracy" around the world.

The divisions within the administration could perhaps be characterized as the gap between reliance on US-dominated multilateralism (imposed by fiat and militarized when needed) and a unilateralist assertion of military power as the first-choice option for an unchallenged superpower that needs to pay little attention to the interests of or pressures facing its allies.

Powell envisioned a US-dominated international "consensus," however artificial or coerced it might be, in whose name US policies could be imposed on the world. On the other side was what the US media quickly dubbed the "Wolfowitz cabal," grouped around the deputy secretary and semi-official Defense Policy Board of hard-line Pentagon hawks. They saw a unilateral assertion of US power, especially military power, as the first-choice option. And their belief in the perks due an unchallenged superpower led to the conviction that the US need pay little attention to the views of its allies.

Under Bush, US military mobilization was joined by the open political legitimation of unilateralism, with specific calls for "unsigning" some treaties (the International Criminal Court), abandoning others (the Anti-Ballistic Missile treaty, the Comprehensive Test Ban Treaty), and rejecting those in the works (the Kyoto environmental protocol, the new protocol to strengthen the bioweapons treaty). Bush's rhetorical shift from Clinton's claimed multilateralism to an overt and official embrace of unilateral power made countries around the world very nervous. Raising a wide range of demands, people took to the streets in capitals around the world challenging Bush's aggressive assertion of US power, and demanding that their governments stand up to growing US pressure. In response, governments around the world made the United Nations a key venue for an ascendant diplomatic challenge to the US. By May 3, 2001, less than five months into Bush's first term, Washington lost its seat on the UN Human Rights Commission, failing to win reelection in the "Western European and Others Group" for the first time since the Commission was created.[9] A month later, the US lost its position on the UN's International Narcotics Control Board.

The governments' moves to unseat the US in the UN agencies did not come in a vacuum. International anger was rising in response to a host of other examples of US unilateralism and hypocrisy. European diplomats explaining the Human Rights Commission vote pointed to the US refusal to sign or ratify numerous treaties and international conventions including those guaranteeing the rights of women and children, the Comprehensive Test Ban Treaty (CTBT), land mine prohibitions, and the International Criminal Court. There was also Washington's abandonment of the Kyoto protocol on global warming and threats (at that time still unrealized) to the Anti-Ballistic missile (ABM) and nuclear Non-Proliferation Treaty (NPT). Then there was the US insistence on maintaining the death penalty. And Washington's rejection of international protection for the Palestinians, most recently seen in the US using its veto to prevent a Security Council resolution calling for unarmed international observers in the Occupied Territories, led to Secretary of State Powell himself admitting that the US veto vote had "left a little blood on the floor."[10]

Unease about the unilateralist tendencies of the Bush administration had shaped international responses right from the beginning of the first term. Fears of this "retreat from international engagement" shaped headlines across the country. Newspaper editorials and pundits, already concerned about Bush's proudly proclaimed ignorance of foreign affairs, expressed discomfort about the consequences of these high-profile withdrawals from global commitments. *New York Times* columnist Tom Friedman described how "America is referred to as a 'rogue state' in Europe now as often as Iraq."[11] Among the public, there was also some unease about the increasingly go-it-alone tendencies of US policy pronouncements.

In August 2001, even some of Bush's right-wing backers were concerned that "going it alone could get very lonely." In a *New York Times* op-ed pleading for the Bush administration to take its relationship with its allies more seriously, analysts from the far-right American Enterprise Institute and the neo-conservative Project for the New American Century criticized Bush for his "almost contemptuous rejection" of the Kyoto Protocol on global warming, and his "small-minded America First" arguments against it. (They were not supporters of the treaty, one should note, but very concerned about how Bush was framing his opposition.) In a notably prescient warning—remember, this was a month before the September 11 attacks—they asked "how does the administration expect to convince the French to forgo lucrative oil contracts with Iraq, for example, if France's own benchmark is such a narrow definition of national interest? How will Mr. Bush persuade the Germans, who are owed billions by Iran, to take a hard line with Tehran for the cause of international security? If America defines its interests too narrowly, it cedes its claim to moral leadership—a remarkable but perishable American asset. Such a definition would also embolden other countries to define their interests in the same way."[12]

By the end of August, the US had failed in its widely publicized effort to orchestrate a global walk-out from the UN's anti-racism conference in Durban, South Africa. Pressure on the empire was mounting.

But then came September 11. Overnight, all of the rising international opposition to Bush's unilateralism collapsed. And in the aftermath of the horrific terrorist attacks, the Bush administration found a new capacity to implement the longstanding goals of the empire builders at its core. Centered particularly in the office of the civilian leadership of the Pentagon and that of Vice President Dick Cheney, the neo-conservative ideologues had for years asserted the legitimacy of a unilateral, military thrust to advance US power around the world. Throughout the 1990s, between their stints in Washington, many of these individuals had drafted a set of working papers outlining a call for increasing the military power of the US. In September 2000, calling themselves the Project for the New American Century (PNAC), they issued their latest version of a plan they called "Rebuilding America's Defenses." It codified their call for massive increases in defense spending, privileging the Pentagon's role over that of the State Department or other cabinet agencies, ratcheting up the military's capacity to fight several major theater wars simultaneously, sidelining the United Nations, and relying on military threats or pressure rather than diplomacy as the first choice of relations with other countries.

Neither PNAC nor the earlier iterations on which "Rebuilding America's Defenses" was based reflected particularly new ideas. But before September 11, 2001, its premises were deemed far too radical to win acceptance among the American people. PNAC's own paper described the need for what it called a "catastrophic and catalyzing event—like a new Pearl Harbor"[13] to win public support for their strategy of global domination. The Bush administration chose to use the destruction of the World Trade Center as just such a tool to win public support for limitless war, making implementation of the right-wing extremist plan possible for the first time.

Support came from the rest of the world too, including many of the same people and governments who had been at the center of trying to build a challenge to US unilateralism only days before. Governments cheered and much of the world stood by as the Bush administration proudly asserted Washington's rights of empire. *"Nous sommes tous les Américains,"* proclaimed *Le Monde*'s September 13 headline in Paris. We are all Americans.

It was as if the Bush White House had taken up the Athenian cause described in the Melian dialogues of ancient Greece. Athens, proud of its claimed commitment to justice but afraid that its fragile new democracy might be imperiled, sent emissaries to the island of Melos announcing its intention to seize the island to increase Athens' strategic reach. The Melians protested, saying "Athenians, you are known for your justice; what about justice?" The Athenians answered simply, "Justice? There is only justice among equals." For Athens, democracy and international law applied; on Melos, the laws of empire were imposed.

The Empire Brooks No Challenge

The US decision to go to war in response to Iraq's 1990 invasion of Kuwait demonstrated that Desert Storm would be a war of choice—and the choice had little to do with what Iraq had done in Kuwait. After all, Iraq was a longtime (if not completely trusted) ally of the US, and for almost a decade Washington had supported Iraq militarily and financially as it waged war against Iran. And Iraq was hardly the first Middle Eastern country, nor the first US ally in the region, to invade and occupy a neighboring state. Long before Iraqi legions marched into Kuwait, Turkey had invaded northern Cyprus, Morocco had seized the Western Sahara, and Israel continued its illegal occupations of the Palestinian territories, of south Lebanon, and of Syria's Golan Heights. In none of those land-grabs had the US president thundered, as George Bush senior did following Iraq's invasion of Kuwait, "this occupation will not stand!"—let alone begun mobilizing US troops to conquer the new occupier.

Certainly the US had some regional concerns regarding the consequences of Iraq's seizure of Kuwait, including the need to maintain domination of the strategic region, consolidating control over its allies' access to Middle East oil, and protecting Israel. But the most important reason for the first Gulf War was not regional at all, but rather international—and it had everything to do with the end of the Cold War. With the Soviet Union already on the skids and about to collapse, the US was concerned that in this newly uni-polar world, without the ideological justification provided by the "Soviet threat," the US lacked a new political/ideological framework to validate its moves toward consolidating international hegemony.

White House and State Department spin doctors in the first Bush administration went to work, replacing the now-outmoded depiction of the superpower US courageously battling the Soviets' evil empire with the cool new image of the US as leader of the brave new free-world coalition challenging an Arab tyrant in the name of all the nations of the world. The US would even manage to coerce key Arab leaders to join its coalition, along with the collapsing remnants of the Soviet Union itself. And in its former ally Iraqi leader Saddam Hussein, whose wars and repressive rule had never bothered the US before, Washington found a demonizable dictator straight out of central casting.

The quick US victory in Iraq—after an air assault had bombed Iraq into what the UN's first inspection team called a "near-apocalyptic... pre-industrial" state[14]—left the United States strategically unchallenged anywhere in the world by any combination of forces. In response, the US intensified its assertion of the legitimacy of unilateral power, which included escalating diplomatic, economic, and political pressures on UN member states, designed to keep the global organization under firm US control. Throughout the next twelve years, US unilateralism and domination of the UN were consolidated in the devastating economic sanctions against Iraq. Decreed in the name of the United Nations, the sanctions were in fact imposed by the United States, with Britain the always-loyal sycophant. Washington's creation, and the Pentagon's regular bombing, of northern and southern "no-fly" zones in Iraq, also with British backing, was never authorized by or even mentioned in any UN resolution, although US officials, including presidents, routinely spoke of "enforcing UN decisions" to justify the bombings. The efforts of both the first Bush and Clinton to legitimize unilateral US attacks by forcing the UN to provide a multilateral cover became a US habit. The pattern was broken only with the aggressive assertion of an extreme anti-UN unilateralism that became the hallmark of the younger Bush's ideologically-driven administration.

The Second Iraq War

It has become famously public that only hours after the September 11 terror attacks, the White House security team that gathered to plan the US response was already discussing the desirability of war against Iraq. War against Afghanistan was an inevitable first step, but for Bush policymakers it was almost a sideshow, insignificant relative to their strategic goal of "regime change" in Iraq. Rationalizations and justifications would come and go, claims regarding Iraq's alleged nuclear programs, its hypothetical weapons of mass destruction, its mythical links with al-Qaeda and Osama bin Laden, all would have their day (or, as it happened, months or even years) in screaming headlines. Only later would the claims be publicly exposed as false in careful, judiciously balanced articles relegated to small-circulation magazines or page A-17 of the mainstream press. But however dubious its justifications, the war against Iraq went forward. This was not a war to eliminate weapons of mass destruction that didn't exist, nor to sever an imaginary Iraqi link with al-Qaeda. This would be a war for oil, for power, and ultimately, for the exigency of empire.

As the Bush administration moved from invasion to overthrow to occupation of Iraq, it continued its broader trajectory toward international expansion of power and global reach. Bush's infamous September 20, 2001, warning that "you're either with us or with the terrorists" sent an unambiguous message to governments around the world: you either join our chosen response to terror, or we will treat you as a terrorist.

Despite the visible failure of its policies in Iraq, despite the false claims of "transferring sovereignty" to Iraqis in September 2004 and "winning democracy" in the January 30, 2005, elections, despite the continuing bloodshed, the brutal siege of Fallujah, the revelations of torture at Abu Ghraib and Guantánamo, and the continuing chaos across the country, Washington continued to declare victory. Defense Secretary Donald Rumsfeld, even while acknowledging in 2005 that the war in Iraq could last twelve more years,[15] never wavered from his early claims that Iraq was on the road to freedom. He blithely ignored civilian carnage and dismissed the destruction of ancient cities because, in his words, "freedom's untidy, and free people are free to make mistakes and commit crimes and do bad things."[16]

However modern its weapons, the arrogance of US triumphalism reflected the hubris once identified with ancient empires. It was only contempt with which the Bush administration looked down on Iraqis and on those peoples, governments, and institutions across the world who dared to defy the US call to war. The 2003 US war in Iraq was certainly not the first time the US had unilaterally, illegally, and without justification attacked another country. But in the recent past—whether Grenada, Panama, the first Gulf War, Bosnia, Somalia, even Kosovo—Washington generally attempted to validate its wars through some kind of claim (however spurious) of international legality. In giving life to Bush's doctrine of preemptive war, the 2003 assault on Iraq represents the first time a US president has claimed—even boasted—that he had the right to launch such a unilateral preventive attack against a country that had not attacked the US and did in fact not pose any imminent threat. International legality, in this new post-September 11 Bush era, was unnecessary, even unwelcome.

Claiming the right of preemptive war would not, by itself, be proof of empire. Even launching this war—which would more accurately be defined as an aggressive preventive war, since a preemptive attack requires an imminent threat—would not by itself represent such proof. But the eagerness of Washington's powerful leaders to launch this war without United Nations authorization and with such reckless disregard for legality or for consequences, with the expressed aim of toppling the government of an independent, oil-rich country (not to mention a country and people mortally wounded from war and twelve years of murderous sanctions), may represent just such proof.

Historian Paul Schroeder, writing some weeks before Washington's invasion of Iraq, concluded that the US "is not an empire—not yet." He described the US as

> at this moment a wannabe empire, poised on the brink. The Bush Doctrine proclaims unquestionably imperialist ambitions and goals, and its armed forces are poised for war for empire—formal empire in Iraq through conquest, occupation, and indefinite political control, and informal empire over the whole Middle East through exclusive paramountcy.[17]

The rapid overthrow of the Baghdad regime within the first weeks after the invasion of Iraq pushed Bush administration officials over that brink. Their gloating "other Middle Eastern governments better learn their lesson" attitude reflected a fortified sense of self-righteousness and of the ostensible justice of their cause. If Washington had not yet consolidated its global empire, the drive toward it was now undeniable.

Ultimately though, what is more important than the debate over whether the US today is already an imperial center ready for global domination or still an almost-empire, is understanding the political significance and consequence of this historical moment. In mid-2005 US tanks still controlled the Euphrates valley and US troops still occupied the sites of the earliest recorded history of humanity. But those US policymakers willing to look beyond their own euphoria will see a devastated, dishonored, and angry Iraq facing at best an uncertain future. And the largest components of the Iraqi population, whom Washington's ideologues believed would welcome US troops with rice and flowers, instead remain adamantly opposed to the US occupation. When Iraqis braved the threats of violence with courage on election day, they voted overwhelmingly for parties promising to ask the US troops to leave. And as Israel's occupation of Palestine is joined by the US occupation of Iraq, the US faces a humiliated and angry Arab world, and a shattered system of US alliances with weakened dictatorships throughout the Middle East.

But at the same time, a constellation of growing governmental opposition, including Washington's closest allies, an emerging global people's movement saying no to Washington's war and no to Washington's empire, and a UN at least for a brief moment joining the global mobilization for peace, rounded out the world's response to Bush's war.

If war in Iraq were the only clear imperial thrust of the Bush administration, it would be tempting to reduce it to the resource-grabbing of an oil-obsessed administration, the actions of an irresponsible hegemon soon to be taken to task by the rest of the global community. Opposition to the war could indeed be reduced to the demand of "no blood for oil." But when taken in the context of long-standing, and more visionary, efforts to reshape regional and global power relations even beyond oil, the Iraq war emerges far more as exemplar of a broad and entrenched pattern than as an isolated case of a US power grab.

This fact is particularly significant in light of the combination of military, political, and economic factors whose collective expansion undergirds the relentless US drive for power and empire. Washington's threats against Iran, for instance, which escalated from 2004 on, made clear that overthrowing Saddam Hussein in Iraq did not signal the end of Washington's oil, strategic, and military ambitions in the region. The hypocrisy of the Bush administration's demand that Iran give up the rights guaranteed to it as a signatory of the Non-Proliferation Treaty (NPT), including the right to enrich uranium for peaceful purposes, was staggering. Iran had kept secret earlier nuclear activities that it later revealed to the UN's International Atomic Energy Agency (IAEA). But even though a new intensive inspection regime by the IAEA found no evidence of illegal weapons activities, and even though US officials themselves acknowledged that Iran's enrichment activities did not violate the NPT, the US launched a virulent anti-Iran campaign based on the Bush administration's "lack of trust" in Tehran.

The US hypocrisy was sharp not only because of Washington's own nuclear legacy as the only country to have used nuclear weapons and the possessor—by a huge margin—of the largest nuclear arsenal in the world. And not only because it was US political and military, including nuclear, support for the shah of Iran, imposed by a CIA-backed coup in 1953 and overthrown by Khomeini's Islamic Republic in 1979, that gave rise to Tehran's nuclear capacity in the first place. But also, as former President Jimmy Carter wrote in 2005,

the United States is the major culprit in this erosion of the NPT. While claiming to be protecting the world from proliferation threats in Iraq, Libya, Iran and North Korea, American leaders not only have abandoned existing treaty restraints but also have asserted plans to test and develop new weapons, including anti-ballistic missiles, the earth-penetrating "bunker buster" and perhaps some new "small" bombs. They also have abandoned past pledges and now threaten first use of nuclear weapons against non-nuclear states.[18]

Militarily, the creation of a network of permanent bases throughout the Middle East and Central Asia, the Pentagon's techno-lethal "revolution in military affairs," the scaffolding of Israel's rise as an unchallengeable regional military and nuclear power, and most especially the public commitment to a new generation of nuclear weapons designed not for deterrence but for actual battlefield use have contributed to a US military capacity so enormous that no combination of other countries could even hope to approach, let alone match or surpass it.

Elsewhere in the world, US military involvement is on the rise in Latin America, particularly in Colombia, despite important emerging gains for popular forces elsewhere on the continent, including Brazil, Argentina, Ecuador, Bolivia, and Uruguay. In Africa, US military aid to oil-producing countries (such as Nigeria) is on the rise. In Asia, the US is rebuilding its military connections with the Philippines, and discussions are continuing with Japan regarding expansion of Tokyo's military capacity and especially eliminating Article IX of Japan's constitution, which once prohibited the use of military force other than in self-defense. Washington is goading an unstable North Korea into consistently higher levels of nuclear brinksmanship, almost daring China to rise to the bait. All over the world, the US is reclaiming access to bases lost earlier to the vagaries of post-Cold War and post-neo-colonial politics—in places such as Yemen, Somalia, Ethiopia, and the Philippines. The fourteen new military bases under construction in US-occupied Iraq are likely part of a Pentagon effort aimed at expanding its network of bases across the Middle East in countries once far from hospitable to US forces. And in once inaccessible arenas, long off-limits to US military forces because of the Cold War or post-Soviet claims of Russian influence, US bases are sprouting like mushrooms. In the oil- and gas-rich countries of the Caspian and Central Asia—in Uzbekistan, Kyrgyzstan, Azerbaijan, Kazakhstan and elsewhere—US bases now surround war-torn Afghanistan.

The Bush administration's September 2002 national security plan, grounded in the earlier documents of the Project for the New American Century, refers directly to maintaining the enormous chasm between the military capacity of the US and that of the rest of the world, calling for the use of military force to ensure that no nation or group of nations ever imagines even matching, let alone surpassing, US prowess. The cavalier dismissal of concerns regarding increasing regional instability as a likely result of war in Iraq reflects a rash acceptance of the PNAC view that every political challenge has a military answer. And earlier, even before September 11, abandoning the Comprehensive Test

Ban Treaty and working to consign the Non-Proliferation Treaty to the dustbin of history were part of Bush's assertion of military unilateralism as a point of legitimate principle.

Both internationally and domestically, it is clear that consolidation of economic power in fewer and fewer hands remains a key strategy of the US drive toward empire. The Bush team exhibited continuing enthusiasm for domestic tax breaks for the rich and for corporations, and a complete lack of concern with the dire domestic economic consequences of their $300+ billion war in Iraq. The contract grabbing and war profiteering by administration-linked companies in occupied Iraq reflected the broader privatization focus of Bush foreign policy. Abroad, the continuing moves to tighten US military control over strategic oil and gas reserves in the Middle East and Central Asia were aimed at providing more economic clout to Washington vis-à-vis its economic competitors and allies. Elsewhere, the United States continued its agenda of advancing corporate trade and investment rights, as it tried to craft a new round of global trade talks in the World Trade Organization. Washington continued its blatant use of economic aid and trade agreements as carrots and sticks to bribe, threaten, and buy coalition partners for the war in Iraq. (It should be noted, however, that it was in this area that Washington's strategic failure was most visible. The fact that the Security Council's "Uncommitted Six" countries—Angola, Cameroon, Chile, Guinea, Mexico, Pakistan—got away with their refusal to sign on to Bush's Iraq war was clearly an important precursor to the emergence of the Brazil-led Group of 20, which stood up against the US and Europe at the 2003 WTO meeting in Cancún.)

Politically and diplomatically, Washington's effort to undermine the United Nations and render it "irrelevant" in the run-up to the Iraq war clearly demonstrated the view of key White House ideologues that UN authorization was not only unnecessary but actually unwanted—damaging to the Bush holy grail of legitimizing the unilateral assertion of US power. Coming on the heels of earlier rejections of treaty obligations and/or negotiations (Kyoto, ABM, the International Criminal Court, etc.) the Bush administration's grudging and dismissive approach toward the UN went far beyond the Clinton administration's instrumentalist view, however cynical, of the global organization. (It was Clinton's then-UN Ambassador Madeleine Albright, after all, who in 1995 famously called the UN "a tool of American foreign policy."[19])

By 2004, going into its second term, the Bush administration was moving more powerfully than ever to expand, rather than compromise, its power. A year later, writing in the London *Guardian*, the perceptive British analyst Julian Borger noted that

> George Bush's Republican party does not rest on its laurels. It is at its zenith in Washington and the world beyond, and yet it is still pushing impatiently against the outer envelope of its power.... Bush's reelection has won the grudging acceptance of European leaders, but here again the administration has shown no taste for mere consolidation. It wants to send as an envoy to the United Nations its bluntest unilateralist, John Bolton, a man who once suggested that the UN Security Council would be better off with a single member, the US... It seems quite possible that the administration's supreme confidence has turned to hubris and that its overreach could yet send the wheels spinning off.[20]

But hubris had not yet brought down the administration. The Bush White House dismissed any notion of accountability to international law or the UN Charter. It operated instead on a litany of assertions that UN resolutions meant only what President Bush said they mean, and that anyway we don't need any UN resolutions—we have the god-given right to go to war when and where and against whom and for however long as we like.

But despite Bush's efforts the United Nations was not rendered irrelevant. To the contrary, for the crucial months in the run-up to the Iraq war and for a brief period after the war began, the UN stood at the center of the global demand for peace. As the British analyst George Monbiot wrote, the US seemed

> to be ripping up the global rulebook. As it does so, those of us who have campaigned against the grotesque injustices of the existing world order will quickly discover that a world with no institutions is even nastier than a world run by the wrong ones. Multilateralism, however inequitable it may be, requires certain concessions to other nations. Unilateralism means piracy: the armed robbery of the poor by the rich. The difference between today's world order and the one for which the US may be preparing is the difference between mediated and unmediated force.[21]

Moving Against Empire: The Second Superpower?
There is no country or group of countries capable of launching a serious—rather than merely disruptive—military challenge to Washington's power. But for perhaps the first time since the end of the Cold War, there is a serious competitor challenging the US empire for influence and authority—the second superpower composed of a mobilized international civil society, key opposition governments, and the United Nations itself. Those forces include not only the protesters who took to the streets around the world to protest the Iraq war, and not only the stalwart Non-Aligned governments of South Africa, Cuba, Brazil, Venezuela, Malaysia, and others, although they are vital to this challenge. Not only the powerful US allies such as France, Germany, or Russia, eager to remain on good terms with Washington, yet clear about the danger of an unrestrained rogue empire. Not only the often beleaguered UN secretary-general and the secretariat that he leads, facing extraordinary pressure to cave in to Washington's will, yet aware that the global organization's real survival depends on its willingness and ability to stand defiant of that pressure and to defend international law and its own Charter.

No one of those three sectors of global society—people, governments, or the UN—can alone successfully defy the US unilateralism and militarism. But when joined, all of those forces together make up the astonishing movement toward a new internationalism that today forms the global challenge to Washington's drive toward empire. The combination of extraordinary events in mid-February 2003—the unprecedented Security Council response to France's then-Foreign Minister Dominique de Villepin's call to defend the UN as an instrument of peace and not a tool for war; the refusal of the Council's member states to accede to US demands to endorse the war, and the outpouring of millions across the globe—provided even clearer evidence that a critical historical juncture was at hand. The *New York Times'* definition of this moment as proof that once again there were two superpowers in the world, made clear that even the most powerful were feeling the blows of those pounding on the empire's walls.

Although that global movement against war in Iraq failed to stop the US onslaught, it did ensure that when the US invasion was launched, there could be no denying that it opened an illegal, unauthorized, unilateral war. This would not be the Gulf War of the senior Bush, whose bribes, threats, and punishments forced sufficient Security Council votes to officially, however reluctantly, authorize the immoral 1991 war against Iraq. This time the effort at legitimation failed, and the US, backed only by Tony Blair in Britain and a few other governments eager to remain in Washington's pocket, went to war alone.

The global movement against war quickly began transforming into a movement against US empire. Many of the speakers at the rallies around the world hit the same point—this war, and this anti-war movement, were no longer just about Iraq. This was about mobilizing the world against US policies and the rising empire they represented. To the shock of ideologically-driven White House policymakers and analysts, European and other governments began to recognize that the need to constrain the US was as urgent—perhaps even more so—as the need to restrain Baghdad, and that effort was reflected in the UN debate. Writing in the *New York Times* magazine, James Traub quoted an unnamed UN official confirming that Security Council "members ended up feeling that they had to stand up to American unilateralism."[22]

It was in this context that the conscious struggle—again with the UN as the primary venue—emerged among Europeans. "Old Europe," led by France and Germany, recognized the danger of ignoring the rise of US power, and came close to admitting publicly the once-hidden goal of building Europe as an explicit counterweight to the US. Anti-war sentiment in France, Germany, and elsewhere made it possible—indeed virtually mandatory—for those governments to stand defiant of the US in the Security Council. Public opinion against the war and against Bush transformed what likely began as the governments' tactical disagreements with Washington into immutable opposition. Even the governments of "new Europe," particularly the weaker and poorer Eastern European states, aspiring to EU and NATO membership and still caught up in the hope of taking advantage of the EU's generous cash benefits while keeping their strategic eggs solidly in Washington's basket, faced 65–80 percent public opposition to their support for Bush's war. Differences over the nature of an expanded Europe, then, emerged as a crucial subtext within international debates over the war.

What happened on February 15, 2003, was not simply a

matter of simultaneous demonstrations: there was the qualitatively greater power that comes from a shared framework (even if spontaneous and rudimentary rather than conscious and comprehensive) of resistance to empire. It was that connection and coordination that set in motion the recognition of the importance of the global movement: an internationalist power that could, when its three component parts were joined in unified defiance, challenge the rise of the 21st century's dominant empire.

2
THE MOVEMENT

The 21st century's first new US and global people's movements against war and empire began to take shape even before that century's first war of empire was launched. In the immediate aftermath of the terror attacks of September 11, 2001, the Bush administration's intention to respond with war, rather than a search for justice, became clear. The first reply to Bush's primitive war cry emerged almost as quickly: grieving mothers, daughters, fathers, and sons whose loved ones perished in the World Trade Center or in the Pentagon or on the doomed flight that crashed in Pennsylvania came together to create September 11 Families for Peaceful Tomorrows. They took their cue from Martin Luther King's venerated statement that "war is a poor chisel for carving out peaceful tomorrows." Motivated by sorrow and rage, "our grief is not a call for war" became their rallying cry. They took the lead in insisting that their loved ones' deaths not be used to justify new US aggression—first in Afghanistan, later perhaps somewhere else.

Challenging Fear
But the "peaceful tomorrows" movement and other components of what would soon become a visible and vocal mobilization of anti-war voices emerged in an extraordinarily difficult context. Within hours after the September 11 attacks, the Bush administration made clear its intention to use those horrific crimes as justification for an even more horrific limitless war. Further, it was clear from the immediate aftermath of the attacks that fear and racism would remain useful and powerful tools for this administration, to be manipulated and exploited at will,

ratcheted up artificially whenever the public level of fear began to diminish.

It would be difficult for someone outside the US to grasp the stranglehold of fear that took possession of the majority of the American population after 9/11. Throughout the world, everyone else knew that such attacks had happened before, that while this one was exceptional in a number of ways (levels of coordination, complete surprise, and especially the high number of casualties) terror attacks on civilians were not invented on September 11, and that throughout much of the world fear of such attack was part of ordinary life.

But the United States was different. Not only in the broad terms of American exceptionalism that still shaped American national identity, but in some very concrete and specific ways. American national identity was shaped by a century-old assumption of American impunity, born of geography and oceans, and now combined with the arrogance of unchallenged power. The US is a huge country, surrounded by oceans on two sides and subordinate countries with long, and for generations peaceful, borders on the other sides. Since the nascent US finished its westward and southward expansions to consolidate its control of what is now its enormous landmass, at the cost of the genocidal slaughter of native peoples across the continent, no one in the continental US has ever faced foreign military occupation. No one alive today can remember a war fought within US borders.

Further, generations of Americans believed themselves immune from any repercussions of their government's actions. Nothing US policymakers did around the world would ever have any serious consequences on their lives at home. So raining bombs on Afghanistan or Sudan during the 1990s, or backing the Contra terrorists who mined Nicaragua's harbors in the 1980s, or claiming Persian Gulf petroleum to be "our oil" as President Carter memorably described it, or providing decades of massive military and economic aid and diplomatic support to Israel's occupation, or imposing crippling sanctions on Iraqi civilians—all this would never, in the popular mind, have any impact here at home.

Somehow most Americans never learned the earlier lesson of an earlier September 11. On that day in 1973, the US backed a military coup d'etat against the democratically elected government of President Salvador Allende in Chile. In the brutality that followed, General Augusto Pinochet's military government murdered or "disappeared" 3,000 Chileans and several foreigners, and imprisoned and tortured tens of thousands more. Those chickens came home to roost back in the United States in 1976, when the exiled Chilean ambassador to the United Nations, Orlando Letelier, and his young American colleague at the Institute for Policy Studies, Ronni Moffitt, were murdered by Pinochet's agents on the streets of Washington, DC. This remained, for a decade and a half, the worst act of international terrorism in US history.

And then, there was American exceptionalism. In the domestic context, that refers most sharply to how the population of the US views itself and its place in the world. Contrary to the reality understood by people in the rest of the world, Americans believe themselves to be not only good global citizens, indeed global do-gooders, but also as people well-loved in the rest of the world. Americans tend to believe that others see them as the source of generous foreign aid, as the model democracy to which other countries aspire, as the overall good guys in a world filled with an awful lot of bad guys.

So when the 9/11 attacks occurred, leaving almost 3,000 people (from 60 countries, it should be noted) dead, it was not surprising that Americans were paralyzed with shock and fear. And fear undermines not only independence of will, but the very capacity to think. Certainly the US population is not, under the best of circumstances, known for an appreciation of critical thinking. But with the 9/11 attacks, many Americans were, for some days at least, rendered virtually incapable of such thought.

And the dominance of fear over law, fear over democracy, ultimately fear over humanity, was not a passing phenomenon. Years after September 11, a *New York Times* reporter analyzing the US public response to torture described how

> an implicit understanding has been reached, or so I would argue, between the governed and those who govern: that the prime task is the prevention of future attacks on our own soil... that extralegal excesses, not excluding kidnappings and physical abuse, may be necessary in the effort to suppress terrorists seeking to implant sleeper cells in our midst and equip them

with deathly substances and bombs; that in pursuit of this goal, much can be forgiven, including big mistakes (the abuse and indefinite detention of innocent people, the tacit annulment— for foreigners, anyway—of legal guarantees, not to mention a costly war of dubious relation to the larger struggle); and that the less we know as a people about our secret counterterrorism struggles and strategies, the less we contemplate the possibly ugly consequences, the easier it will be for those in authority to get on with the job of protecting us.[1]

The "ugly consequences" were of course easier to tolerate because those who were the victims of those consequences were not white, were not Christian, were not Americans. They were overwhelmingly (though not entirely) Arabs, Afghans, South Asians, and European hyphens—Arab-Europeans, Asian-Europeans, etc. And crucially, they were Muslims. The immediate "ugly consequences" of the Bush response to 9/11 played out dramatically within the United States, where hundreds, then thousands of Arabs, Arab-Americans, South Asian-Americans, Muslim-Americans and anyone who looked like they might come from one of those suspect categories were rounded up for interrogation, arrest, deportation; many disappeared, held incommunicado for months; others were attacked on the streets, their children harassed at school. Mosques were attacked.

Any person, all US communities, and ultimately several countries, who could be portrayed as being somehow linked to "them"—the Other, the bad guys, the terrorists—paid the price. Only days after September 11, the powerful Palestinian-American poet Suheir Hammad, author of *Born Palestinian, Born Black* wrote

fire in the city air and i feared for my sister's
life in a way never
before. and then, and now, i fear for the rest of us.

first, please god, let it be a mistake, the pilot's
heart failed, the
plane's engine died.
then please god, let it be a nightmare, wake me now.

please god, after the second plane, please, don't
let it be anyone
who looks like my brothers.[2]

The racism inherent in the Bush policy remained constant. Careful claims that "this is not a war against Islam" and carefully orchestrated visits to carefully selected mosques could not mask the anti-Arab, anti-Muslim, anti-immigrant fever that was at the core of the building support for the war. From the beginning, the racist impact of the war meant that immigrant communities, Arabs, Muslims, and communities of color in general would play central roles in the emerging peace and justice movement that would simultaneously challenge both the international and the domestic versions of Bush's war without end.

The Bush administration was quick to take advantage of the fear-driven paralysis of thought that affected so many Americans. With a public politically paralyzed and desperate for leadership, Bush chose the moment to rally the population behind one chosen response to the September 11 attacks: war. It was posed as inevitable, as necessary, and as fervently desired by the American people. But no alternative response was ever offered: the choice was limited to two: to go to war, endlessly and everywhere against the amorphous concept of terror, or to "let 'em get away with it." Given the very real horror of grieving families, unknown numbers of victims and uncertainty about who might have been responsible, it is not surprising that "let 'em get away with it" was not a viable choice. Certainly neither President Bush nor anyone else in his administration—nor virtually any other political leader—mentioned the alternative vision of responding to the terror attacks on the basis of international law, international jurisdiction, and international cooperation to find and bring to justice the perpetrators and those who backed them.

Instead, the only choice the US and the world were offered was a demand for war.

The Peaceful Tomorrows' movement was initially small, but with its insistence that "our grief is not a call for war," it held a moral credibility and legitimacy that could not be gainsaid. Made up largely, though not entirely, of new activists galvanized into their first anti-war actions by outrage over Washington's manipulation of their anguish, the group quickly moved to the center of a fast-growing mobilization already in place, led by experienced organizers and longstanding peace and justice organizations.

On the morning of September 13, only 48 hours after the World Trade Center was attacked, Congress passed the administration's authorization for use of military force. The bill gave up congressional power and handed the president a virtually unlimited mandate to

> use all necessary and appropriate force against those nations, organizations, or persons he determines planned, authorized, committed, or aided the terrorist attacks that occurred on Sept. 11, 2001, or harbored such organizations or persons in order to prevent any future acts of international terrorism against the United States.

The reference to preventing future acts certainly indicated that no restraints were envisioned; Bush's Pentagon now had congressional authority to use its power in preemptive attacks anywhere for an unlimited period of time. Of 535 legislators, only one, the brave California Congresswoman Barbara Lee, voted no.

The first demonstration against the looming war in Afghanistan brought a couple of hundred protesters to Lafayette Square in downtown Washington on September 24, less than two weeks after the attacks. Also by that time, longtime activists were at work in New York City, at the epicenter of what was already being called "Ground Zero." They were calling for a major mobilization demanding justice and international law, not war, in response to September 11. That demonstration was set for October 7, 2001, with "not in our name" as the centerpiece of a call for peace. It was less than a month since the World Trade Center had been attacked. New York City authorities balked, but eventually gave in and granted permits for the Union Square rally. No one knew what to expect. The ruins of the twin towers were still smoldering—would the demonstration be sabotaged by angry New Yorkers? Would even committed anti-war activists be afraid to come out? As it turned out, the protest brought out 5,000 people, their tone somber, angry, determined.

In Washington, 200 miles south of the protest that same morning, I watched President Bush announce that his war against Afghanistan had begun. US bombers were winging their way toward Kabul. I telephoned Leslie Cagan, one of the country's preeminent anti-war organizers, who was coordinating the demonstration, to tell her the war had started. I reached her by cell phone, backstage at the Union Square assembly. Leslie told the crowd that Washington had begun its new war in the very face of the thousands of demonstrators demanding peace. It would be the first of this new century's US wars launched in direct and utter disregard of international law and of US and international mobilizations against exactly such actions. Despite a consistent rise in anti-war activities, it would not be the last.

But those early demonstrations held a significance that belied their ultimate failure to prevent or later halt an aggressive war. According to Achin Vanaik, an Indian anti-nuclear campaigner and fellow of the Transnational Institute, "I think it is unfair as well as unrealistic to… expect that movement to have stopped the invasion. The US was going to go ahead regardless. But the importance of the movement is that it robbed the US of the legitimacy that they wanted."[3]

Public protests, even in the form of the first rather modestly sized and politically somewhat tentative demonstrations, gave visibility, legitimacy, and collective voice to the large numbers of people in the US who were outraged, distressed, or at least mildly uneasy about the war trajectory of Bush's response to September 11. Internationally, as the initial outpouring of post-September 11 human solidarity toward the US was quickly squandered by the White House's aggressive military attacks and by its hard-line "you're either with us or against us" stance, the existence of even small US protests reassured the world that not all Americans agreed with the government's policies.

At the global level, the urgency of the peace movement's mobilizations reflected the growing recognition that September 11 had brought about major qualitative changes in world politics and power. It took a bit more time, but soon US activists, along with some intellectuals and others, recognized what so many around the world had seen instantly: it was not the terror attacks themselves that had transformed the world, but the Bush administration's response to the attacks. The attacks provided a gift to the neo-conservatives occupying powerful positions in the administration. Years earlier, drafting the Project for a New American Century (PNAC) those same neo-cons had identified what would be necessary for achieving their political goal of US domination of the world: a "catastrophic and catalyzing event—like a new Pearl Harbor."[4]

In the words of Chalmers Johnson, the noted historian of empire, the PNAC team members ensconced in power throughout the Bush administration believed that such a catastrophic event "would mobilize the public and allow them to put their theories and plans into practice. September 11 was, of course, precisely what they needed."[5] Similarly, according to the *New Yorker*'s Nicholas Lehman, then-National Security Adviser Condoleezza Rice asked members of the National Security Council to think about "how to capitalize on these opportunities to fundamentally change American doctrine, and the shape of the world, in the wake of September 11th." Rice had then told him, "I really think this period is analogous to 1945 to 1947," and Lehman noted those were the years "when fear and paranoia led the United States into its Cold War with the USSR."[6]

Crucially, the war on Afghanistan was, from the moment of Bush's decision to attack, understood to be a sideshow to the real story: an invasion of Iraq and the overthrow of Saddam Hussein. In *Washington Post* reporter Bob Woodward's 2002 book *Bush at War*, he describes Secretary of Defense Donald Rumsfeld insisting at the September 12, 2001, cabinet meeting that Iraq should be "a principal target of the first round in the war against terrorism."[7] The president allegedly replied that "public opinion has to be prepared before a move against Iraq is possible," and instead chose Afghanistan as a much softer target.[8]

But even as the US public began to grasp the Bush administration's determination to attack Iraq, opposition to the ongoing war in Afghanistan remained the key focus of the nascent anti-war movement. In the US, small demonstrations grew into large and widespread protests. Members of the growing Peaceful Tomorrows network traveled widely, speaking in London, Italy, Japan, Canada, aboard the Japanese Peace Boat on its round-the-world crossing, as well as throughout the United States.

Internationally, particularly in Asia and Latin America as well as much of Africa and parts of Europe, the powerful movements challenging corporate-driven globalization began investigating, exposing, and building opposition to the economic interests at stake—involving Afghan oil pipelines, control of Central Asian natural gas, past US collusion with the Taliban and more—in Bush's Afghanistan crusade. Those global justice protesters soon joined traditional peace forces to demand, though at first largely fruitlessly, that their governments resist US pressure to endorse Washington's war.

By early 2002 the pace of US anti-war organizing was picking up. While the Afghanistan war was lethally underway, the Bush administration was moving more and more toward open acknowledgment that war in Iraq was topping their agenda. Plans began to take shape for a major national mobilization in Washington, DC in April to protest the existing and coming wars, and the broader US "war against terrorism." Numerous organizations, national and local, including both longtime anti-war opponents of Iraq sanctions and new constituencies finding Afghanistan on the map for the first time, joined the campaign, many of them moving in and out of informal and fluid coalitions.

In the meantime, US anti-corporate and anti-globalization activists found themselves suddenly thrust into the mainstream of political debate and even mainstream protest, as scandals brought down wealthy executives and CEOs from a host of major corporations, including some with embarrassingly close ties to top Bush administration officials. Enron became the poster company for profiteering and cronyism, and Enronitis the new codeword for corporate greed. Anti-corporate protesters, flush with unexpected media access and credibility in wider-than-normal circles, brought new energy and new faces to the growing anti-war mobilizations. They would form a vital contingent at the April 2002 demonstration.

And then, just as preparations were getting underway for the Washington protest, a separate rising crisis was pushing the Afghanistan war off the front pages. Publicly, at least, all of the debates within the administration and inside the Pentagon regarding whether and how to mobilize a military strike against Iraq faded, for a moment, in the face of what would quickly become the biggest temporary obstacle to any such US attack. That new challenge erupted a thousand miles west of Baghdad, in Israel and the occupied Palestinian territories.

Palestine and the Israeli Occupation
The second Palestinian intifada (uprising), which began in September 2000 after the collapse of the failed Camp David summit and the collapse of the Oslo-driven hopes of

Palestinians, had been escalating through much of Bush's presidency prior to September 11. Israeli settlements were expanding, while Palestinians faced an upswing of collective punishment, including curfews, closures of towns and cities, house demolitions, destruction of thousands of ancient olive trees and huge swathes of agricultural land. Palestinians were held, often for hours and sometimes even for days, at checkpoints that sprang up across the West Bank and Gaza; dozens of women gave birth at checkpoints and several died in childbirth when soldiers refused to let them cross to nearby hospitals. Palestinians in huge numbers met with arrest, beatings, shootings, and killings by Israeli troops. Incidents of Palestinian resistance to occupying soldiers and settlers continued; Israel's military forces throughout the West Bank and Gaza increased their firepower; and Palestinians were dying in higher numbers. More Israelis, too, were dying, though nowhere near as many as Palestinians. Many of the Israelis killed were occupation soldiers or armed settlers, but Israeli civilians, inside Israel itself, began to be among the victims of Palestinian resistance.

The Bush administration continued flip-flopping over its Israel–Palestine policy. In the first months of its term, before September 11, the administration had adopted a policy of essentially ignoring the rising intifada—keeping up existing levels of diplomatic protection and economic and military aid to Israel, but keeping their heads down and their hands off peace talks. This was not terribly surprising—Bush was, after all, part of a family and an administration whose economic and political power was thoroughly enmeshed in the oil industry, with close ties to Arab states where so much of the world's oil is located.

Certainly the existing close ties between the United States and Israel had not disappeared or even diminished when Bush came to power. Nevertheless, despite the continuity of close to $4 billion in annual military and economic aid to Israel, and the continued use or threat of use of UN vetoes and walk-outs to protect Israel in the United Nations, the Bush policy became known as "disengagement" from the Middle East. Europe, Arab states, and others around the world began crying for "greater engagement," as if Washington's billions in aid, the protective UN vetoes, and the diplomatic privileging of Israel did not constitute intimate engagement. What was needed, of course, was not more engagement, but an entirely different kind of engagement. And that was not on Bush's Middle East agenda.

Immediately after the World Trade Center attacks, the Bush administration appeared to distance itself, at least a little bit, from Israel. The need for maintaining Arab and Islamic governments' support for Bush's new "war on terror" trumped the administration's longstanding embrace of Israel, although US economic and strategic backing for Tel Aviv remained quietly unchanged.

Fearing precisely that kind of cooling reaction after September 11, Israeli spokespeople and supporters launched a near-frenzied campaign of linkage, claiming unparalleled unity with Americans as victims of common terror and with common Arab/Islamic enemies. Despite the clear differences in context, their goal was to push for a US military response to the attacks, among other things to provide new legitimacy for Israel's persistent military escalations in the West Bank and Gaza.

The *New York Times*'s Clyde Haberman, writing within hours of the attack on the World Trade Center, weighed in on Israel's behalf. On September 12, he wrote:

> Do you get it now? It is a question that many Israelis wanted to ask yesterday of America and the rest of the finger-pointing world. Not in a smart-alecky manner. Not to say, "We told you so."... The American criticism of Israel has been *sotto voce*. But it is there. And in this Black September, after the worst act of terrorism in history, the question arises from Israelis... Do you get it now? It was simply a question for those who, at a safe remove from the terrorism that Israelis face every day, have damned Israel for taking admittedly harsh measures to keep its citizens alive.[9]

Similarly, Israeli Prime Minister Ariel Sharon called the World Trade Center and Pentagon attacks an assault on "our common values," and he declared, "I believe together we can defeat these forces of evil." For his part, asked what the terrorist attack meant for Israel, former Prime Minister Benjamin Netanyahu blurted out, "It's very good." Then, catching himself and editing his words more carefully, he added, "Well, not very good, but it will generate immediate sympathy." He predicted that the attack would "strengthen the bond between our two peoples, because we've experienced terror over so many decades, but the United States has now experienced a massive hemorrhaging of terror."[10] (Later, fearing that the Bush administration effort to seek Arab support for its anti-terrorism war would lead to a move away from a clear embrace of Israel, Sharon would accuse the United States and the West of "appeasement," conjuring up images of Neville Chamberlain's acquiescence to Hitler.)

Overall, however, the Israeli effort to link its occupation of Palestine with the looming anti-terrorism war of the United States did not work very well beyond the punditocracy and Israel's own American supporters. By November 2001, the administration was determined to win and maintain Arab and Muslim government support. Secretary of State Colin Powell, speaking at the University of Kentucky in Louisville, and Bush himself at the UN General Assembly were paying more attention to words the Palestinians and—more strategically— Arab governments and their angry populations wanted to hear. Bush's UN call for a "state of Palestine" and Powell's assertion that "the occupation must end" appeared, for a moment, to herald a new, maybe even-handed, approach for US diplomacy.

But this approach was not to last. The "war on terror" was now primary in Washington. The Bush administration was prepared to weather Israel's displeasure, and that of Israel's backers in the United States, as long as winning Arab compliance was at the top of its regional agenda. For a while the administration appeared unconcerned with the escalating violence of the occupation, appearing to believe, against all evidence to the contrary, that Palestine could burn and somehow the crisis would stay contained and US allies in the region would not be harmed.

But soon the situation on the ground in Afghanistan, then the major center of the "war on terror," changed. As major Afghan cities under Taliban rule began to fall to US military assault, the need for regional support, particularly from the Arab world, changed. As the goal of maintaining international support for the Afghanistan war became less urgent, the need for winning and keeping Arab and broader international support for a coming war in Iraq took center stage. That meant emphasizing the US role as an "honest broker" intent on supporting a peace arrangement in Palestine and Israel. But to do that, the US had to reclaim its traditional links with Israel, in case anything that looked like even a mild criticism of the Israeli occupation later became necessary. So the tactical pendulum swung back and Washington returned to its usual public embrace of Israel and General Sharon. The shift was announced as a plan for Washington to "re-engage" in the "peace process." The first messenger to the region was former Central Command chief General Anthony Zinni, whose two earlier visits at the end of 2001 had ended in failure.

When Bush made his State of the Union speech in early 2002, he explicitly included the Palestinian organizations Hamas and Islamic Jihad, as well as the Lebanese resistance movement Hezbollah, in his litany of "terrorist" organizations. His purpose was not so much to signal a new campaign by the United States aimed directly against those groups. Rather, the US sought to pressure Iran, backer of several of the groups, as well as the Palestinian Authority, the putative "government" in whose territory two of them operated, as "sponsors of terror" or governments "harboring" terrorists. But in addition, the message regarding the Palestinian Authority was widely seen as a green light to Sharon. It was a signal that anything Israel did to the PA would be viewed in Washington as a legitimate attack on a "government" (however disempowered) that was harboring terrorists—drawing a direct parallel from Israel's escalating occupation to what the United States was doing in Afghanistan.

By February 2002, however, Iraq was already publicly replacing Afghanistan as the central target of US regional efforts. The stakes were going up and a new round of regional shuttling was required to lay out the expectations of support and lay down the law to Washington's Arab allies. General Zinni was not considered quite high enough in the Bush administration hierarchy for this one, so into the breech stepped Vice President Dick Cheney, an experienced Middle East hand from his years as secretary of defense in the first Bush administration.

In fact, Cheney had carried out a virtually identical Middle East regional roundup once before—on the eve of the 1991 Gulf War more than a decade ago, and for a similar purpose: to ensure Arab and broader regional (read: Turkish) support for a strike against Iraq. In the wake of September 11, with dependent and already compliant Arab regimes frightened of their own angry populations and falling over each other to win Bush's support by boarding the anti-terrorism train, the administration seemed to anticipate Cheney's job would be a pushover. Sure, there might be some unease in the palaces regarding how Arab populations were raging over the rapidly deteriorating crisis in the West Bank and Gaza, but it was assumed that however much they twitched and weaseled, Washington's Arab allies would stand with Washington.

As it turned out, Cheney's job was not quite so easy. While there was little doubt that at the end of the day the Arab kings, emirs, princes, and presidents would indeed do as their patron ordered, public opinion throughout the Arab world had hardened not only against Israel and its occupation, but against its global backer, the United States. Arab governments, already facing severe crises of legitimacy, would pay a very high price for their alliance with Washington, especially as war with Iraq loomed. Israel's military escalation in the occupied territories afforded what seemed to provide an easy dodge for the Arab royals looking for a way out of supporting Bush's planned attack on Baghdad: "How can you even talk to us about supporting an invasion of Iraq when Palestine is burning and you are doing nothing?"

Some time before Cheney took off for the Middle East, someone in Washington realized what was about to happen, and General Zinni was sent back to the region ahead of the Vice President, hoping to smooth the way for Cheney's visit. Zinni's mandate had not changed and there was little chance he would succeed, however that elusive word was defined (a ceasefire, a diminution of violence, whatever), but that was okay. Although he began his shadow shuttle in Jerusalem and Ramallah, Zinni's real role had far more to do with developments in capitals of the Arab states. Zinni was Cheney's political cover. "What do you mean we're doing nothing about the Palestinian crisis—we're sending General Zinni!" would be the vice president's new mantra.

As it turned out, that plan did not work either; while Arab regimes were still likely to cave in to pressure from the United States when it was finally exerted, shaky governments were simply not willing to concede prematurely and risk further destabilization or even potential threats to their regimes. One *Washington Post* article reported on Cheney's next-to-last stop in the Arab world, Bahrain:

Crown Prince Salman bin Hamad al Khalifa made clear that Arabs have little patience for considering a strategy to confront Iraq, with pictures of Palestinians killed during clashes with Israelis that continue to dominate newscasts and front pages across the region. "The people who are dying today on the streets are not a result of any Iraqi action," he said at a joint news conference with Cheney. "The people that are dying today are dying as the result of Israeli action. And likewise, the people in Israel are dying as a result of action in response to those actions that are taken. So the perception of the threat in the Arab world really focuses around that issue and we are preoccupied by it, deeply so."[11]

Cheney's trip fizzled, and the vice president's response was to try to re-spin a new rationale for his trip, denying that winning regional support for striking Iraq was his goal at all. "I sense that some people want to believe that there's only one issue I'm concerned about or that somehow I'm out here to organize a military adventure with respect to Iraq," he told reporters in Bahrain, "That's not true."[12] But the Arab world was not convinced.

Then it was Secretary of State Powell's turn. Following Cheney's failed trip, the Bush administration had called a brief time-out in the new game of Middle East engagement. Pundits turned to the Washington version of Kremlinology to sort out what might come next, examining tea leaves and photo ops to judge who was up and who was down in the Bush entourage. The early splits that had characterized the administration were still in place: once shaped by policy disagreements over Iraq, the same division between the Powell pragmatists and the Rumsfeld/Wolfowitz ideologues were now playing out over Palestine. Should any US official higher than an acting assistant deputy under-secretary of something ever sit in the same room with Yasir Arafat? Could any US official criticize anything that General Sharon did since he was fighting terrorism just as the United States was in Afghanistan?

The US press, watching the failure of the shuttle diplomacy, focused largely on the messenger. Was General Zinni simply too low in the Bush hierarchy to have the requisite clout with Sharon and/or Arafat? Would Bush send General Powell again, ratcheting up the four-star factor? What was largely left out of the debate was the reality that it was not the messenger but the message that would determine the success or failure of the mission. Zinni did not fail because he was not of high enough rank, but because he had no mandate to seriously dictate terms to Israel.

As it would turn out, though, neither did Powell.

Even before the decision was made to send the secretary of state back to the region, the situation on the ground turned even grimmer. Israeli attacks escalated sharply in March. Palestinian resistance escalated as well, with several deadly suicide bombings against civilian targets inside Israel, including one in Netanya, on March 27, the first night of the Jewish holiday of Passover, in which 26 Israelis, including children, were blown up as they sat down to a Seder dinner. On March 28, the Arab League endorsed a new proposal from Saudi Crown Prince Abdullah, that offered a peace agreement and full diplomatic relations with Israel in response to full Israeli withdrawal from all the occupied territories, a just solution to the refugee problem in accordance with UN resolution 194 (insuring Palestinians their right to return), and establishment of a sovereign Palestinian state in all of the West Bank and Gaza with East Jerusalem as its capital.

Israel did not even respond to the new diplomatic initiative. Instead, on the day after the Arab League offer, Israel's military invaded and re-occupied Palestinian cities, towns, villages, and refugee camps across the occupied West Bank. The assault that began March 29 was by far the largest operation of the Israel Defense Forces (IDF) since General Sharon led Israeli tanks into Lebanon twenty years earlier. Peace movements around the world—including in the US—would have to respond.

Israel had long used collective punishment in answering Palestinian resistance to its illegal occupation, whether that resistance was in the form of legitimate actions against Israeli military targets or attacks that violated international law by targeting civilians. But its March–April assault was an unprecedented action, destroying the last vestiges of the Oslo Accord's mythology of Palestinian authority in the major population centers across the West Bank. IDF troops punched into the cities of Ramallah, Bethlehem, Nablus, Jenin, Tulkarem, and tiny villages in between, with Apache helicopter gunships, Hellfire missiles, Caterpillar armored bulldozers, and

F-16 fighter-bombers. Almost all the weapons were made in the US. It looked, said UN Secretary-General Kofi Annan, like "a conventional war." Israel claimed its goal was to find and arrest "terrorists," but the scale of the military strike made clear it was designed to punish the entire Palestinian population.

At that point, with sharp images of Israel's reliance on US-provided missiles, helicopter gunships, fighter-bombers, and other military hardware filling television screens across the region, the Bush administration realized it could no longer avoid a direct response. Bush himself jumped into the fray. In a major speech in the White House Rose Garden on April 4, he announced he was sending Powell to the region and outlined a vision, if a bit skimpy and more than a bit blurry, of what a peaceful settlement might look like:

> This could be a hopeful moment in the Middle East. The proposal of Crown Prince Abdullah of Saudi Arabia, supported by the Arab League, has put a number of countries in the Arab world closer than ever to recognizing Israel's right to exist. The United States is on record supporting the legitimate aspirations of the Palestinian people for a Palestinian state. Israel has recognized the goal of a Palestinian state. The outlines of a just settlement are clear: two states, Israel and Palestine, living side by side, in peace and security.[13]

In fact, of course, it was not anything remotely resembling "a hopeful moment." Referring to the Arab League proposal, Bush conveniently ignored the inconvenient fact that the Saudi crown prince had called for Arab recognition of Israel to take place only after a complete Israeli withdrawal to the 1967 borders, creation of a Palestinian state, and recognition of Palestinian refugees' right of return. The United States may have been on record supporting Palestinian aspirations, but everything Washington was doing, before as well as after September 11, only helped prevent those aspirations from becoming reality.

According to Bush in his Rose Garden speech that day, if a Palestinian state had not been achieved yet, Palestinian leader Yasir Arafat had only himself to blame:

> The situation in which he finds himself today is largely of his own making. He's missed his opportunities, and thereby betrayed the hopes of the people he's supposed to lead. Given

his failure, the Israeli government feels it must strike at terrorist networks that are killing its citizens.[14]

Bush acknowledged that Israel's military actions might "run the risk of aggravating long-term bitterness and undermining relationships that are critical to any hope of peace," but, despite that, Bush would not criticize Sharon's assault, except to hope that Israel's "response to these recent attacks is only a temporary measure." Some of the most important words were present in Bush's speech: Israel must stop settlement activity, and "the occupation must end through withdrawal to secure and recognized boundaries...." Four days later Bush claimed he told Sharon, "I expect there to be withdrawal without delay." But while he talked the talk of serious pressure, he refused to walk the walk.

Bush was sending Powell back to the region without authorizing him to actually pressure Israel using any of the myriad tools available to the administration. There would be no cut in the billions of dollars in military or economic aid to Israel; no brake on the pipeline of military equipment the IDF was using against civilians (despite potential violations of the US Arms Export Control Act[15]); no reversal of the veto in the Security Council preventing the deployment of international protection or even observer forces; not even a public reprimand.

Given the lack of any action to match Bush's strong words, it should have surprised no one that General Sharon paid little attention. As veteran *Washington Post* columnist Mary McGrory described Bush's posture, "the leader of the free world lolled in a lounger in Crawford, Texas, and told Sharon to go to it."[16] For anyone who still harbored any optimism regarding Bush's intentions, the harsh reality was made clear in the timetable announced for Powell's ostensibly urgent journey to the region. Powell would indeed go to Israel and Palestine, but he would take his long sweet time getting there. Arriving first in Morocco, several days after Bush's speech, its young king Mohammed VI welcomed Powell with the question "Don't you think it would be more important to go to Jerusalem first?"[17] The night before Powell arrived in Morocco, half a million people demonstrated in the streets of Rabat, protesting the Israeli military attacks and US backing for the Israeli occupation. According to the

Washington Post, "that demonstration was the first pro-Palestinian rally that authorities have allowed since the latest round of violence erupted in late 2000 and was described by Moroccan authorities as one of the largest protests in the kingdom's history. Similar demonstrations have swept the Arab world in recent days, from Egypt, a crucial US ally and keystone of the Middle East peace process, to Bahrain, home of the Navy's 5th Fleet."[18]

Powell continued his languid pace, first from Morocco to Madrid to convene the diplomatic fiction known as the "Quartet"—the US backed by the largely supine Russia, the European Union, and the UN—and then on to Jordan and Egypt, until finally arriving almost a week later in Jerusalem. Powell's long delay had been, without doubt, seen as a week-long green light for Sharon's assault on the cities, villages, and especially refugee camps of the West Bank, and that assault continued its violent progression. Powell's visit accomplished nothing.

The situation was explosive enough that the usually cautious UN Secretary-General Kofi Annan called for a multinational force under the provisions of the UN Charter's Chapter VII, which would authorize the use of military force, to protect Palestinians in the occupied territories. He said he did not favor an official UN force of Blue Helmet peacekeepers, but rather a "coalition of the willing," made up of member states of the UN, who would have, he hoped, a "robust mandate" from the UN. It was the first time the UN leader had called for Chapter VII to be applied to the Israeli occupation of Palestine. But the Security Council, accustomed to US vetoes whenever there was a possibility Israel might be held accountable for its violations of international law, ignored his proposal.

When Powell returned from the Middle East, nothing had changed. President Bush welcomed him home with the astonishing claim that the goals of the United States had been met and that the secretary of state's trip had been a success. All was well with the world. It was an Alice in Wonderland moment, with Bush announcing straight-faced that "I do believe Ariel Sharon is a man of peace."[19] He then went on to claim, "Israel started withdrawing, quickly after our call... History will show that they have responded and as the prime minister said, he gave me a timetable and he's met the timetable."[20]

In fact real withdrawal—even from the Palestinian cities newly reoccupied in April 2002—was not on Sharon's or Bush's agenda.

Of all the Palestinian areas Israel attacked, the IDF assault on the Jenin refugee camp in the northern West Bank showed more graphically than anywhere else the horrors of military occupation. Israeli tanks and armored bulldozers had crushed houses, cars, and even people trapped inside. Resistance to the occupying forces had been fierce; 23 Israeli soldiers were killed in the fighting. Over 50 Palestinians were killed, pulled from the moonscape-like rubble of what had once been a crowded warren of a camp. At least 22 were civilians. Harsh debate broke out over whether the Palestinian claim of a "massacre" was accurate; Israeli officials accused anyone using the term of "blood libel." Human Rights Watch, which sent in a forensic team, indicated in a preliminary finding (that also urged a full international investigation) that they had not seen evidence of an identifiable massacre. That claim was a lead story, making front-page headlines in the American press. Few media outlets, however, picked up on the Human Rights Watch report's first point: Israeli troops had committed at least ten separate war crimes in Jenin.[21]

The UN quickly took up the issue. The UN's special envoy to the Middle East, Terje Roed-Larsen, called conditions in the Jenin refugee camp following the Israeli assault, "shocking and horrifying beyond belief... It looks as if an earthquake has hit the heart of the refugee camp here." Larsen, who went into the camp with representatives of the Palestine Red Crescent and UNRWA, the UN's Palestinian relief agency, described "the large-scale suffering of the whole civilian population here. No military operation could justify the suffering we are seeing here," he said. "It's not only the corpses, [it's] children lacking food." Larsen called on the Israelis to give fuller access to the camp to aid agencies trying to distribute food and water to the residents. Journalists accompanying Larsen reported the air filled with the stench of decaying corpses. An earlier report that day had indicated that two boys, ages six and twelve, had been pulled alive from beneath the rubble of their house at the camp. Palestine Red Crescent and other rescue officials, however, told journalists the boys were already dead.[22]

According to the preliminary report of Physicians for

Human Rights, who sent a forensic team into Jenin:

Children under the age of fifteen years, women and men over the age of 50 years accounted for nearly 38 percent of all fatalities.... One out of three fatalities was due to gunshot wounds with vast majority sustaining fatal wounds of head, or head and upper torso. Eleven percent of the total fatalities were due to crush injuries in addition to a 55-year old male crushed by a tank in the township of Jenin.

Of the one hundred-plus patients the PHR team interviewed at the Jenin hospital with gunshot and other traumatic injuries from the siege, "women, children under fifteen years, and men over the age of 50 years accounted for a total of over 50 percent of all admissions.[23]

Human Rights Watch investigators documented the deaths of numerous residents of Jenin camp. They included:

fifty-seven-year-old Kamal Zghair, a wheelchair-bound man who was shot and then run over by IDF tanks on April 10 as he was moving in his wheelchair equipped with a white flag down a major road in Jenin; thirty-seven-year-old Jamal Fayid, a paralyzed man, who was crushed in the rubble of his home on April 7 after IDF soldiers refused to allow his family the time to remove him from their home before a bulldozer destroyed it; fourteen-year-old Faris Zaiben, who was killed by fire from an IDF armored car as he went to buy groceries when the IDF-imposed curfew was finally lifted on April 11.[24]

One case study documented by Physicians for Human Rights involved a 42-year-old Palestinian employee of the United Nations. Their report read:

Review of pre-surgery X-rays revealed shattered distal left tibia and fibula with compounded comminuted fractures. The fracture pattern was consistent with high velocity gunshot injury. During the interview the man related that he was a schoolteacher employed by UNRWA, teaching in an elementary school in a nearby village... On the evening of April 4, 2002, when he went to the second floor of his two-story dwelling to get milk for his young child, he was shot, reportedly by an IDF sniper. The bullet struck his left leg above the ankle along the inner side and there was a dark hole on the outer surface of his left leg. According to this report, he collapsed and his wife dragged him down to the lower floor. He had no painkillers or antibiotics, but he applied a tight homemade bandage. He made many attempts to obtain help from the Palestinian Red Crescent and the Jenin Hospital but, because the camp was sealed off, no one could come to help him. He even begged an Israeli foot soldier to help him, showing him his UNRWA identity card. The soldier told him that if he needed help he should call Kofi Annan. After his house was demolished, he was allowed to go to Jenin Hospital by Red Crescent ambulance on April 11, 2002.[25]

Secretary-General Kofi Annan, appalled by the reports of his special envoy, called for an international investigative team to be sent. A draft Security Council resolution sponsored by the Arab Group at the UN called on Annan to investigate "the full scope of the tragic events that have taken place in the Jenin refugee camp." It also called on Israel to respect the 1949 Geneva Convention for protecting civilians in times of war, and called for "an international presence that could help provide better conditions on the ground."[26]

In the Council, however, those initial efforts to craft a tough resolution condemning Israel's actions collapsed. The United States immediately made clear it would veto any resolution with strong language or any enforcement clout. After days of squabbling, a weakened resolution was finally passed, at least supporting the secretary-general's initiative in sending a fact-finding team to Jenin. Israel had earlier denied entry to UN High Commissioner for Human Rights Mary Robinson, who had assembled a team to implement her Commission's decision to investigate the human rights aspects of the Israeli incursions into the West Bank. Along with Robinson, the high-profile team excluded by Israel included former Spanish Prime Minister Felipe Gonzalez and the former secretary-general of South Africa's African National Congress, Cyril Ramaphosa.

At first Israel announced it would accept a UN team to investigate the crisis in Jenin. Foreign Minister Shimon Peres told the UN secretary-general that Israel "has nothing to hide" and would welcome an investigation. But as soon as the Council actually voted to support the secretary-general's fact-finding team, Israeli opposition began. First came complaints about the composition of the team; it was to be led by Finnish president and experienced UN envoy Maarti Ahtissari, joined by Sadako Ogata, former UN High Commissioner for Refugees, and Cornelio

Sommaruga, former head of the International Committee of the Red Cross (ICRC). The team also included retired United States general William Nash, initially as a military adviser but raised to full participatory level at Israeli insistence, and leading Irish police official Peter Fitzgerald as police adviser. Next Israel wanted additional "anti-terrorism" experts to be added. Then Israel demanded the right to determine which Israeli witnesses would be allowed to testify, as well as guarantee ahead of time that any witnesses would be immune from war-crimes prosecution that could arise from their testimony. Ultimately Israel made clear that unless its demands were met, it would not allow the fact-finding team to enter the country at all.

Hanny Megally, executive director of the Middle East and North Africa division of Human Rights Watch, was very clear: "Suspects shouldn't be able to choose their investigators."[27] But Israeli rejectionism prevailed. And the United States provided Israel with protection in the Security Council, effectively preventing any Council action to hold Israel accountable, to impose some kind of sanction, or even to condemn the Israeli action. The Council issued only a mild statement of "regret" that the fact-finding team was not able to work. No blame apportioned, no condemnation. On May 2, the UN secretary-general officially disbanded his investigation team, whose members had been cooling their heels in Geneva waiting for Israeli authorization.

April 20, 2002

But despite the failure of the UN investigation, the slow process of internationalization of the Palestinian–Israeli conflict seemed to be under way. In the Middle East itself, Arab anger toward the Israeli occupation and US support for it was a longstanding reality. But the powerful street demonstrations spreading throughout the Arab world were for the first time in a generation giving internationally visible expression to that anger. The demonstrations also made clear that Washington's goal of using the Powell visit and Bush's speech to stabilize the region sufficiently for US-backed Arab regimes to safely endorse a future US military strike against Iraq without fearing domestic upheaval, had roundly failed.

And far beyond the Middle East, the demand for Israel to

end its occupation, and for the US to end its uncritical support for Israel's occupation, was emerging not only in the UN and other diplomatic centers, but at the very heart of the burgeoning global peace movement. Throughout the global south, the question of Palestine had from the beginning been a central feature of the growing movement against the US "war on terror." People across the world recognized US support for the Israeli occupation and its denial of Palestinian rights, as key links in US global strategy and in Washington's drive toward empire. The call to end the occupation was a centerpiece of anti-war mobilizations. Only in the US, and in a few parts of Europe, was there reluctance, sometimes even fear, to include the demand to end Israel's occupation as a necessary component of the peace and justice movements' call.

But still, on April 20, 2002, more than 100,000 Americans did something that, in the wake of the terrible aftermath of September 11, seemed very brave: they packed the Washington Mall, marching and chanting from the Washington Monument and the White House to the Capitol, and they filled the streets of San Francisco. Across the US, the intersection of the re-occupation crisis across the West Bank (especially Jenin) with the April 20 demonstration against the "war on terror," brought about, once and for all, the normalization of the Palestine issue at the heart of the peace movement.

In Washington the protesters gathered in four separate mobilizations, each focused on a different, though related, primary cause—the war in Afghanistan and the assault on Arabs and Muslims and broader civil liberties attacks within the US; the Israeli occupation of Palestine; the war in Colombia; and corporate-driven globalization and the destruction wrought by its institutional backers, the IMF and the World Bank (which were holding their annual meeting in Washington that same weekend). The plan was for each group to hold its own protest, and then march to join all the others at the main rally.

But what actually dominated the entire mobilization was opposition to the Israeli occupation of Palestine, and the demand to end US support for Israel's occupation, US backing of Ariel Sharon, and US funding of Israel's war machine.

One unforeseen result was perhaps an under-emphasis on the Afghanistan war and the devastation it was causing to the

Afghan population. But the significance of the demonstration lay in its integration, for the first time, of the issue of Palestine and the demand to end US support for the occupation into the broadest components of the peace and global justice movements. For the first time, the issue was not kept marginalized for fear of alienating supporters of Israel within those movements. For the first time, the call to end US support for Israeli occupation joined the call for a law-based, not war-based, response to the attacks on the World Trade Center.

Opposition in the Streets and in the Suites

Throughout the winter and into the spring of 2002 debate and dissension swirled across Washington policy circles and in the pages of major newspapers across the country and around the world. The war against Afghanistan was widely popular in Washington (the brave Barbara Lee of California was the only member of Congress to vote against its authorization), but government and other powerful circles were divided over Iraq. For months the elite debate raged in an unusually public way. The Colin Powell-led pragmatists in the State Department battled the neo-conservative cabal based in the vice president's office. The uniformed military brass disagreed with the Pentagon's civilian leadership. The White House overrode the State Department. The *Washington Post* emerged as a major cheerleader for war, while the *New York Times* urged caution.

There was little debate over the economic costs. The $48 billion addition to the Pentagon budget requested by the Bush administration in January 2002 by itself was more money than any other country spent on its military—and that was on top of the existing $379 billion military budget.[28] In US terms alone, it was by far the biggest defense increase since the Cold War.[29] Few in Washington raised questions.

But there was a debate among the powerful, largely over how and when, though not about whether, to go to war against Iraq. Much of it focused on the role of the United Nations. How much should the US rely on the UN arms inspections? How important would be UN authorization for war? But while the elite debate was narrow in its framework, it was hard-fought and bitter for its protagonists. The extremism of the Bush administration, visible from its first pre-September 11 months in office, had frightened centrists as well as the few official progressives in Washington, moderate Republicans as well as Democrats. They understood the stakes were high.

The fierceness of the battle, far beyond ordinary partisanship, was evident in the willingness of adherents on both sides to wage their battle in public, in the full glare of the major media. One effect, beyond showing the raw public divide among the Washington elite, was the opening of usually closed mainstream media outlets to alternative, progressive, critical voices. For months from early 2002 until perhaps late summer, voices of the US peace and justice activists and analysts were heard—if not frequently, at least not as rarely as usual, on mainstream US television and radio talk shows, quoted in mainstream US newspapers, participating in mainstream "town meetings" and debates.

Usually such voices are relegated to the alternative media. I had spent months of the post-September 11 period doing virtually constant media interviews—but the majority of them were for the international media and the growing US alternative and independent media. Those outlets—Pacifica Radio, the range of IndyMedia operations, Air America, journals such as the *Progressive* and the *Nation* remained crucial, providing background information and analysis to activists and anti-war partisans across the United States. Amy Goodman's extraordinary *Democracy Now!* radio show became a kind of national bulletin board and newsletter for those opposed to the rising war.

While some slighted the alternative press for "preaching to the converted," the stark reality was that the converted desperately needed the serious analysis necessary to back up their instinctive or spontaneous or emotional or spiritual or habitual position against the war, especially in their efforts to win new converts to an anti-war position. What is the real history of the relationship between the Taliban and US oil companies? What are the real US interests in Iraqi oil? How do we talk about Saddam Hussein's massive human rights violations? The depth of analysis was available almost exclusively within the independent media.

But the alternative media reached a limited—though growing—percentage of the American people. So it was particularly important when mainstream outlets opened up to voices against which they had long been closed. From early spring until late summer, then, the US press appeared to be quite a different phenomenon, coming close to (if never quite matching) the kind of "free press" people in many democratic countries take for granted, but which has rarely been a feature of US media. Instead of having access mostly to the alternative press, I was suddenly discussing Iraq policy with White House advisors on National Public Radio, being quoted in the *Washington Post*, and debating the neo-conservatives' own "Dark Prince," Richard Perle, on the prestigious Lehrer News Hour television show.

But that opening was not to last. By late summer, much of the elite debate was muffled. Administration critics were silenced, congressional opponents were suddenly subdued. A decision had been made. The press mostly retreated to its usual Washington talking heads, with critical voices largely locked out.

Into the Streets

Parallel to but on a separate trajectory from the elites' widely publicized but narrow criticism of the Iraq war, a huge peace movement saying a clear no to war in Iraq took shape. From early 2002 the movement was mobilizing not only to stop the Afghanistan war, but to prevent a war in Iraq. By the time the April 20 demonstration was over, Iraq had emerged as the dominant focus. The Bush administration pretended to take no notice, but activists from many different constituencies began the difficult work of developing ties with other governments standing defiant of the war, with key forces in the UN who were leading the international organization's opposition to war, and crucially, with their counterparts in the emerging global peace movement, throughout Europe and Canada and especially in the global South. In the US, work began aimed at identifying potential congressional critics and opponents of the war, to help strengthen both their arguments and their backbones.

Throughout the period of elite division and public criticism of the Iraq war, anti-war mobilization in the US took a wide variety of forms, including demonstrations and protests, teach-ins and other educational fora, and a wide range of campaigns to pressure members of Congress. Especially as the summer's critical opening narrowed what was emerging as an inevitable congressional vote to approve an increasingly inevitable war, the congressionally-focused advocacy work moved into a fever pitch.

The congressional hearings, under the auspices of the Senate Foreign Relations Committee, were as one-sided on the issue as the Bush White House, despite being controlled by the Senate's (then) Democratic Party majority. Officially, according to the State Department, the committee would examine four themes: the nature and urgency of the Iraqi threat to the region, the US, and its allies; appropriate responses and policies to meet the threat; regional considerations, including US interests and regional stability; and prospects for democracy in a post-Saddam Hussein Iraq. But the committee's Democratic leadership, working hand in glove with the congressional Republicans and with the full support of the White House, refused to allow any testimony from serious critics of the administration's war drive.

On the question of the "Iraqi threat," for instance, a key witness was Richard Butler, former head of the UN arms inspection agency in Iraq. He told the Senate committee that Iraq still maintained nuclear, chemical, and biological weapons, and said that Iraqi officials' claims that Iraq does not have such weapons are false. He did admit that the exact status of these weapons are unknown.[30]

Witnesses were limited to Iraqi expatriates, including some responsible for various frightening scenarios involving Iraq's alleged nuclear capacity, supporters of "regime change" from the usual assortment of right-wing and pro-military think tanks, and academics (including such notables as virulent supporter of regime change professor Fouad Ajami) known for their support of war. The tone was careful; the ideologically driven neo-cons of the White House were not participating. But the basic tenets at the core of the Bush administration's justifications for war remained unchallenged: Iraq represents a major threat (maybe to the US, maybe to our allies, maybe in the region...); the US has the right to respond to the "Iraq problem"; non-military solutions are not likely to work; the White House shouldn't go to war without asking Congress; it would be nice to get the world on our side but as long as Congress agrees the Bush administration can do pretty much whatever it wants.

Slightly dissenting voices came from cautious moderates, mainly from Democratic Party faithful, urging that more careful thought be given to issues of timing, efforts to find international support, etc. Interestingly, however, the main caution regarding civilian casualties came not from the Democratic Party, but from noted military analyst and former Pentagon official Anthony Cordesman, senior analyst of the Center for Strategic and International Studies and long a supporter of military solutions to most global problems. Cordesman acknowledged that "even with our precision weapons, we cannot guarantee that civilians will not be struck," and added that to be careless about this possible war would be a disaster. He didn't, however, argue against going to war.

No one challenged the notion that Iraq was still somehow a military threat to the US, despite being devastated from a dozen years of crippling economic sanctions and qualitatively disarmed by UN inspectors even before they left Iraq (at the White House's suggestion) in 1998. No one acknowledged that a US war to overthrow the Iraqi regime was likely to cause far more suffering, would cost hundreds of billions of dollars and would violate international law and make the US an outlaw state. No one questioned the "right" of the US government to launch a war against a nation that had not attacked us. No one testified directly, clearly, and unequivocally that the war was wrong and should be rejected. The late Senator Paul Wellstone, a member of the Committee (and known by his own description as representing the "democratic wing of the Democratic Party") attempted to place me, as a critical voice from the Institute for Policy Studies, on the witness list, but was rebuffed. At the end he was allowed only to enter my written testimony into the record, but it is highly unlikely that any of the senators actually read it.

But while the Senate hearings showed clear bipartisan support for the administration's main position, rarely had a political divide (however lopsided) been as bitter as in the run-up to the September vote to authorize Bush's planned invasion. The number of House and Senate members prepared to directly challenge the Bush war was never high enough to threaten a congressional endorsement. But for those who did stand against the war—about a quarter, eventually, of House and Senate members—the battle was hard-fought and politically brutal. But despite the attacks by congressional colleagues, screaming talk show hosts, and mainstream pundits, for those prepared to resist the war tide, popularity with constituents was high.

The popular mobilizations underway were of course one-sided, since supporters of Bush's war, confident of an overwhelming vote to endorse the coming invasion, felt no need to pressure Congress. And at the end of the day, the enormous, powerful campaign targeting Congress had its impact. Most people, from mainstream pundits to activist organizations, anticipated a level of congressional opposition only slightly higher than Congresswoman Barbara Lee's lone "no" vote on the Afghan war a year earlier. But the final vote to give up congressional oversight power to the Bush administration and allow them to go to war was very far from unanimous. When the resolution authorizing Bush to use "all necessary means" in Iraq finally came to the floor of the Congress, 133 members of Congress and 24 senators voted against the war. If all those whose districts were strongly against the war had actually voted as their constituents demanded, the anti-war vote would have been even stronger. But given the level of White House-driven media propaganda regarding Iraq's alleged weapons of mass destruction, links with al-Qaeda, and nuclear capacity (much of which had only just begun to be exposed as lies), and given the escalating pressure from both the administration and the Democratic congressional leadership, it was extraordinary that so many members of Congress said no.

The Global Justice Movement Joins the Anti-War Movement

As the administration ratcheted up its preparations, the war's opponents also moved into high gear. Over the summer, taking advantage of the openings provided by the divisions among Washington policymakers and the media, experienced anti-war organizations and new activists mobilized by outrage joined in discussions of strategy, tactics, ideas. One coalition alone listed thirteen separate national and international anti-war mobilizations in 2002 in their website's archive of past actions (see note for a round-up of these events).[31]

As school came back into session and student activists geared up their activities, the fall's demonstration calendar quickly took shape. First on the agenda was the annual meeting of the World

Bank and the International Monetary Fund (IMF) in Washington, DC, set for early September. This meeting, and the protests that inevitably confronted the Bank and IMF officials, was particularly important.

The global justice movement, which focused on the inequality and injustice perpetuated around the world by unfair trade, aid, and loan policies imposed by the US-dominated international financial institutions, was trying to recover from a year-long crisis stemming from September 11, and the cancellation of the major protest that had been planned for the following week. That movement's September 1999 protests in Seattle during the meeting of the World Trade Organization (WTO), despite disruption by police, had succeeded beyond anyone's expectations. The "battle of Seattle" had simultaneously mobilized the widest range of protesters ever (from the environmentalist "Turtles" to the job-focused Teamsters), and had had the strongest immediate impact in forcing a halt to Washington's efforts to expand the WTO's mandate and power. The Seattle mobilization reflected how the global justice movement was moving past its relatively small origins to consolidate its place as the key vector of mobilization against economic disempowerment throughout the world. Organizers had anticipated the largest, most diverse demonstration yet for their September 2001 protest.

So the return of the global justice movement to the US, in the fall of 2002, was eagerly watched around the world. For this sector of progressive activism, more than any other, had already created a global consciousness and an on-the-ground international reality that dwarfed that of other movements. It was also a movement whose primary raison d'etre, even with war in Iraq looming, remained a matter of utmost urgency. By the beginning of the year, global inequality—the income gap between rich and poor households—had skyrocketed. According to the BBC,

> the gap is so big that the richest 1 percent of people (50 million households), who have an average income of $24,000, earn more than the 60 percent of the households (2.7 billion people) at the bottom of the income distribution... The biggest source of inequality is the difference between the income of people in the five major economies (USA, Japan,

Germany, France and Britain) and the poor in rural India, China and Africa. ... In the five years of the study, world per capita real income increased by 5.7 percent. But all the gains went to the top 20 percent of the [global] income distribution, whose income was up 12 percent, while the income of the bottom 4 percent actually declined by 25 percent.[32]

Anyone in official Washington who wondered what possible connection there could be from their own vantage point between issues of global poverty and global justice, and the questions of terrorism, war, and security dominating the agendas of both policymakers and protesters, had only to look at the last part of the BBC article. "The huge gap between rich and poor—with 84 percent of the world receiving only 16 percent of its income—has become more worrying since the world has faced the threat of organized terror from groups based in some of the world's poorest countries," the BBC reported.

And the spread of global communications may make the income gap—with the richest 10 percent receiving 114 times the income of the poorest 10 percent—more difficult to maintain. However, with the world's richest countries on the verge of recession, there appears little hope that an ambitious development agenda will emerge from the most recent round of negotiations.

The global justice movement's early September 2002 demonstrations brought several thousand protesters, fewer than many hoped, to Washington for the annual IMF and World Bank meetings. The organizers of the Washington protest planned for a large and peaceful rally. Many of the demonstrators hoped they would be able to essentially paralyze Washington non-violently by clogging major streets in the downtown area near the Bank and the IMF headquarters. But instead the earliest gatherings of protesters on the street were met with a massive police presence. Washington, DC had mobilized not only its own police and other security agencies, but had called in reinforcements from surrounding cities, states, and various federal jurisdictions. The result was an overwhelming police domination of the streets. Huge numbers of people in the area—including many tourists, workers and shoppers in local businesses, journalists, as well as protesters, were cordoned off, caught in enormous police sweeps that surrounded whole blocks without giving people an opportunity to leave the area. By the end of the day, over 600 people had been arrested, and the protest message of global justice instead of global profits had been superceded first by fevered police accusations of protesters out of control and taking over the city, and later, when photographs and video of what really happened began to surface, charges of police brutality. (Two years later, protesters and others caught up in the sweeps would begin to collect large damage awards from the Washington, DC police and other agencies.)

From the beginning of the post-September 11 Afghanistan- and Iraq-focused peace movement, activists in the global justice arena took up the anti-war banner as their own. Globally, many of the national peace mobilizations were rooted in and organized by the groups for whom economic justice and fighting corporate domination had been the main point of unity. In the US that convergence between the global justice and anti-war movements was slower. While the September 2002 demonstrations against the World Bank and the IMF included lots of placards, banners, and chants against Bush's call for war, few traditional peace organizations had brought their activists and supporters into the streets.

Next in the fall calendar came the September 29 "Don't Bomb Iraq" anti-war events in Washington, which included a march to Vice President Dick Cheney's home. The demonstrators then made stops at several embassies either to protest those countries' support for Bush's call for war (Britain), or to thank them for statements against the war (South Africa, Egypt, Japan, Turkey). The second week of October brought a nationally coordinated series of local and state-wide protests across the country.

At the same time, planning went on for what would become the largest demonstration yet of the post-9/11 period and the largest peace protest since Vietnam, which brought over 100,000 protesters to Washington, DC on October 26. International ANSWER (Act Now to Stop War and End Racism), a group known for its ability to bring large numbers of protesters into the streets, was the primary organization mobilizing the march from the Vietnam Memorial on the Mall to the White House. Tens of thousands more marched in San Francisco. While ANSWER also had a reputation for excluding others from decision-making and for often setting the level of unity for their demonstrations so narrowly that relatively small percentages of potential participants would show up (such as their policy during the sanctions years of refusing to criticize Saddam Hussein's repression), this event was different. Along with a wide political range represented among the speakers, the crowd was diverse, including significant numbers of people of color, as well as the largely white "first time protester" sectors the US press continued to identify as evidence of a broader movement.

The *Washington Post* described how

> "Nebraskans for Peace" and "Hoosiers for Non-Violence" chanted alongside silver-coiffed retirees from Chicago and a Muslim student association from Michigan. Parents could be seen enjoying a sunny, picnic-perfect afternoon by pushing a stroller with one hand and carrying a "No War for Oil" sign with the other.[33]

Consolidating the Protests, Building a Movement

On the Friday before the October 26 demonstration, one group of activists arrived in Washington, DC with an agenda beyond marching in the Saturday protest. Called together by a collection of organizations and individuals who had worked together for years in peace and justice campaigns, the meeting was chaired by longtime anti-war organizer Leslie Cagan and Bill Fletcher, the president of TransAfrica, whose office hosted the gathering. These were groups with a long history of collaboration in the peace, solidarity, anti-apartheid, and global justice movements. They included the Institute for Policy Studies, TransAfrica, Global Exchange, Peace Action, the Middle East Research and Information Project (MERIP), the Quaker American Friends Service Committee, Black Voices for Peace, the American-Arab Anti-Discrimination Committee, Iraqi-Americans for Peaceful Alternatives, the National Council of Churches, New York City's Racial Justice 9/11, Business Leaders for Sensible Alternatives (led by Ben Cohen of Ben & Jerry's ice cream fame), Veterans for Peace, and dozens more peace, anti-racist, women's, environmental, and global justice organizations.

The goal was to unite the broadest anti-war coalition possible around a clear peace and justice platform. But just as the discussion began among the 120 or so organizers, the ubiquitous ring of cell phones began to travel around the room. The first few, grabbing their phones with apologetic murmurs and quickly heading for the back of the room, were soon joined by dozens more. Then the first finished their calls, returning ashen-faced to their seats, some barely holding back tears, whispering to their friends as the meeting threatened to collapse. News had just broken that the plane carrying Minnesota Senator Paul Wellstone, longtime champion of many in the peace movement, had been lost in a violent early-winter storm. Soon we would learn there were no survivors.

But the discussion was pulled back together. After a round-up discussion about the various anti-war events that had occurred already, as well as what was planned for the coming period, the group reached agreement on a new call, to form the United for Peace coalition. Soon the name would be changed to United for Peace and Justice (UFPJ), reflecting the early-on commitment to including a clear anti-racist, economic justice, and defense of civil liberties component, particularly in regard to the Arab and Muslim communities.

From the beginning, UFPJ defined its mission broadly, building opposition to the looming US war in Iraq but shaping that in the context of challenging the US policy of permanent warfare and empire-building. It was already clear that while some sectors of the Democratic Party, particularly in the Congressional Black Caucus and the Progressive Caucus, might disagree with some or even much of the Bush administration's strategy, this was ultimately not going to play out as a partisan issue. Some of the conservative leadership of the Democratic Party and even some "moderate" Republicans might chafe at some of the most extremist policies of the Bush White House, but the post-September 11 fear-dominated political culture in Washington insured that there would be little or no public opposition. There was simply too much pressure on, and too little backbone in, many of those potential critics among Washington's elite.

The creation of a people's movement that would pressure Congress as well as the Bush administration, but remain independent of Washington, was urgently needed. Throughout its first year, UFPJ operated through a set of working groups, each focused on a different element of the broadly defined peace and justice agenda: preventing the war in Iraq; fighting against the post-September 11 erosion of civil liberties, with a particular emphasis on defending immigrant communities and others specifically targeted; opposition to the Israeli occupation of Palestine; and joining the global justice movement to fight against the corporate-driven globalization that leads to so much impoverishment in the world.

From the original 70 or so organizations that came together to form the new coalition, UFPJ quickly grew to hundreds more members. They were diverse, including small grassroots committees organizing weekly anti-war vigils in front of the post office in small towns across the United States, and huge national organizations and networks with hundreds of thousands of their own members. By early 2005 there were more than 1,300 member organizations. UFPJ emerged as the centerpiece of the growing peace movement, within which a host of longstanding campaigns renewed their energy, and a plethora of new and creative mobilizations took shape.

There was Code Pink Women for Peace, visible from blocks away whenever they showed up in their trademark baby-blanket-pink to hot-magenta-pink outfits, and who took their name from the color-coded "threat alerts" that Washington's new Homeland Security Department instituted, to great public ridicule. They quickly became known for their ability to slip unnoticed into congressional hearings and official Washington soirees, only to strip off a top layer of clothes to reveal pink slogans, unfurl pink banners, remind viewers of civilian victims of the war, and for their willingness to chant at the top of their lungs until escorted out of the room.

Black Voices for Peace, begun in the immediate aftermath of September 11, would become the first national organization working specifically within the African-American community on peace issues. It quickly became a key component in UFPJ's and the broader peace movements' efforts to link peace and justice issues, and to integrate the historically segregated peace coalitions.

And Cities for Peace, initially the brainchild of Marc Raskin at the Institute for Policy Studies, soon reached hundreds of city officials, mayors, and city council members, and hundreds of thousands of active city residents, during the run-up to the Iraq war. The officials worked to pass city council resolutions against the war, and by the time of the February 15 mobilization just before the war, over 165 cities had said no to the Iraq war. They ranged from tiny progressive and student enclaves such as Berkeley; Madison, Wisconsin; Ann Arbor, Michigan; and Boulder, Colorado, to the biggest industrial cities of the country, including New York, Chicago, Los Angeles, Seattle, St Louis, Baltimore, Atlanta, Milwaukee, Cleveland, and more.

Other key constituent organizations included the newly formed US Labor Against the War, and its local off-shoot New York Labor Against the War. While small, USLAW demonstrated a vital change in the traditional reluctance of the US labor movement to challenge foreign policy, particularly foreign wars. Initially based in union locals, USLAW took a significant step forward when the national Service Employees International Union, or SEIU, the largest union in the United States, and later the AFL itself passed anti-war resolutions.

Links with the Iraqi and Iraqi-American communities were difficult, as those exile-based communities tended to be divided over support for the build-up to war in Iraq. Some, particularly among those Iraqis who still had family in Iraq and had spent years fighting against the repression of Saddam Hussein's regime, resented the absolutism of the anti-war opposition that refused to acknowledge the illegitimacy of the regime.

The UFPJ coalition focused much of its organizing work on education—providing to local and state-based groups the resources, information, and material to train organizers and to provide activists with the fundamental background necessary in building a broader peace movement. Production and distribution of speakers bureaus, films and videos, articles and talking points, teach-ins and background briefings, all remained part of its agenda. One national UFPJ teach-in, in May 2003, focused on war and empire and drew a standing-room-only crowd of over 2,000 people to Washington, DC to hear Arundhati Roy, Howard Zinn, Edward W. Said, and many others. Another set of simultaneous teach-ins, coordinated by UFPJ and put together by IPS in Washington, Global Exchange in San Francisco, and other UFPJ activists in Ann Arbor, was produced in March 2005 on the 40th anniversary of the first Vietnam-era anti-war teach-in, held at the University of Michigan in 1965.

But much of UFPJ's most visible work was in the streets, keeping up the pressure on the Bush administration to stop the war. Two days after the invasion of Iraq began, UFPJ brought more than 300,000 people into the streets of New York City to protest the war. Other major mobilizations included the October 25, 2003 national march and rally in Washington, DC against the occupation of Iraq, and the November 9, 2003, national day of action against Israel's apartheid wall, with events in 11 cities around the US coordinated jointly with the US Campaign to End Israeli Occupation.

That same fall, UFPJ helped coordinate—in an unprecedented coming together of the US anti-war and anti-corporate globalization movements—more than 60 demonstrations around the United States to protest what the US and its allies were doing in the World Trade Organization meeting in Cancún, Mexico. The September demonstrations also expressed solidarity and support for the efforts of the Brazil- and India-led Group of 20, which stood defiant against the wealthy countries' efforts to impose new trade regulations. And continuing its work linking opposition to war and empire with the global economic justice agenda, UFPJ played a major role in the November 18–20, 2003, mobilizations in Miami against creation of the NAFTA-inspired Free Trade Area of the Americas.

One year after the war began, UFPJ initiated the call to action for a global day of protest on March 20, 2004. More than 3 million people worldwide took to the streets that day, holding over 575 protests in more than 60 countries. In cities across Spain, hundreds of thousands joined rallies against the war only days after the horrific bombings of the Madrid subway system. The crowds celebrated the election of a brand-new government committed to bringing Spanish troops home from Iraq. In Italy, over a million protesters thronged the streets of Rome, where tens of thousands of rainbow "PACE" (peace) flags flew surrounding the ancient Coliseum.

At the end of that summer, the Republican Party came to New York for their convention, to anoint the Bush–Cheney ticket as official standard-bearers for the November elections. The UFPJ-coordinated New York protests were huge, and it was particularly significant that the US election process had become very much a global issue. "The World Says No to

Bush!" resonated around the world as the peace and justice movements filled the streets of their own capitols. The subjects of the empire were casting the only vote they could.

And in March 2005, on the second anniversary of the start of war, UFPJ coordinated local and regional protests in all 50 states. The effort was a powerful success, with demonstrations, teach-ins, vigils, rallies, sit-ins, and other anti-war actions in more than 750 cities across the United States. While the national press largely ignored the actions, or in some cases dismissed them as failures because of the lack of a single huge mobilization in New York or Washington or San Francisco, across the country the grounding of the anti-war movement into the very fabric of mainstream US society was becoming evident. Polls bore that out—by the time of the March 2005 protests, over 58 percent of Americans believed that the war had been wrong from the beginning. And by May 25, 2005, 128 members of Congress voted to begin the process of bringing the troops home.

The Movement Online

Throughout this period, new internet-based lobby and advocacy campaigns emerged, led by MoveOn, a small group of liberal activists whose messages mobilized hundreds of thousands of supporters to sign online petitions, send email letters to members of Congress demanding that they refuse to endorse Bush's war, and send commensurate amounts of donations to pay for newspaper and television ads. Experienced Washington campaigners knew that emails, precisely because they are so easy to send and re-send, have the lowest impact level of any forms of congressional pressure (visits, letters, petitions, etc.). But somehow the enormous numbers of online messages rendered that conventional wisdom irrelevant.

The approach of MoveOn, and other similar but smaller campaigns, was to keep the message simple and non-challenging, ostensibly to avoid alienating "mainstream" voters. According to founder Eli Pariser, MoveOn's constituency "are not longtime activists who are being reactivated." Things like signing online petitions and fundraising for anti-war ads, he said, "provide them with a safe first step."[34] Clearly, anti-war activism was reaching broadly into mainstream America—and the easy tasks led to MoveOn claiming 350,000 new members in the six-month period beginning with the congressional hearings of August 2002. That translated to a huge, if politically cautious, mobilization of cyber-activists.

During the period leading up to the congressional hearings on war in Iraq, mainly through the late spring and summer of 2002, the new breadth of the movement, particularly its online component, brought about unprecedented pressure on members of Congress. The beleaguered staffs of some anti-war congresspeople called activist organizations, urging them to call off their email and phone campaigns, sometimes reminding them that their member was already against the war and they should focus their energy somewhere more urgent. Many also begged for a respite from literally tens of thousands of messages, overwhelmingly calling for a "no" vote on war in Iraq.

Though Congress did vote for the war, still the refusal of Congress to entirely give in to Bush's pressure represented a much-needed victory for the developing peace movement. Congress members across the political spectrum spoke openly of the overwhelming numbers of messages, personal visits, letters and emails, petitions, and other forms of pressure they had received urging them to oppose the war. But winning more votes against an ultimately victorious war resolution was not enough. The focus on Congress had been appropriate for that period, but it did not provide the comprehensive strategic framework the US movement still needed.

Mainstreaming the Movement
The relationship between recognizing the breadth of anti-war sentiment within "mainstream" public opinion in the US and the efforts of the peace movement to sharpen the movement's message and demands was often contentious. There was a tendency within key sectors of the movement to emphasize the importance of winning broader and broader sectors of US society to some version of an "anti-war" or "peace" position, without worrying too much about the details of the message itself. That meant, for example, that linking the anti-war argument to the fear that war in Iraq would undermine Bush's so-called war on terror was a perfectly sufficient approach. Among those sectors there was little discussion about why an anti-war movement, albeit a movement

focused primarily on the looming war in Iraq, should support as legitimate the "war on terrorism." There was also little debate over who constituted the new "mainstream" components of the anti-war forces, elements already beginning to be noticed by the mass media: it was the participation of white and middle-class sectors that provided the significant new and important reasons the movement was being taken seriously.

But this definition of "mainstream" carried its own limitations and created its own problems. The people in the US most immediately and directly affected by the "war on terror" and by the coming Iraq war were mostly not white and not middle class. They were Muslims and other immigrants, caught up in the nightmarish consequences of the Patriot Act and other attacks on civil liberties; they were Arabs, Arab-Americans, and South Asians, targeted on the streets by racist thugs and in the courts and the jails by a newly overt race-based system of repression and control; they were poor and working-class youth, disproportionately people of color, for whom the cutbacks in educational funds and employment opportunities meant the "poverty draft" pushed them into the military almost as inexorably as the legal draft did a generation before. Those communities—Muslims, Arabs, immigrants, working-class youth—had never been strongly represented within the traditionally defined peace movement. Yet their participation this time around, however critical, was not defined by the mainstream press or by some key activist organizations as representing the critical "mainstreaming" of the movement.

Writing in the *Middle East Report* in the spring of 2003, analysts noted that

> the mainstreaming of anti-war dissent, as it has been understood, runs the risk of reproducing the racial, class, and cultural divides that historically have been the bane of American social movements. The breadth of anti-war sentiment helped force the major media to correct its notoriously bungled coverage of the first mass protests, and it is clear that the mainstreaming of the peace movement gave permission even to sympathetic reporters to treat dissent respectfully. But when reporters quote high-school Spanish teachers from Rice Lake, Wisconsin and mid-level insurance executives from Hartford, Connecticut as evidence that anti-war marchers are "not your parents' protesters," it is equally

clear to an American reader that "mainstream" is coded as middle-class and white. Several press reports on the January 18 demonstration in Washington explicitly mentioned the presence of three khaki-clad suburbanites bearing a placard identifying themselves as "Mainstream White Guys for Peace" as proof positive of the mainstreaming thesis.[35]

One of the other organizations that reflected that popular view of "mainstream" was called Win Without War, a title which itself reflected the ambiguity of their position. This group, initiated by activists who had defended a new version of "smart" economic sanctions in Iraq as an acceptable substitute for war (despite acknowledging that economic sanctions had been responsible for the deaths of hundreds of thousands of Iraqis) was quickly taken up by a number of internationally known artists. Some of them expressed their own concerns regarding the failure of the organization's founders to adequately criticize the kind of brutal economic sanctions that had led to so many deaths in Iraq throughout the 1990s, but the call for "winning" against Iraq without actually going to war proved popular. The organization played an important role in bringing an anti-war message, particularly through a variety of creative newspaper ads and media appearances by well-known Hollywood figures, to a wide sector of Americans who would otherwise perhaps never have heard an anti-war position voiced by anyone with whom they could identify. But Win Without War was hesitant to join organizations or coalitions whose members might include forces to their left, fearing it would alienate their perceived base.

Here again was the operative assumption that the crucial constituency to be reached was largely middle class, cautious, and being exposed to anti-war ideas for the first time, as opposed to poorer communities, largely people of color, and other sectors of the population who might have long been opposed to this and other wars but had never been urged into active resistance. Win Without War certainly played an important role in the broadly defined campaigning in the run-up to the invasion of Iraq. Once the invasion took place, however, its role and identity lost crucial focus.

Within other sectors of the movement, however, longer term goals remained central. Many were concerned about broadening the traditionally white peace movement to those communities of color that had traditionally opposed US foreign interventions in far greater numbers, but who were not always organized or very visible within the identifiable anti-war movements. Anti-racist organizations, especially in New York and other major cities, took the lead, joined by longtime organizers whose political activism encompassed a "peace and justice" framework. In a letter to their counterparts in the movement, these activists urged a renewed commitment to broadening the predominantly white peace movement to include far more representation of people of color, and a rethinking of the whole definition of "mainstream" that had for so long undermined national anti-war organizing in the US. One of the signers of that letter, Hany Khalil, who later became the national outreach coordinator for UFPJ, described the "intense discussions and negotiations" involved in UFPJ's efforts to respond to the needs of and, even more importantly, to mobilize the enormous anti-war potential within communities of color. The result, according to Khalil was "great strides" in UFPJ's work.[36]

The goal was not acquiescence to some sort of politically correct demand. Rather, the articulation of a clear commitment to an anti-racist agenda and mobilization strategy was understood to be critical for building a strong anti-war movement. It had long been recognized, but far too rarely acted on, that spontaneous anti-war sentiment in the US was much higher in communities of color, most especially in the African-American community, than in predominantly white communities. It was not hard to understand why. Beyond a generally more progressive political framework, the costs of war, both human and economic, exact a higher price in poor communities, disproportionately for people of color. So real integration of the anti-war mobilization—reaching far beyond the usual effort to include people of color among the speakers—was a vital task for the emerging national peace movement.

Military Resistance
But the problem of how to define and deal strategically with the "mainstreaming" of the movement was not only a question of race. Throughout 2002, even before the US invasion of Iraq was launched, a new sector of the peace movement began to take

shape. This was made up of families of military servicepeople, who challenged the legitimacy of the war build-up with a personal credibility unmatched by the rest of the movement. With the help of some longtime organizers whose loved ones were on active duty, they cohered as Military Families Speak Out (MFSO). The impact on the movement was almost instantaneous. In one moment the movement as a whole could no longer be sidelined as "outside of the mainstream" or accused of "not supporting the troops." In fact, MFSO took that pro-war slogan as their own, transforming it into the far more precise "Support the troops—Bring them home!"

The emergence of MFSO also made possible a broader analysis of how the war fit into the "national security" and "national interests" of the US. That is, by focusing on how the US troops in the field were themselves victims of the war, it demonstrated how the illegal war was being waged in the interests of only a small group of economically and politically powerful Americans. It was not serving to protect Americans at home. From the beginning, MFSO worked closely with September 11 Families for Peaceful Tomorrows, the two organizations sharing the particular credibility that derives from being the loved ones of those made victims or at risk from US policies.

The threat to active-duty servicepeople for criticizing the war openly was very high, with the possibility of harassment and assignment to especially dangerous duties by angry superiors, and the potential of legal consequences, up to and including expulsion from the service, court-martials, or other criminal proceedings. While most of the criticism came from lower-ranking troops, those most directly affected by the war strategy's failures, service people in the highest ranks were not immune. Even before the war began, when top army General Erik Shinseki stated, in direct contradiction to official Bush administration claims, that occupying Iraq would require several hundred thousand US troops, he was harshly criticized, sidelined, and soon resigned. In another example, in the spring of 2005, a three-star general was summarily dismissed, lost one star, and was denied any sort of hearing—apparently because of his criticism of the Iraq war. According to the *Baltimore Sun*, three-star General John Riggs was told by senior Army officials that he would be retired at a reduced rank, losing one of his stars because of infractions considered so minor that they were not placed in his official record. He was given 24 hours to leave the Army.... His Pentagon superiors said he allowed outside contractors to perform work they were not supposed to do, creating 'an adverse command climate.' But some of the general's supporters believe the motivation behind his demotion was politics. Riggs was blunt and outspoken on a number of issues and publicly contradicted Defense Secretary Donald H. Rumsfeld by arguing that the Army was overstretched in Iraq and Afghanistan and needed more troops. 'They all went [crazy] when that happened,' recalled retired Army Lt. Gen. Jay M. Garner, a one-time Pentagon adviser who ran reconstruction efforts in Iraq in the spring of 2003. 'The military part of [the defense secretary's office] has been politicized. If [officers] disagree, they are ostracized and their reputations are ruined.'[37]

The cashiering of General Riggs, like the sidelining of General Shinseki, confirmed the danger to any active-duty military officials who dared criticize US policy. So the role of the military families became particularly important. But as the months passed, despite the risk, some of the troops themselves began to take on a more public role. In many cases, this was the result of growing scandals regarding the lack of protective gear for troops in the field, the Pentagon's efforts to hide the numbers and severity of US casualties, and increasingly, the sense that the top military and political officials trumpeting the war's virtues cared little about the troops actually fighting it. That view was later exacerbated with Secretary of Defense Rumsfeld's infamously callous remark in early 2004. Asked by a US soldier at a Kuwait staging area waiting for deployment to Iraq, "Why do we soldiers have to dig through local landfills for pieces of scrap metal and compromised ballistic glass to up-armor our vehicles?" Rumsfeld responded breezily that "you go to war with the army you have, not the army you wish you had."[38] The questioner, Army Specialist Thomas Wilson of the 278th Regimental Combat Team of the Tennessee National, became a national hero. The anger among troops and their families at home grew even more intense.

Abu Ghraib

The level of anger and nascent resistance escalated within the military and among families with the early 2004 disclosure of what would soon become known as the Abu Ghraib torture scandal. The scandal first broke in the US press after an appalled soldier turned over photos circulating on the internet of what had clearly been a pattern of physical, sexual, and emotional abuse and torture of Iraqis and Afghans, both military and civilian, by US guards. The abuse was being perpetrated at US-run prison and detention facilities in countries and territories illegally occupied by the United States, from Guantánamo Bay, Cuba, to Afghanistan and Iraq.

The extent of the abuse and the torture did not become known right away. It started in Guantánamo, where prisoners were brought who were sometimes captured in battles with the Taliban in Afghanistan, but more often snatched from the street or from home in Pakistan or from mountaintop villages across the Hindu Kush. They were held for months or years, under terms set by the Bush administration, which announced that Taliban or al-Qaeda detainees would not be considered prisoners of war but rather "illegal combatants." That meant that they would not be provided with the protections guaranteed to POWs by the Geneva Conventions, and despite the requirements of international law, they would not even be granted a hearing to determine what their legal status would be. While top-level Bush cabinet members claimed that the Guantánamo prisoners would be treated "humanely," the effect of officially stripping the prisoners of their POW status was to tell the guards, interrogators, and military officials that they could use whatever kind of abusive treatment—up to and including torture—that they wished, with no fear of accountability.

Only later, when the Abu Ghraib photos were revealed, did it become clear that the official White House position regarding mistreatment of prisoners in the so-called war on terror had expanded from Guantánamo Bay to prisons across Iraq and Afghanistan and to a network of secret US-controlled detention facilities scattered across the world. By May 2005, Amnesty International would issue their most serious condemnation of US violations of human rights, labeling the network of US prisons around the world an American "gulag." After Bush called the Amnesty report "absurd" and Rumsfeld called it "reprehensible," Amnesty's international Secretary-General Irene Zubaida Khan noted:

> The administration's response has been that our report is absurd, that our allegations have no basis, and our answer is very simple: if that is so, open up these detention centers, allow us and others to visit them... What we wanted to do was to send a strong message that... this sort of network of detention centers that has been created as part of this war on terrorism is actually undermining human rights in a dramatic way which can only evoke some of the worst features of human rights scandals of the past.[39]

Along with Washington's global network of secret prisons, the White House-sanctioned Pentagon practice of "extraordinary rendition" was also largely hidden. This was a stratagem designed to take advantage of the practice of many countries— mostly close US government allies—who were known for carrying out overtly the kind of torture that US officials were afraid might be discovered if they did it themselves. The Pentagon, when faced with prisoners they deemed unwilling to talk or perhaps who simply did not have the information US military interrogators sought, would thus send these prisoners, "rendering" them in Pentagon-speak, to Egypt, Uzbekistan, Syria, or other countries known for their regular practice of torture as a normal part of interrogation.

One of the most egregious known cases involved a Canadian citizen, Maher Arar. A 34-year-old engineer with two young children, Arar was arrested by US agents in New York on September 26, 2002, while changing planes on his way home to Canada. He was held incommunicado by US officials for thirteen days, then flown to Jordan and handed over to Syrian intelligence agents. Transferred to Syria, he was held in a tiny cell for ten months, and beaten with metal cables. Eventually, Syria released him. Bush administration officials refused to cooperate with a Canadian governmental investigation and cited a "state secrets privilege" to defend against Arar's lawsuit in New York. Administration sources told the *New York Times* that his name was on a "watch list," but they found no evidence to justify holding him. Nonetheless, "they decided it would be irresponsible to let him go home to Canada.... With insufficient evidence to hold Mr. Arar, one way to have him interrogated was to deport him to Syria."[40]

Why was Arar on the watch list to begin with? US and Canadian officials cited his links with others in Ottawa's 40,000-strong Muslim community, in a city with only one central mosque. According to Arar, he met one person under official suspicion, Ahmad El-Maati, while waiting to get his car repaired. Some time later, El-Maati was detained in Syria where, under torture, he falsely confessed to a non-existent plot to destroy the Canadian Parliament, and identified Arar as an acquaintance. He was later released from Syrian prison. Arar's other "connection" was with Abdullah Almalki, who was also later arrested and tortured in Syria. In that instance, Arar was arranging a discount on ink cartridge purchases. Both Almalki and El-Maati are living in Canada, facing no charges. According to Representative Edward J. Markey, the Democratic congressman from Massachusetts, the real reason "the US sent Mr. Arar to Syria and not Canada is that Syria tortures people and Canada doesn't."[41]

Aside from the clear violation of international and US domestic laws inherent in sending detainees to a country where they would invariably face torture, there was a particular irony in that though most of the cooperating countries were close allies of the US, their illegal practices of torture had been analyzed and exposed in the annual country reports of the US State Department. The practice made a further mockery of international (as well as US domestic) law through its reliance on those governments—Uzbekistan was especially egregious here—whose close relationship with Washington was rooted in the post-September 11 Bush administration crusade to recruit strategic (read: oil-rich or well positioned for military bases) countries for assistance in the "war on terror." The new relationship would be cemented by Washington not only offering money, but granting a kind of international impunity for some of the world's worst human rights-violating governments, in return for access to oil, base rights, or the work of experienced and accomplished torturers.

In its defense of ordinarily shocking practices, the Bush administration counted on a combination of fear and the same kind of collective demonization that had made it possible for the US government to get away with imposing economic sanctions in Iraq that were responsible for killing hundreds of thousands of Iraqis, particularly children and vulnerable elders, from 1990 to 2003. During that period, Washington's then-ambassador to the UN, Madeleine Albright, memorably announced, in reference to the sanctions-caused deaths of 500,000 Iraqi children, that "we think the price is worth it."

By simply asserting that every detainee brought to Guantánamo from Afghanistan or neighboring countries was obviously an enemy Taliban soldier or a disciple of Osama bin Laden out to slaughter Americans, without having to provide any evidence to anyone of who the prisoners actually were, what they were doing in Afghanistan or Pakistan or the Philippines, or the circumstances under which they were captured, the Bush administration played to that same set of racist prejudices that had shaped US policy in Iraq for a decade, exacerbated by the post-September 11 blanket of fear that continued to smother the country. And given that rising level of fear across US society and after so many years of dehumanization of Iraqis and Muslims, it was not surprising that ordinary American soldiers would be affected as well. As a result, it was also not surprising that the young and often inexperienced soldiers assigned to guard Afghan or Iraqi prisoners would find the criminally sadistic abuse in the prisons acceptable behavior, especially when applauded and urged on by military intelligence operatives.

Once the Abu Ghraib photographs became public, in early 2004, the broader issue of mistreatment and torture of prisoners became key components in the growing disenchantment among military personnel themselves. That spring Bush himself created a new level of outrage when, on the first anniversary of his infamous May 1, 2003 "mission accomplished" speech, he ignored the growing torture scandal and claimed that "one year later, despite many challenges, life for the Iraqi people is a world away from the cruelty and corruption of Saddam's regime. At the most basic level of justice, people are no longer disappearing into political prisons, torture chambers...."[42] Given the then-new revelations of exactly that, it was a lie of breathtaking audacity. But it wasn't the last. In his 2005 State of the Union address, Bush went even further. Ignoring the recent round of publicity exposing the US policy of "extraordinary rendition" of detainees to expert torturers in countries such as Egypt and Uzbekistan, he declared: "Torture is never acceptable, nor do we hand over people to countries that do torture."

Over time outraged responses to torture increased within the military. By mid-2005, when accounts of torture by US military personnel had become commonplace, a new report focusing on the role of military medical professionals complicit in torture brought a renewed level of outrage. One response came from Burton J. Lee III, a former Army Medical Corps doctor and later the personal White House physician for Bush senior. He began by recounting his military and White House history, noting that

> I might be expected to bring a skeptical and partisan perspective to allegations of torture and abuse by US forces. I might even be expected to join those who, on the one hand, deny that US personnel have engaged in systematic use of torture while, on the other, claiming that such abuse is justified.

But, he went on, "It's precisely because of my devotion to [my] country, respect for our military and commitment to the ethics of the medical profession that I speak out against systematic, government-sanctioned torture and excessive abuse of prisoners during our war on terrorism."[43]

What was perhaps even more remarkable was that Lee, a high-ranking veteran and strong supporter of the military, went on to lament how

> our government and the military have slipped into Joseph Conrad's *Heart of Darkness*. The widespread reports of torture and ill-treatment—frequently based on military and government documents—defy the claim that this abusive behavior is limited to a few noncommissioned officers at Abu Ghraib or isolated incidents at Guantánamo Bay. When it comes to torture, the military's traditional leadership and discipline have been severely compromised up and down the chain of command.

But responsibility for the torture stalled at the lowest ranks, and the lack of accountability of higher ranking military forces remained a serious problem. The widespread publicity of the Abu Ghraib photographs and the resulting international scandal forced the Pentagon to initiate various investigations of the abuse of prisoners. But the investigations were sorely limited—examining only lower ranking soldiers, focusing largely on the publicly exposed incidents from Abu Ghraib, excluding how top-level announcements regarding the inapplicability of the Geneva Conventions and related claims had spread to other prisons, and crucially, excluding the accountability of the highest levels of authority. That accountability should have been investigated up the chain of command up to and including Secretary of Defense Rumsfeld, as well as Bush himself as the commander in chief of the US military. Both knew or should have known that their public pronouncements regarding the non-POW status and non-applicability of the Geneva Conventions to the prisoners would inevitably lead to widespread abuses by lower ranking military personnel.

The torture issue created a difficult challenge for the growing anti-war forces in and around the military. There was clarity in the understanding that the top of the military hierarchy bore primary responsibility for creating the climate leading directly to the abuse. It was clear that the troops' lack of specific training in exactly what the Geneva Conventions require represented a further indictment of the military's failure to take international law seriously. But most recognized that it does not take detailed familiarity with the intricacies of the Geneva Conventions to know that sexual humiliation and torture are never acceptable. As a result, while everyone agreed on the fundamental complicity of top Bush administration and military officials, questions remained whether the lower ranking soldiers, those who actually carried out the torture and abuse at Abu Ghraib and elsewhere, should themselves be held accountable for their actions when their superior officers were treated with absolute impunity. For many in the anti-war movement, the solution was a call for accountability—including criminal liability—for "Bush and Rumsfeld First."[44]

Conscientious Objectors

For some of the growing number of war opponents within the military, the torture scandal was just the last strand in a web of outrages that led to decisions to apply for conscientious objector status, and refusal to participate in the war while their CO applications were pending. For others, in at least four public cases, anti-war opposition meant leaving the service altogether, including decisions to travel clandestinely to Canada and to seek political asylum there.

In Canada, peace forces quickly began to mobilize to support the new generation of resisters. Calling for a return to Canada's Vietnam-era role as the protector of huge numbers of US draft and military resisters throughout the 1960s and 1970s, Canadian activists urged Parliament to reverse post-Vietnam immigration laws that tightly restricted Canada's asylum policies. The first of the asylum hearing rulings, in March 2005, denied asylum to former soldier Jeremy Hinzman, but Canadian activists and parliamentarians continued what was anticipated to be a long-term effort to put Canada back on the side of opposing war.

In his December 2004 hearing, Hinzman argued the US war in Iraq was criminal, and that if he killed or injured anyone in Iraq, he would be guilty of war crimes because the conflict was illegal. The ruling, reflecting the political shift in Canadian law and politics since the Vietnam war, claimed that extradition to the US "would not subject [the Hinzman family] personally to a risk to their lives or to a risk of cruel and unusual treatment or punishment" because, the judge found, "Hinzman has brought forward no evidence to support his allegation that he would not be accorded the full protection of the law pursuant to the court-martial process."[45] In fact, Hinzman's entire case was not based whether or not he would have access to a court-martial, but on the claim that the US war in Iraq was illegal. After the Canadian government intervened directly in his case, the hearing judge ruled that the entire issue was irrelevant to his case.

Though Hinzman didn't get the ruling he'd hoped for, still he felt that his case, with the testimony of former Marine Staff Sergeant Jimmy Massey, had made an impression on Canadians: "It was very powerful," Hinzman told Amy Goodman. "You could hear a pin drop in the room when he [Massey] was giving his accounts of what happened." Hinzman, part of a growing number of soldiers leaving the ranks of US forces, articulated for *Democracy Now!* listeners why he had decided not to go to Iraq:

Every justification or rationale that we have ever offered for going to Iraq has been bogus. There were no weapons of mass destruction there. There have been no links established between Saddam and international terrorists, and then the notion that we're going to bring democracy to Iraq is—we'll see if that comes to fruition, but I don't think we'll see it, unless it's convenient to America's agenda. So anyway, I felt that we had attacked Iraq without any defensive basis, and I think it's been well established at Nuremburg that in those instances, you cannot simply just say that you're following orders, but you have a duty and obligation to disobey.[46]

As the war in Afghanistan proceeded and the war in Iraq began, and as soldiers started to rotate home (often to prepare for a second or even third deployment to Iraq or Afghanistan), another military organization emerged, Iraq Veterans Against the War. Taking its name and its mission from its predecessor of an earlier generation, Vietnam Veterans Against the War, IVAW captured the intensity of opposition within the ranks of the US military itself. While the organization was not launched publicly until July 2004, during the Veterans for Peace annual conference, it clearly reflected an already high level of resistance within the military. While some spoke of parallels to the GI resistance during the Vietnam war, in this case, opposition sentiments and soon an actual organization emerged at a far earlier stage in the war's progress.

Another difference between the Vietnam and Iraq wars was the anger generated by the indifferent attitude of the Pentagon brass and the White House toward the needs of US troops; the IVAW was committed to addressing this problem. Beyond the inadequate medical care for returning soldiers, insufficient body and vehicle armor on the front lines caused anger within the military. That had to do with the massive deployment of reserve and National Guard troops, whose ostensible mission was to protect the US at home, to long and all-too-frequent tours in Afghanistan and Iraq. And further, implementation of the so-called Stop-Loss laws, which allow the Pentagon to keep active duty personnel in the military even after their legal contracts have expired, continued to infuriate servicepeople and their families across the political spectrum.

In recognition of the multiplicity of reasons for which servicepeople and veterans might come to oppose the war, the

Iraq Veterans Against the War mission statement includes a range of goals, to bring the troops home, to support the reconstruction of Iraq, and to support the US troops and veterans:

> Iraq Veterans Against the War (IVAW) is a group of veterans who have served since September 11th, 2001 including Operation Enduring Freedom and Operation Iraqi Freedom. We are committed to saving lives and ending the violence in Iraq by an immediate withdrawal of all occupying forces. We also believe that the governments that sponsored these wars are indebted to the men and women who were forced to fight them and must give their Soldiers, Marines, Sailors, and Airmen the benefits that are owed to them upon their return home.[47]

Inevitably, as US military casualties (which still only amounted to slightly more than 1 percent of the number of Iraqi civilian casualties) mounted, members of growing numbers of MFSO families faced the loss of their loved ones, killed in Afghanistan or Iraq. In response, a few families came together to form the somber organization, Gold Star Families for Peace (GSFP), in reference to the "gold star" designation the Pentagon awards to families of those killed in war. Started originally as a sub-group within Military Families Speak Out, the Gold Star Families for Peace soon became an independent organization. They identified their goals as bringing an end to the occupation of Iraq, and providing a support group for Gold Star Families. It was a reflection of the time of their origin that they spoke specifically of the "occupation" of Iraq, rather than the war or invasion.

But GSFP went further. In the words of founder Cindy Sheehan, whose son died in Iraq, the members of the organization "demand that George W. Bush honors our family's sacrifices by admitting to the 'mistakes and miscalculations' (*Washington Post*, 17 January 2005) of this invasion and occupation of Iraq by ending the occupation immediately and bringing our troops home now. This is not a request and it is not negotiable."

Then, referring to the Downing Street memo, the leaked documents confirming that British leader Tony Blair had agreed to join Bush's Iraq war many months before either government acknowledged its intention, the GSFP went on:

We individually, and as a group, are dismayed and broken-hearted anew as the memo from Great Britain dated 23 July 2002 has recently surfaced. This invasion and occupation of a sovereign country was prefabricated and has resulted in the deaths of tens of thousands of human beings, has destroyed the lives of millions, and demolished a country that was no threat to the USA. In addition to withdrawal of the troops, we call for the immediate resignation of George Bush, Dick Cheney, and the entire Cabinet. [They must be] held accountable to the laws of our land and for damaging humanity so thoroughly.[48]

The Movement Goes Global

Around the world, many people agreed with Cindy Sheehan. And from the beginning of the US peace mobilizations challenging the looming Iraq war, the US movement identified itself as part of the emerging global peace movement. That international people's movement, rooted equally in the traditional peace forces and the newer, often younger global justice campaigners, had already outstripped the efforts of its US counterparts from the first moments of Bush's crusade for war in Iraq. In the US it was primarily the UFPJ coalition, the largest and broadest of the anti-war forces, that developed strategic ties with key international activists and became recognized as the central US component of the global movement.

It was particularly notable that in key countries whose governments were, at least temporarily, standing defiant of the US war—including France, Germany, Brazil, the Philippines, and many other countries—the self-defined anti-war movements were made up of largely the same constituents as the anti-corporate globalization or global justice movements. Their understanding of the economic basis key to Bush's oil and empire drive, and their demands for a more equitable, just, and sustainable global order, even while pressing the need for peace, provided a key framework for global mobilization. But the immediate demands of the international movement, and soon the global agenda of resistance, were set first by events most clearly visible in New York, at the headquarters of the United Nations.

Within days of Congress concluding its narrowly defined hearings into the Iraq war, Bush announced his intention to go to New York to address the General Assembly. His real goal was to threaten the United Nations with US-imposed "irrelevance" if they did not get on board his war train by granting a UN imprimatur of legitimacy to what would otherwise be recognized as a unilateral war.

Pressure began immediately at UN headquarters, as the US mission to the UN and the State Department sent their minions, mimicking what the first Bush had done in 1990 in the run-up to another war against Iraq. The son's operatives had the same arsenal of bribes, threats, and punishments to force recalcitrant countries to support the war. But this time it wasn't so easy. A decade earlier the US moves toward war against Iraq were justified, however hypocritically, by Iraq's occupation of Kuwait. Officially, at least, UN member states claimed they believed the US war was supposed to end an occupation acknowledged as illegal by virtually every UN member, and many governments were reluctant to openly challenge Washington's claimed intention to reverse the illegal occupation.

More important than the false justification in 1990, however, was the timing. The Iraq crisis had emerged simultaneously with, and in important ways linked to, the collapse of the Soviet Union, the end of the Cold War, and the emergence of a host of often-competing micro-nationalisms that all clamored for both public and official attention. The post-Cold War era had not yet begun, Cold War rivalries remained, and while there was widespread international opposition to the US war plans (stronger of course at the popular than governmental level), Washington's allies, junior partners, and dependents all hesitated to cross their patron. Also, the US moves at the UN were largely invisible in the international press and on the global stage, so the US could offer irresistible bribes (cheap Kuwaiti oil and new arms deals for poor countries on the Council, diplomatic rehabilitation and a resumption of long-term development aid for China) and mete out harsh punishments (cutting all US aid to Yemen after its "no" vote) largely without domestic or global consequence.

But a decade later, instead of a Cold War-era Security Council scenario, with a compliant Britain and France, a collapsing Soviet Union, an isolated China, and a host of weak and impoverished Southern countries among the ten non-permanent Council members, George W. Bush faced an entirely different scene. Of the Council's five permanent members only Britain, led by Tony Blair (whom the British press unaffectionately dubbed "Bush's poodle"), could be counted on to support the war. Among the ten rotating Council members, things were not too much better. Despite extraordinary pressure, including herculean US efforts to bribe, threaten, and bully Council members, Washington never achieved more than its original three supporting votes (Britain, Spain, and Bulgaria). With permanent Council members France, Russia, and China, as well as Germany and Syria, clearly opposed and not interested in compromising, the pressure campaign focused on the "Uncommitted Six"—Chile, Mexico, Cameroon, Guinea, Angola, and Pakistan. To win Council support, the US needed at least five of the six, but in fact it never got the commitment of a single vote. (See Chapter 3 for more about these governments' resistance to US pressure.)

A second, crucial distinction from the 1990–1991 period had to do with the rise of the international media. Certainly the new 24-hour commercial news stations that had popped up around the world (although only those in the Arab world provided a dramatically different kind of coverage, for those who had access to al-Jazeera, al-Arabiyah, al-Alam, and the others) transformed the instant-access news, with new challenges to producers to fill huge blocks of time. But more important by far was the explosive expansion of the global independent media networks that made possible, indeed made inevitable, a much more probing, investigative coverage of events at the UN, in Washington, on the ground in Iraq and neighboring countries, and more.

For the global movement, this access to developments in real time at the UN or the Pentagon or the White House made strategic responses far easier and more timely. It also ensured that a new level of knowledge and coordination about events, analyses, and approaches from movement activists would be quickly shared via the internet. The result, for peace activists in countries across the world, was a clearer link to developments involving their own governments—in the capital, at the United Nations, or in response to US pressures. This enabled activists in each country to craft a much sharper strategy, targeting their government's actions and responding immediately to diplomatic or other governmental moves.

And for the movement as a whole, it meant an entirely new level of communication with each other, and as a result, a newly conscious and articulated self-identity, within each national movement, of being part of a global mobilization. It wasn't just that easier email communication allowed quick coordination of demonstration dates or slogans. It was the emerging consciousness of a shared political framework, even if spontaneous and rudimentary rather than conscious and comprehensive. It also meant that a growing number of people within the peace movement understood its work as part of a global mobilization against a much bigger threat even than devastating war in Iraq—the broader economic, political, environmental, social, and military threat of the US drive toward empire.

The arguments shaping that global movement are only now being woven into a coherent whole. They start with condemning the civilian lives lost and massive destruction in Iraq, the links between the "dual occupations" of the US in Iraq and Israel in Palestine, exposing the skyrocketing economic and human costs of the war and their impact on the poorest strata in the US and globally, including the virtual abandonment of already insufficient economic aid to Africa. Even before the war began, the movement was developing clarity on issues of US hypocrisy regarding its WMDs and its own role in creating Iraq's WMD programs; US double standards in response to violations of UN resolutions; and challenging the massive Iraq resource-grab inherent in the hand-out of multi-billion dollar contracts to Bush administration corporate cronies.

As the global movement's parameters expand, its broader articulation frames the Bush administration's US and global trajectories and explains the connections within and between them. Those include the links between Iraq and Israel-Palestine; between oil, Central Asia, and the unfinished Afghanistan war; between preemptive war doctrine and aggressive preventive wars; between potential North Korean nukes and Israel's nuclear arsenal; between Syria and Iran and weapons of mass destruction; between corporate domination and military spending; between US power projection and cut-backs in local budgets; between forced imposition of a global neo-liberal economic agenda (characterized by ruthless privatization and shredding of social protections) and the false US claim of democratization; between building a new internationalist movement and the role of the United Nations.

The issue of the UN role in the Iraq crisis alone has been widely misunderstood and confusing for many activists around the world. The question of whether the UN, dominated by the US, is primarily a villain or a victim in situations like that surrounding the Iraq war, remains unresolved in many parts of the peace movement. Should the goal be to defend the global organization from US attack and domination and try to reclaim the UN as ours, or to target the UN as "imperialism with a global face"? Many activists do not recognize that while there are constraints imposed on the UN, it has potential to be a venue of opposition to hegemony, and there is an urgent need for civil society to defend it from the ravages of US power.

The organizations created to defend the UN, particularly in the United States, have served largely as cheerleaders for the UN, without articulating the organization's potential role in defying US power. They have generally not challenged whatever administration was in power in Washington, and were unable or unwilling to articulate the political context of the rising anti-UN crusades of the early 21st century. And many within both the US and the broader global peace movement remained uncertain about the UN, seeing its early silences in the face of the US war build-up as evidence of unchallenged collaboration with the war. The eight-month period of 2002–2003 UN defiance, including the refusal of the six Non-Aligned Security Council members to cave in to Washington's extraordinary pressure to endorse the US war, changed the perspective of many about the UN's potential. But the UN collapsed again in mid-May 2003, under enormous US pressure, and the concocted "scandals" involving Kofi Annan and the oil-for-food program, used by right-wing elements in the US Congress and media, made it unclear whether and when the UN could reclaim its role within global opposition to empire.

What remained very clear was the vital role that civil society and the mobilized peace and justice movements would have to play if there was to be any chance of reclaiming the UN. The Italian-initiated but quickly globalized "Reclaim Our UN" campaign, which emerged in 2003 but gained important new momentum in the meetings of the World Social Forum in Mumbai and Porto Alegre in 2004 and 2005, has begun one such effort. Starting from a sophisticated understanding of the role that the UN has all too often been forced to play as an instrument of US policy, a defender of neo-liberal agendas, and a legitimator of unilateral wars, the mobilization moved to the next step of calling for a transformation of the global organization to one that will represent people's, rather than only governmental, interests.

This transformation meant understanding the need to reshape what reform of the UN would look like, to replace budget cuts and corporate partnerships with calls for transparency, democratization, a real role for civil society and accountability to the global South and the poorest peoples and nations. It also meant understanding the need for a nuanced and complex relationship between popular forces, social movements and civil society, and the UN. That relationship would have to recognize the necessity for a range of responses to the United Nations: to challenge the UN directly when it supports neo-liberal economic policies and legitimates war; to criticize constructively the inadequacies and shortcomings of more-or-less acceptable UN practices and the occasional spinelessness of more-or-less well-intentioned UN officials; to demand serious reforms of the UN, focusing on transparency and democratization; and to defend the global institution from de-funding, political attack, and domination by the US.

From 2002 until the first few months of the Iraq war, for instance, such an approach to the United Nations meant criticizing the willingness of some top-level UN officials to initiate serious planning for a UN role in post-invasion Iraq even while they acknowledged the illegality of a US invasion. It also meant condemning the Bush administration efforts to undermine the UN and render it irrelevant, and continuing to demand that UN arms inspectors be allowed to continue their work and that the build-up to war be officially deemed illegal. Further, understanding the UN role meant providing whatever level of support possible for the member states, particularly the governments of the weak and impoverished "Uncommitted Six," whose opposition to the US war made possible the UN's own broader resistance.

New Challenges: Building a Global Movement

As the world's attention focused on what was happening at the UN as well as in Washington, the pressure from the street on both ratcheted up. From the angry protesters across the Arab world, who linked their opposition to war in Iraq with the 2002 Jenin massacre and Israel's reoccupation of Palestinian towns and cities, to the passionate street demonstrations in the capitals of Security Council members by their own people demanding that their governments stand firm against US pressure, to the singing crowds led by Code Pink carrying flowers to the Washington, DC embassies of resisting countries to urge them to continue to say no, people around the world gave voice to a rising global movement.

In what turned out to be the last weeks before the war began, the pace of protests ratcheted up. By the end of 2002 the global sense of urgency had risen to new heights. Word spread, first from the European contingent of the World Social Forum, and rapidly taken up by UFPJ in the US, that February 15 would be a day for a huge global mobilization. UFPJ put out the slogan: "The World Says No to War." It was translated into scores of languages, painted and printed and silkscreened on signs and banners and t-shirts and streets around the world.

In only six weeks, UFPJ in New York and coalitions around the world went to work to make it real. The networks of the World Social Forum process took on a huge task of pulling global justice activists, indigenous organizations, and others of their networks into action. The goal was enormous: to organize unified protests, under a unified slogan and calling for a unified demand—to stop the drive toward war—in virtually every country of the world. Internet communications made the global collaborations possible, but human energy and commitment were still required to bring the hundreds of thousands and then millions into the streets to say no to war.

In the US, short of funds, time and sleep, the tiny national organizing staff of UFPJ, bolstered by a host of energized volunteers flooding the office, and backed by the mobilized work across the country of small local campaigns and well-financed national organizations, took on the herculean work of putting on a major national demonstration. It meant struggling to get police permits, fighting with New York City officials over venues, finding and funding the giant video-screens to project the stage program to an expected record-breaking crowd, arranging for artists and political leaders to speak, printing signs and stickers and leaflets in a dozen languages, and holding together a huge, diverse, and often unwieldy coalition. It was impossibly hard, breathtakingly challenging, and no one involved in the work ever regretted a moment. How could we? February 15 represented the birth of a global peace movement.

The demonstrations on that day transformed the political terrain in which movements were being built. But that single day, with all its drama and energy, could not, by itself, translate into the creation of a conscious, coordinated international mobilization with the capacity to build a powerful global movement with the staying power to successfully challenge Bush's Iraq war and the drive toward empire that shaped it. The slogan that brought together the legions of protesters around the world, "The World Says No to War," certainly reflected an international consensus that united diverse peoples with disparate interests and varying analyses and different long-term goals. Certainly the logistical coordination that made possible the seeming coherence of the international sweep of protests took enormous amounts of work. But the strategic political ties remained sporadic, almost accidental, and long after February 15, the question of how to institutionalize and make permanent those ties remained. How does an international movement, with enormous visibility but little ongoing collaboration or shared leadership, transform itself from a largely spontaneous eruption into a conscious, grounded movement able to speak with one voice even if in different languages? How does the leadership of those historic protests, scattered around the world, help to transform diverse groups of committed activists into participants in a self-consciously defined internationalist movement that shares short- and long-term political goals? How does a movement characterized by both peace and anti-war, global justice and anti-corporate sectors create a common framework that speaks equally of peace and justice?

The challenges were and remain enormous. Earlier periods of widespread anti-corporate organizing, such as the 1990s movements against neo-liberalism that targeted the injustices wrought by the IMF, the World Bank, and later the World Trade

Organization, saw more consolidated international links. Movements in different countries developed close strategic ties because each was engaged in more or less the same effort of undermining the legitimacy of the same international financial institutions and attempting to craft alternatives to those corporate-dominated fixtures of neo-liberal control. In contrast, the 21st century's drive toward war and empire was led by a single individual government in a single country, albeit a government more powerful than any that has ever existed in history. It was easy to mobilize public opposition to the Bush administration in other countries, but beyond intense street protests, implementation of a viable anti-war agenda had to take the form of pushing other, diverse governments to reject US demands for troops, endorsements of war, and legitimation of the empire. And that meant that national anti-war or anti-Bush or anti-US mobilizations necessarily looked very different, reflecting the specificities of each country.

Just looking at the European arena, for example, demonstrations against the Iraq war in France and Germany, whose governments (for their own opportunist reasons) had led the multilateral opposition to Bush's war, were shaped by very different political dynamics than those in Britain, where outrage at Tony Blair's embrace of Bush's policies bolstered some of the biggest mobilizations in the world. In Spain alone, the political realities in which anti-war organizers functioned were vastly different during the Aznar period, when Spain was closely allied with the US and Spanish troops were deployed to Iraq, and then later, after the March 2004 subway bombings in Madrid, and the defeat of Aznar and election of Zapatero with an overwhelming mandate to bring the troops home.

Earlier examples, from periods when anti-war mobilizations also took on a global cast, differ qualitatively from the movements created in the run-up to war in Iraq. One of the most significant differences is rooted in the nature of the Iraqi resistance itself. In the 1960s and 1970s, important sectors of the Vietnam-era anti-war movement in the US, and even more strongly internationally, identified closely with the goals of national independence and the vision of economic egalitarianism and socialism that the Vietnamese resistance articulated. Though there was plenty of romanticism, most activists eschewed any slavish idealization of Ho Chi Minh, the National Liberation Front of South Vietnam (known as the "Viet Cong") or the North Vietnamese, but there was also a strong appreciation for both the national legitimacy of those forces and the social program for which they fought. Certainly the existence of a popular neutralist opposition, largely Buddhist in identity, was recognized as part of the national liberation movement. But it was equally understood that the military resistance as well as most of the social/political mobilization opposition within the country was led by the communist forces, and their social, economic, and political program was widely known.

In the 1980s the international mobilizations against US intervention in Central America, focusing on the contra war in Nicaragua and the US counter-insurgency war in El Salvador, were largely initiated by exiles and other supporters of the revolutionary movements and governments in that region, the FMLN (Farabundi Marti National Liberation Movement) in El Salvador and the Sandinistas in Nicaragua. They were soon widely backed by faith-based and other progressive organizations around the world. Legions of activists traveled to Central America to observe first-hand the accomplishments of the Sandinista revolution, and the impact of US support for the counter-revolutionary "contras" in Nicaragua, as well as the consequences of the US war in El Salvador. They returned to Europe, Japan, Latin America, and especially the US itself, identifying closely with the struggles they had witnessed. The activists, organizers, resistance fighters they had come to know and embrace became their counterparts.

Even more dramatically, the anti-apartheid movement built its global breadth and credibility largely through the leadership of the African National Congress and the person of Nelson Mandela. Although other anti-apartheid organizations were active in South Africa (including the Pan-Africanist Congress, the Black Consciousness Movement, and others) and had numerous supporters abroad, the moral stature of the imprisoned ANC leader provided an indisputable center for the movement as a whole. Internationally, a sophisticated media and organizing campaign led by ANC exiles across Europe and the US brought about a close identification with the people of South Africa, especially among African Americans and others of the

African diaspora. Backed by the image of Mandela, the students of Soweto braving attack by the apartheid army became the counterparts, however idealized, of a whole generation of student activists in the rest of the world.

But while Iraq has been the centerpiece of much of the international activists' work for more than a decade, it never came to symbolize a political counterpart of the global peace and justice movements fighting against the US wars and occupations of the country. Of course, the recognition that "Saddam Hussein is not Nelson Mandela" was a clear understanding of the anti-sanctions and earlier anti-war movements even before Bush's war began. The single most important reason for the longstanding divide within the US movement against the 1990–1991 US war in Iraq, the movement against economic sanctions, and the peace movement challenging the 2003 war was the split over how to understand and talk about Saddam Hussein and Iraq's Ba'athist regime. The vast majority of the anti-war (and later the emerging anti-empire) movements' supporters viewed Saddam Hussein's regime as a brutal government responsible for serious violations of political and civil rights of Iraqis, particularly of the Kurds. It was also understood, among those same sectors, as one of the many dictatorial regimes around the world that were armed, financed, and protected by the United States. A few, on the other hand, refused to criticize the regime.

Few within the movements were aware of the extraordinary accomplishments of Iraq in the area of economic and social rights, under that same Ba'ath Party leadership and after 1979 under the control of Saddam Hussein. Throughout the 1970s and 1980s the Ba'athists had used Iraq's oil revenue not only for vast military expenditures, but for social spending that led to the country becoming a regional leader in secularism, education, health care, science and technology, women's equality, and more. On the eve of the 1990 Gulf crisis, for example, UNICEF was on the verge of closing its operations in Iraq, because the social indicators for children's lives—health, education, social development—were deemed too high to need UNICEF's assistance.

Political activists in the US had worked hard, against great odds, to educate Americans about Washington's role in Iraq, particularly during the 1980s, when the US had consistently backed Baghdad in its war against Iran. The US provided Saddam Hussein with military financing disguised as agricultural credits, and direct military support including the sale of seed stock for biological weapons programs including anthrax, botulinum, E. coli, and more,[49] as well as satellite targeting information for chemical weapons Iraq used against Iranian troops.[50]

But with the exception of the post-occupation oil workers' unions in Basra, with whom US Labor Against the War developed strong ties, there were few such identifiable organizational or political counterparts in Iraq. Despite a decade-long effort by the US and European anti-sanctions movements to give a human face to the usually invisible Iraqi victims of the economic sanctions, Iraqis, and especially Iraqi civil society, remained largely unknown. There were no widely known and respected individuals, potential counterparts for international activists, associated either with the Ba'athist regime or civil society before the war, or with the largely unidentified military resistance once the war began. A few names emerged within the opposition to the US occupation, most notably Moqtada al-Sadr, the fiery young Shia cleric whose forces challenged the US military in Najaf and elsewhere, and the Ayatollah Ali al-Sistani, Iraq's revered Shia religious leader. But the influential al-Sistani largely made his peace with the US occupation through winning reluctant support from Washington for more rapid elections in occupied Iraq, and Sadr's military resistance appeared unaccompanied by a broader social program (although some evidence of a regressive set of social policies particularly regarding women's role in society did emerge from some of Sadr's forces). So while acknowledged and respected, neither leader engendered anything like the international deference commanded by earlier revolutionary figures. Their religious identities also separated them from the largely secular anti-war activists, though they were claimed more closely by Muslim and particularly Islamist sectors of the global movements.

And the level of violence during the US occupation made it difficult for international activists, even those with longstanding ties in Iraq, to travel and spend time in Iraq. Knowledge of an emerging civil society of resistance, of students organizing in the universities, of new media efforts, of women's mobilizations against the US occupation remained largely abstract. The important focus continued to be on understanding that resistance to occupation in Iraq involves many people, and takes many forms, most of them not military.

After the Search for Counterparts

Certainly it is the Iraqi military resistance that in the first years of the war imposed the highest costs on the US occupation. Those costs were exacted first in human terms, in the deaths and injuries of US and "coalition" troops (many of whom survived with far more serious injuries than in any other war). They were exacted in financial terms, in the loss of anticipated Iraqi oil income because of consistent attacks on oil pipelines and in the escalated US costs of the vast military deployment aimed at wiping out the resistance. They were exacted in political terms, as the military resistance prevented the kind of "stability" in Iraq that would allow Washington to consider withdrawing many of its troops under the terms set by the White House, meaning a post-occupation Iraq still under US economic and military control. And they were exacted in moral and legal terms, by preventing the Bush administration from being able to claim unmitigated "victory" for "freedom and democracy" in occupied Iraq.

Under international law, the people of Iraq living under occupation have the right to resist. Their right of resistance against the US and "coalition" forces arguably extends as well to resistance to the Iraqi government and military forces created and kept in power by the occupying forces, since even the 2005 election that brought Iraq's transitional government to power was held under the dominion of the occupying army. And in the context of a military occupation, such as that which exists in Iraq, the people of Iraq have the right to use military force to resist that military occupation—though, also under international law, they are prohibited from targeting military force against civilians.

Protocol I of the 4th Geneva Conventions (Protection of Victims of International Armed Conflicts) governs the conduct of war. In describing the obligations of combatants, Article 57(2), the Protocol says:

(a) those who plan or decide upon an attack shall: (i) do everything feasible to verify that the objectives to be attacked are neither civilians nor civilian objects and are not subject to special protection but are military objectives...; (ii) take all feasible precautions in the choice of means and methods of attack with a view to avoiding, and in any event to minimizing, incidental loss of civilian life, injury to civilians and damage to civilian objects; (iii) refrain from deciding to launch any attack which may be expected to cause incidental loss of civilian life, injury to civilians, damage to civilian objects, or a combination thereof, which would be excessive in relation to the concrete and direct military advantage anticipated;

(b) an attack shall be cancelled or suspended if it becomes apparent that the objective is not a military one or is subject to special protection or that the attack may be expected to cause incidental loss of civilian life, injury to civilians, damage to civilian objects, or a combination thereof, which would be excessive in relation to the concrete and direct military advantage anticipated;

(c) effective advance warning shall be given of attacks which may affect the civilian population, unless circumstances do not permit.

There is no question that US violations of this Protocol, and indeed US violations of all of the Geneva Conventions' protections of civilians, far outweigh any violations carried out by Iraq's military resistance forces. But those US violations, however egregious, do not, should not, legitimize other (even smaller) violations by the otherwise lawful resistance. While it is vital that we understand the pressures of years of war, sanctions, invasion, and occupation that give rise to unlawful actions, it is equally important that we recognize the universality of international law even if the forces of empire and occupation do not. That is certainly true politically, in determining whether to embrace any particular resistance movement regardless of its social program or its military strategy, but it is also true legally.

The US (along with Turkey, Afghanistan under the Taliban, Iraq under Saddam Hussein, and a few other countries) has refused to ratify Protocol I, precisely because it would require that the militants the Bush administration calls "unlawful combatants" would have to be accorded the privileges of any prisoners of war. The Protocol was drafted specifically to include the obligations of anti-colonial and anti-occupation resistance fighters. Article 2 (4) of the Protocol extends its authority to

> include armed conflicts which peoples are fighting against colonial domination and alien occupation and against racist regimes in the exercise of their right of self-determination, as enshrined in the Charter of the United Nations and the Declaration on Principles of International Law concerning Friendly Relations and Co-operation among States in accordance with the Charter of the United Nations.

It is especially tragic, though perhaps inevitable, that the overwhelming majority of victims of the continuing war in Iraq, including the victims of the Iraqi resistance forces, continue to be Iraqis, most of them civilians. The common resistance tactic of targeting groups of Iraqi civilians lining up to join the occupation-backed military or police forces (unsurprising, despite the danger, while unemployment hovered near the 70 percent mark) carries its own sad logic, but remains a violation of international law. And so the targeting of those unarmed civilians (despite their intended future in the occupation-backed military or police) remains a crucial part of the reason for the lack of international support for the resistance, including among key sectors of the global anti-war movement. While some sectors do espouse an uncritical "support the military resistance" stance, they are a minority of those in action within the anti-war mobilizations. Most activists acknowledge that US imperial violations of international law—those responsible for most of the death and devastation in Iraq—must be condemned first and most aggressively, but that resistance forces who violate international law should be criticized as well.

There is also concern regarding the nature of the disparate organizations that make up "the Iraqi resistance." US intelligence officials speak of a patchwork of groups, with varying assessments as to their levels of coordination and cooperation. Some of the most incendiary attacks, particularly the car bomb and suicide attacks that generally have caused the highest level of casualties, especially among bystanders, are often blamed on non-Iraqi Islamist radicals, including those claimed to be linked to al-Qaeda. But US officials indicate that only about 10 percent of the resistance is actually thought to be what one former military intelligence officer called "foreign jihadis."[51]

The problem, of course, is that while opposition to the US occupation is widespread in Iraq, and resistance to it takes many forms, little is known about who really makes up the factions of the armed resistance. They almost certainly include some former Ba'athist military forces, who had access to weapons even before the moment of the US invasion. That some component of the resistance forces operates within an extremist Islamist framework appears undeniable. How many of those or other military factions willing to attack civilians are in fact made up of non-Iraqis remains unclear, but it is certain that the war has transformed Iraq into something it never was before: a center for global terrorism. Again it is not clear how many of the non-Iraqi fighters in Iraq hold to an Islamist agenda as opposed to a broader set of anti-US or anti-empire goals.

But the uncertainty about who makes up the Iraqi resistance does not seem to be a concern of the US occupation authorities, who acknowledged in June 2005 that US military commanders and diplomats were meeting with representatives of the Iraqi resistance. In what the press called "an apparent softening of the Bush administration's opposition to negotiations," US officials decided that "the insurgency has to be addressed."[52]

Crucially, it is virtually certain that a large component of Iraq's armed resistance, and even more of the unarmed followers and supporters, are simply Iraqi nationalists outraged by the occupation of their country by foreign soldiers. The problem is that along with the lack of clarity about who makes up the armed resistance, even less information is available about what they stand for beyond an end to the US occupation. Their social program, their political goals—if indeed they exist at all— remain obscure. Without clarity about who they are and what they stand for, it becomes meaningless to endorse or encourage those unknown armed resistance forces. Additionally, the illegitimacy of the tactics that have become hallmarks of this resistance movement, particularly the car and suicide bombings that target Iraqi civilians, takes on a far greater significance, and makes such endorsement inappropriate. It remains unclear whether the US negotiators were meeting with Iraqi nationalists as well as former Ba'athists and Islamist elements.

Recognizing the right of the Iraqi people to resist illegal occupation, including the right to use arms to counter a military occupying force, does not require endorsement of any particular resistance movement, whether or not it is negotiating the occupation forces, let alone endorsing any particular tactics or leader. And the ambiguity of the identity of the armed Iraqi resistance organizations, combined with a propensity for tactics that violate international law, mean that few anti-war activists are prepared to wholeheartedly embrace the military resistance.

In earlier movements that situation was different. Certainly the sectors of the global anti-apartheid movement who recognized the right of South Africans to use military force to challenge apartheid still disagreed with or even condemned some military actions carried out during the liberation struggle (such as "necklacing," the widely condemned tactic of killing opponents by placing flaming tires around their necks). But their overarching support for the African National Congress was not withheld or withdrawn, since that support was based on an understanding and endorsement of a well-known and public social and political program that represented the real centerpiece of the resistance to apartheid. In South Africa, in Vietnam, in El Salvador, and elsewhere, opposition to particular tactics (including criticism regarding possible violations of international law by resistance forces) was overshadowed by the much broader support for the political program that underlay the resistance. Ultimately those resistance movements were themselves understood not only as nationalist or anti-occupation forces, though those were key components of identity, but as organizations committed to social transformation as well.

In Iraq, where neither the identity, nor existence of social programs or political goals, of the armed resistance factions is known, opposition to illegal military tactics has become far more prevalent. As a result, relatively few anti-war activists around the world, and very few within the United States, including the large number who recognize and support the right of Iraqis to resist, are prepared to embrace, champion, or endorse specific Iraqi military resistance forces.

Civil society in Iraq faces enormous challenges in its efforts to create ways of defying the US occupation with political, economic, social, and other forms of resistance. But small examples are emerging, gaining influence in Iraq, and, as is the case with the oil workers' unions, making links with global activists to strengthen their work and to provide the international anti-occupation movement with crucial on-the-ground information regarding developments in the country.

Common Agendas

One of the most creative uses of international law by the global movement was in the creation of a series of World Tribunals for Iraq. Modeled after the War Crimes Tribunal for Vietnam created by Bertrand Russell in the 1960s, the Iraq tribunals were initiated at the April 2003 meeting of what became the Jakarta Peace Consensus. The major tribunals were eventually held in Brussels, New York, and Turkey, with smaller sessions in more than twenty countries. Opening the final session in Istanbul at the end of June 2005, Indian novelist and anti-war activist Arundhati Roy, spokesperson for the jury of the tribunal, explained its value:

> The Jury of Conscience at this tribunal is not here to deliver a simple verdict of guilty or not guilty against the United States and its allies. We are here to examine a vast spectrum of evidence about the motivations and consequences of the US invasion and occupation, evidence that has been deliberately marginalized or suppressed. Every aspect of the war will be examined—its legality, the role of international institutions and major corporations in the occupation, the role of the media, the impact of weapons such as depleted uranium munitions, napalm, and cluster bombs, the use of and legitimation of torture, the ecological impacts of the war, the responsibility of Arab governments, the impact of Iraq's occupation on Palestine, and the history of US and British military interventions in Iraq. This tribunal is an attempt to correct the record. To document the history of the war not from the point of view of the victors but of the temporarily—and I repeat the word temporarily—vanquished.
>
> There are remarkable people gathered here who in the face of this relentless and brutal aggression and propaganda have doggedly worked to compile a comprehensive spectrum of evidence and information that should serve as a weapon in the hands of those who wish to participate in the resistance against the occupation of Iraq. It should become a weapon in

the hands of soldiers in the United States, the United Kingdom, Italy, Australia, and elsewhere who do not wish to fight, who do not wish to lay down their lives—or to take the lives of others—for a pack of lies. It should become a weapon in the hands of journalists, writers, poets, singers, teachers, plumbers, taxi drivers, car mechanics, painters, lawyers—anybody who wishes to participate in the resistance...

The assault on Iraq is an assault on all of us: on our dignity, our intelligence, and our future. We recognize that the judgment of the World Tribunal on Iraq is not binding in international law. However, our ambitions far surpass that. The World Tribunal on Iraq places its faith in the consciences of millions of people across the world who do not wish to stand by and watch while the people of Iraq are being slaughtered, subjugated, and humiliated.[53]

While recognizing the lack of official jurisdiction under international law, the tribunals' organizers were committed to using the precepts of law for its work. As Princeton University's noted scholar of international law Richard Falk described it, the tribunals were "filling in the gaps" between national laws, the International Criminal Court, and other established institutions.[54] The seriousness of the tribunal process reflected a growing understanding within the global movement that international law was not simply a rhetorical abstraction, but could be seized and turned into a tool of resistance.

Along with the claiming of international law, the overlap between the global justice and the peace or anti-empire movements has been a crucial factor in the success of the mobilizations and in the rising internationalist consciousness of activists in both movements. But the more difficult challenge lies in linking not only movement activism and mobilizations, but in working to link the analytical frameworks that shape the two movements as well.

Historically, particularly through its major emergence in the 1990s and into the new century, the global justice movement focused its critique on the international neo-liberal economic system of privatization and opening of trade without protections that has threatened to become the norm across the globe. The movement highlighted the role of corporations and targeted the international financial institutions that reflect and magnify corporate interests—most notably the World Bank, the

International Monetary Fund, and the World Trade Organization. As its work expanded from critique to the search for alternative economic models, the role of states and governments came into the equation, but the focus remained rooted on the global economic system, and the key actors to be challenged remained corporate-driven globalization and the depredations it caused throughout the world, especially in the global South. The US, Europe, and Japan were understood to be the primary beneficiaries of neo-liberalism, but wars and military occupations in the global South were often overlooked and the movement's most important targets were the financial agencies themselves.

The peace and anti-empire movement, on the other hand, traditionally focused on the issues of war and militarization, political domination and unilateralism; the primary target of the global peace movement remained the US government and military. While many individual activists and key organizations within the peace movement operated from a core analysis of the primacy of economic factors, the immediate economic issues were often not at the centerpiece of their mobilization.

In the context of building the global movement to prevent war in Iraq, one of the most important strengths lay in the operative intersection between the economic and the political/military factors as the basis for opposition and resistance. That linkage was made far more consistently and clearly outside of the US—it remained particularly constant in the anti-war mobilizations in Africa and in some parts of Asia, Latin America, and Europe. In May 2003, for example, participants in the conference that would issue the Jakarta Peace Consensus statement represented both a range of organizations and activists focused on challenging corporate globalization, and those based in the conventional peace and solidarity movements. The Jakarta document took on greater significance than many anti-war conference declarations precisely because its challenge of the Iraq war provided a framework for mobilization and movement-building directly relevant to the anti-globalization activists who had not traditionally been involved in anti-war efforts.

In the US, many of the global justice activists whose primary focus was the role of corporations and the international financial institutions participated in the demonstrations, and speakers regularly addressed the economic linkages, but the two movements never completely cohered as they did in other parts of the world.

What was new and especially important for maintaining the analytical links was the crucial issue of war profiteering and corporate greed in Iraq—the economic invasion of Iraq.[55] Iraq was the first war in US history in which Congress did not pass a specific set of laws to prevent war profiteering. Instead, the government-corporate links were open, often celebrated. The links between the Bush administration and the corporations winning the multi-million, sometimes billion-plus dollar contracts for "reconstruction" projects in Iraq quickly became public in the US, although mainstream media outlets were cautious at the beginning. The international press was far less restrained in covering the scandal. One example from the Australian press:

> All the American firms to get Iraqi reconstruction contracts have bankrolled George Bush and the Republican Party or have direct links to USAID, the department of state handing out the Iraqi contracts. All the contracts are being negotiated in secret—in the interests of national security—and all the contracts will go to US firms. British firms are only allowed to bid for sub-contracted work.[56]

From Anti-War to Anti-Empire

As the international movement challenging empire evolves, it will need a strategy linking other key challenges facing the world's people, challenges beyond the occupation of Iraq, which remains the centerpiece of US domination. The links between the dual occupations now shaping the Middle East, the US occupation of Iraq and Israel's occupation of Palestine, must be clarified. The significance of potential European resistance to a threatened US invasion of Iran must be explored. The links between oil, US bases in Central Asia and the unfinished Afghanistan war; between ostensible US concerns about nuclear proliferation and Israel's undeclared nuclear arsenal; between Pentagon budgets and corporate profits; between US wars and global poverty—all must be better explored and brought to the center of the anti-war agenda.

The global movement for peace and justice that cohered in the run-up to the US war in Iraq was born in a new kind of world, under conditions far different than those shaping earlier global anti-war mobilizations. It requires a newly defined global strategy. It has taken some time for a unifying agenda for the global peace and justice movement to emerge, and many components of that agenda remain uncertain.

For example, there is recognition of the need for, but uncertainty about how to craft, the kind of nuanced political framework required to build a movement that can take advantage of the anti-empire stance of unreliable and often hostile tactical allies. Specifically, the global movement as well as its US counterpart has begun to recognize the importance of recognizing the role Paris or Berlin might play as part of the global front against US empire, as they did in the UN during the run-up to the war in Iraq, while continuing to rigorously challenge their corporate-driven economic trajectory. But the nature of that recognition—how to take advantage of those powerful anti-empire or anti-war forces while not conceding them strategic legitimacy—remains unclear. Another example would be how to interact with the emerging progressive governments of Latin America, most notably Venezuela and Brazil and Uruguay, as well as those of South Africa and a few others. In those situations, governments may take strong positions against war and in defense of the UN and international law, but their opposition to neo-liberal policies being pushed by the US through the IMF, the World Bank, and the WTO may be less than consistent. The relationship between those governments and the global social movements will always be complex and precarious; there will often be sharp disparities between inside and outside strategies carried out by activists inside those countries and regions, and those working in other parts of the globe or within United Nations arenas.

It is certain that one feature of the global movement's agenda will have to include universal disarmament, focusing on the extraordinary dangers posed by the largest nuclear/military powers, including the US. There is an urgent need to challenge the common assumption operative in the US and many European capitals that "non-proliferation" among small, impoverished, often unstable countries will resolve the global threat of war without the nuclear weapons states doing anything. That will have to include broadening our defense of the Non-Proliferation Treaty to include a new emphasis demanding implementation of Article VI of the Treaty, which requires the US and the other four "official" nuclear weapons states to move toward full and complete nuclear disarmament.

Another aspect will need to be the focus on economic justice as a linchpin of the struggle against war and empire—not only to strengthen the unity of the two components of the international mobilization against empire, the peace and global justice movements, but because economic injustice lies at the root of almost all wars and certainly all bids toward empire.

Other issues will have to include the primacy of internationalism and the centrality of the United Nations in all our work. That means claiming the UN as our own, as part of the global mobilization for peace, and working both to empower and transform the UN into a center of multilateral power and governance that can challenge the United States empire. Bishop Tutu's words to UN Secretary-General Kofi Annan on the morning of February 15, 2003, bear repeating: "We are here on behalf of the people marching today in 665 cities around the world... [W]e claim the United Nations as our own, we claim it as part of our global mobilization for peace."

Internationalism can only include the United Nations if the people's mobilizations for peace and for justice claim the global organization as part of our movements, and fight to reclaim the UN from US domination. It also means we must move beyond celebrating the creation of the International Criminal Court, to fighting to expand the Court's jurisdiction to those powerful Northern leaders who arm, finance, and enable the South's dictators—not only General Pinochet but Henry Kissinger, not only Saddam Hussein but George Bush should be in the dock.

The global mobilization against empire is operating in a new era, in which aggressive war based on lies, unilateral security policies that put the entire world at greater risk, a US national security directive officially authorizing preventive as well as preemptive war—all are newly legitimized, indeed publicly lauded, by Washington's powerful. The drive toward empire is no longer hidden, but rather celebrated.

The first stage of challenging the US drive toward empire

lies in stopping the war in Iraq—beginning with the withdrawal of US troops and an end to occupation. Once the occupation is over and US troops are gone—and only after those preconditions have been met—the US will have to face the other obligations it owes to Iraq. Those include massive reparations to begin the serious reconstruction of the shattered country, and financial and political backing for the international assistance missions that will follow. The initial UN estimate for repair of war damage to Iraq, not including reconstruction from sanctions-caused damage, was $200 billion. With the additional damage of escalating US attacks in 2004–2005, particularly the destruction of Falluja, Washington must be prepared, perhaps with British, Australian, and other "coalition" help, to pay at least the equivalent to what the US and its allies have already paid to destroy Iraq.

But paying what it owes for Iraq's real reconstruction does not give the US the right to control how those funds are used, nor to keep US or "coalition" soldiers, US mercenaries or military contractors, or US corporations, on the ground in Iraq. The principle must be that Iraqi workers and companies are the primary recipients of US funds, and only those Iraqi entities would have the right to subcontract or recruit regional or broader international assistance based on their own assessment of needs.

Accomplishing even that first goal of ending the occupation and ending Washington's massive violations of international law will require a series of difficult steps. By the middle of 2005 more than 58 percent of Americans said that the war in Iraq was not only wrong but should never have been waged. But there remained serious reluctance at both the public and official (including congressional levels) to move to the obvious consequence of that view: that if the war was wrong, we should end it. The advice of the late retired Admiral Eugene Carroll of the Center for Defense Information should have been taken more seriously: "There is an old military doctrine called the First Rule of Holes," he often said. "If you find yourself stuck in one, stop digging."

Those who continued to advocate "staying the course" or "internationalizing the war" were still stuck in their holes, too busy digging deeper. A real solution to the Iraq war must start with ending the US occupation. Then, and only then, we can talk about internationalizing the peace.

This war has, like the Vietnam War of a generation ago, seriously divided the people of the United States. Too many people continued to believe, in the face of all evidence to the contrary, that somehow US occupying troops were making things better for the people of Iraq, and that ending the occupation would bring chaos. In fact, of course, the occupation itself is characterized by a brutal chaos—and Iraqis continue to suffer. Their country has been shattered by military assaults, and continues to languish under a violent occupation and brutal war. Cities such as Falluja have been virtually destroyed by US military forces claiming to "liberate" the city, leading to the forced expulsion of 300,000 residents, most of whom remain unable to return home. The ruin of Falluja, and so much of Iraq, by US forces recalls the words of the great writer Tacitus, who followed Rome's legionnaires as they laid waste to that empire's far-flung cities. "The Romans brought devastation," he wrote, "and they called it peace."

Despite the June 2004 so-called transfer of authority to the Iraqi interim government, and despite the January 2005 elections of the "transitional government," the US military occupation forces and political representatives remain in control of Iraq's people and its economy and social and political systems. The result has been a serious deterioration in the lives of the Iraqi people. By mid-June 2005 the British-based Iraqi Body Count had documented 22,248–25,229 specific civilian deaths caused by military violence.[57] And according to US researchers from Johns Hopkins University, publishing in the British journal the *Lancet*, over 100,000 Iraqi civilians had perished by October 2004 as a result of the US invasion, occupation, and war.

The *International Herald Tribune* reported:

"We were shocked at the magnitude but we're quite sure that the estimate of 100,000 is a conservative estimate," said Dr. Gilbert Burnham of the Johns Hopkins study team. He said the team had excluded deaths in Falluja in making their estimate, since that city was the site of unusually intense violence. In 15 of the 33 communities visited, residents reported violent deaths in the family since the conflict started in March 2003. They attributed many of those deaths to attacks by coalition forces—mostly airstrikes—and most of the reported deaths were of women and children. The risk of violent death was 58 times higher than before the war, the researchers found... "The fact that more than half of the deaths caused by the occupation forces were women and children is a cause for concern," the authors wrote. ... "From a purely public health perspective it is clear that whatever planning did take place was grievously in error," Horton wrote. "The invasion of Iraq, the displacement of a cruel dictator and the attempt to impose a liberal democracy by force have, by themselves, been insufficient to bring peace and security to the civilian population. Democratic imperialism has led to more deaths, not fewer."[58]

Fighting a war launched in defiance of the United Nations and in violation of international law as well as the US Constitution, the US and coalition forces are engaged in a pattern of lawlessness that violates both US and international law. US officials and many Americans brag of the US being a great democracy, living under the rule of law with a government accountable to the will of its people. If that is true, citizens are liable for the US government's actions, putting even greater responsibility on the US peace movement to work to stop the war.

Around the world the vast majority of people and governments stand opposed to this war. In the US, a majority of people, and increasing numbers of political and military leaders, believe the war was wrong from the beginning or is not worth the price. Ending the US occupation of Iraq is the only solution to this escalating crisis. Ending the US occupation of Iraq means bringing the US troops home. All of them. Immediately. The nearly 150,000 US troops in Iraq in 2005 remain the primary cause of violence in Iraq; they are not the solution to the violence.

Iraqi history provides some useful lessons. The British ruled Iraq, officially, under a League of Nations mandate from 1922 until 1932, and unofficially through pro-British generals and the monarchy from 1932 until the 1958 revolution. London's emphasis was on controlling Iraq's oil through a strong, pro-British Iraqi military. The resulting primacy of the military within Iraqi society helped set the political stage for the ascendancy of the Iraqi Ba'ath party and eventually that of Saddam Hussein.

To the extent that the armed resistance is unified at all

among its disparate ethnic, religious, and political sectors, the unity appears limited to shared opposition to the US occupation. Once the occupation is withdrawn, the much smaller sectors of the resistance that are motivated largely by religious fundamentalism and extremism rather than by nationalism or anti-occupation views, and who are responsible for some of the worst violence against civilians, will likely become isolated from the broader sectors of the resistance. One probable result will be a significant reduction—though not an immediate end—of violence, with the departure of the key targets of the violence, the US occupation and its Iraqi backers.

It is likely that the withdrawal of US troops may lead to the collapse of at least some parts of the US-imposed "transitional government," though some of its institutions, including the police, the military, and other security agencies, could well survive with new leadership untainted by association with the US occupation. And without an outside enemy occupying the country, it is also more likely that the kind of secular nationalism long dominant in Iraq would again prevail as the most influential (though certainly not sole) political force within the emerging Iraqi polity, as opposed to the virulent Islamist tendencies currently on the rise among Iraqis facing the increasing desperation of occupation, repression, and growing impoverishment. The role of the US peace movement must be to maintain and strengthen the demand for US troops to be withdrawn and the US occupation ended.

But in the longer term it will no longer be sufficient for the challenging movements to say no—to war, to empire. Those movements must offer an alternative vision of global human security. Such security must be rooted in a new internationalism that links people, through global social movements; governments, in different combinations and for different reasons; and the world, through the United Nations, in a far more comprehensive challenge to empire—and to the wars, poverty, inequality, and injustice on which that drive toward empire is based—than any challenge we have brought so far. In the United States the peace movement will have to broaden its demands beyond calling for an end to war and unilateralism, to call for completely replacing Washington's war-based government and economy with a set of foreign policies based on international law, the UN Charter, the Universal Declaration of Human Rights, global equity, and complete disarmament. Internationally the peace movement will be fighting not only for an end to war and occupation and neoliberalism, but for a shift of national priorities away from war, military spending, and corporate profits, to new emphases on human security, human priorities, environmental protection. We will fight for open societies characterized by respect for all human rights—economic, civil, social, political, and cultural—aimed at creating a new internationalism to replace the rising empire.

3
GOVERNMENTS

A lexander Hamilton, who might have been commenting on the evils of the 21st-century US empire, famously recognized that the "spirit of moderation in a state of overbearing power is a phenomenon which has not yet appeared, and which no wise man will expect ever to see."[1] A variety of forces, among which the social movements for peace and global justice hold the pride of place, stand defiant of that power. Certainly no government in power can be counted on as an absolutely unwavering, principled, strategic ally of those progressive global movements, nor is any government a consistent, unequivocal backer of internationalism and international law. But it is certainly true that some governments—those that do not represent a "state of overbearing power"—on occasion will choose to challenge precisely those states that Hamilton described. And in so doing, those defiant governments will find themselves confronting the exigencies of empire and standing, however reluctantly, alongside the social movements that are leading the global resistance.

The resistance of governments to the rising and already over-arching dominion of the world's "hyper-power" will never be unconditional and reliable; it will always be tactical, hesitant, and fraught with narrowly defined self-interests. Governments, led by France and Germany, played a crucial role in the global opposition to the US war in Iraq. But those same governments, while opposing the war and even while adamantly claiming to oppose the Bush administration's policy of "extraordinary rendition" of detainees to countries known for brutal torture, continued close collaboration between intelligence agencies and the CIA aimed at analyzing "the transnational movement of terrorist suspects and develop[ing] operations to catch or spy on them." The top-secret agency, known as Alliance Base, opened in 2002 and is funded by the CIA but located in Paris; the working language is French, in order to "play down the US role." And the intelligence agencies involved in the center include those of France, Germany, Canada, as well as staunch US war-backers Britain and Australia. Judge Jean-Louis Bruguiere, France's top counter-terrorism magistrate, said that "the relations between intelligence services in the United States and France has been good, even during the transatlantic dispute over Iraq, for practical reasons."[2]

Those "practical reasons" for the tenacity of strategic ties between the US and other governments should come as no surprise, and the ties certainly go even beyond intelligence cooperation. But nonetheless, the task of winning other governments to oppose, at least officially, the key features of the drive toward militarism and unilateralist domination through pressure and protest campaigns remains a vital component of any successful anti-empire movement—however reluctant, tactical, and inconsistent the governments' resistance.

State or governmental opposition to the second Bush administration's unilateralism and militarism began even before September 11. In the first months of Bush's first term (and indeed even before the new administration took office in January 2001) international public and official anger was already rising.

It was not surprising. From their first moments in office, Bush officials brought to the White House not only an aggressive brand of unilateralism, but absolute disdain for global opinion and contempt for international law and institutions. This was not an administration uneasy about or embarrassed by their chief's utter lack of foreign policy experience, an attitude applauded by the isolationist contingent in Congress. It was only three years, after all, since the National Security Caucus Foundation reported that a full one-third of the members of the House and Senate did not even have passports.[3]

From the beginning of 2001 on, the Bush administration followed, and certainly expanded, a powerful unilateralist inclination in foreign policy. But it was a pre-existing trend—Bush didn't invent it. Eight years earlier, the Clinton administration came into office claiming "assertive multilateralism" as their basis for foreign policy. But that commitment was always more rhetorical than real, and Clinton was far more committed to the appearance of "leading a global coalition" than to any real power-sharing in global decision-making. In fact, during eight years of Clintonian "multilateralism," the US rejected or sidelined treaties on everything from the rights of children to the International Criminal Court to the prohibition of anti-personnel land mines. The US repeatedly violated the United Nations Charter and circumvented Security Council decision-making. US dues to the UN remained billions of dollars in arrears.

After the *Black Hawk Down*[4] Somalia debacle of 1993, the slogan "assertive multilateralism" dropped off the Clinton administration agenda. But versions of the catchphrase continued to surface on occasion, because it somehow continued to resonate with the American people. The idea, if not the reality, of the US moving in concert with the international community, participating with, rather than isolated from, other countries, shaped a popular paradigm for post-Cold War foreign policy. And many people believed the rhetoric. They were prepared to accept the Clintonites' claims that most of official Washington was on the right track, that only the right-wing in Congress or a few recalcitrant senators were responsible for the US failing to pay its UN dues or to ratify treaties on the rights of children or to support the International Criminal Court.

But it was rhetoric, not reality. It was in 1999, during the Clinton years, after all, that France's then-Prime Minister Lionel Jospin first publicly acknowledged that "we're confronted with a new problem on the international scene. The United States often behaves in a unilateral manner." His foreign minister, Hubert Vedrine, went even further, asserting that "the predominant weight of the United States and the absence for the moment of a counterweight... leads it to hegemony, and the idea it has of its mission to unilateralism. And that's inadmissible."[5]

Vedrine described an initial approach to challenging US unilateralism. "There are two opposing approaches: on one side, the dominant power with its means of influence; on the other side, a system both multilateral and multipolar associating all or part of the 185 countries of the world."[6] Vedrine's proposals regarding the United Nations reflected the limitations of France's definitions of multilateralism. He focused only on "reform or reinforcement" of the Security Council, and the international financial institutions including the WTO, the World Bank, and the IMF, ignoring the urgent need to strengthen the General Assembly, the UN's Economic and Social Council (ECOSOC), citizens' rights, human rights, labor, women's and environmental movements, and more. But he was raising the right idea: that unilateral power must be fought with engaged internationalism, not isolationist retreat.

And that was during the Clinton administration. In the first months of his presidency, George W. Bush's unilateralism differed less in substance, and more in rhetoric and emphasis, from Clinton's approach. But the multilateral gloss of the Clinton years had captured a certain part of the public imagination, both in the US and internationally, so Bush's shift toward a more overt unilateralism seemed more significant than perhaps it really was. When Bush came into office in 2001 following his bitterly contested and ultimately false claim of victory, it was against the image and the rhetoric of the "multilateral" Clinton years, not their reality of emerging unilateralism, that Bush foreign policy would be measured.

So there was little public recognition of the pre-existing roots of Bush's supposedly "new" approach, nor of how much its origins could be found within the broad parameters of US foreign policy in recent years. When the Senate had voted against ratification of the CTBT in October 1999, many claimed then that the "new isolationism" of the Republican Party's right-wing had triumphed over Clinton's multilateralism. That so-called isolationism, though, was already a more malignant version of the longstanding US propensity for unilateralism. What would change with the Bush administration would be that Washington's solitary decision-making, including decisions to send troops to other countries and to ignore or violate international laws on a whim, would be asserted as a point of pride rather than implemented in the shadows.

From the start Bush asserted a boldly unilateralist voice, one that catered to both the far-right social conservatives and the most belligerent military hawks of the Republican Party. After the election, one of the first decisions of the new administration was to reimpose an international gag order, known colloquially as the "global gag rule," withholding US aid to any family planning service provider anywhere in the world if its staff (with separate, non-US funds) provided, lobbied for, or even mentioned abortion or abortion rights to its patients. Many in the US, women in particular, and many in UN and other international health agencies, were outraged.

Bush had inveighed against Clinton-style "nation-building" during his campaign, condemning US participation in Balkan peacekeeping and hinting at a unilateral withdrawal from Bosnia and/or Kosovo. Europe, in particular, was not pleased. Some of the new administration's earliest foreign policy prescriptions further antagonized allies—especially its high-handed withdrawal from the Kyoto Protocol and its announced intention to abandon the Anti-Ballistic Missile treaty (ABM), long viewed as the linchpin of the global, especially US–Russian, arms control regime. The Comprehensive Test Ban Treaty (CTBT), for which the Clinton administration had failed to win Senate ratification, was taken completely off the agenda. In March 2001 the US suspended missile talks with North Korea. And from the first moments of his presidency, George Bush took on the role of cheerleader for the so-called missile defense shield, a science fiction-based effort to protect against mythical future missiles that might be fired some day from North Korea or Iran or Iraq. The plan was rooted in the long-discredited Star Wars of Ronald Reagan, and soon became emblematic of Bush administration extremism and militarism.

There was broad trepidation right from the beginning. Fears of a US abandonment of alliances and international obligations shaped headlines around the world. Newspaper editorials and pundits, already concerned about Bush's proudly proclaimed ignorance of foreign affairs, expressed discomfort about the consequences of these high-profile withdrawals from global commitments.

The Bush administration's first international crisis, involving a US spy-plane over China in the spring of 2001, at first seemed to reflect the preeminence of the hard-line, militarize-the-diplomacy faction led by Deputy Secretary of Defense Paul Wolfowitz (later appointed by Bush as president of the World Bank). The rhetoric was tough and uncompromising, and fear of further confrontation settled over Washington and the US media. The slow-cruising US EP-3 spy-plane, bristling with the most advanced surveillance gear in Washington's arsenal, was flying off the Chinese coast in an area Beijing has long claimed as within its territorial waters, but which the US claimed was in international jurisdiction. China dispatched two F8 fighter jets to intercept the spy-plane. Sources differ about what happened next, but according to the *Guardian* in London,

it seems that the Chinese jets "hemmed in" the much bigger American plane, in an apparent manoeuvre to make it change course. According to the Chinese foreign ministry, the US plane suddenly veered to the left, hitting one of the single-seater jets on its tail. The Chinese machine crashed into the sea and the pilot is missing, presumed dead.[7]

The damaged US plane limped to the closest airstrip, on China's Hainan Island, where Beijing took the crew and the plane into custody. Tensions mounted. Bush demanded immediate return of the crew and the plane, saying the incident threatened severe damage to US–Chinese relations. But China stood firm, demanding an apology for the pilot's death and for the unauthorized landing on Chinese territory; the US refused. Stalemate ensued, and rhetoric remained tough.

Then it appeared that Chinese defiance paid off. One week into the crisis, Secretary of State Colin Powell, emerging as the point man for the crisis, expressed "sorrow" for the incident, and three days later China's official media reported his statement. Eleven days after the crash, the crisis ended. The Bush administration claimed that they did not apologize, but the US letter of understanding, relying on an artful use of the past tense as a diplomatic dodge, provided a different story. According to China's Xinhua News Agency, the letter read "Both President Bush and Secretary of State Powell have expressed their sincere regret over your missing pilot and aircraft... Please convey to the Chinese people and to the family of pilot Wang Wei that we are very sorry for their loss." In what Chinese Foreign Minister Tang Jiaxuan called a "humanitarian gesture," the crew was then released.[8] It was the first direct challenge to the Bush administration's aggressive rhetoric, and the challenger won.

But the spat with China was only the beginning. Several other factors began to emerge that marked ways that distinguished the new White House from its predecessor. Those differences may have reflected more style than substance, more rhetoric than reality, but they soon became major indicators of a new US view of its role in the world. One had to do with the Bush administration's public pride in its assertion of unilateral US power—a far cry from Clinton's determination to appear as an international actor. One example was Colin Powell's approach to the US–British military attacks in the "no-fly zones" in northern and southern Iraq. Powell distanced himself from Bill Clinton's mendacious claim that "enforcement" of the zones was somehow a US obligation under UN resolutions, to justify the attacks in thoroughly unilateral terms. In fact, of course, no UN resolution on Iraq ever authorized, or indeed even mentioned, the creation of such zones, let alone authorized their enforcement with warplanes and bombing raids. But Clinton, the ostensible multilateralist, remained determined to legitimize the unilateral military policy by claiming a UN imprimatur. Powell, on the other hand, had no such compunction. Instead, in testimony before the Senate, Powell identified the "no-fly zone operations" as being "essentially between US and the United Kingdom,"[9] thus acknowledging unabashedly that the no-fly zones and the bombing of the zones were not authorized by UN resolutions.

But within the hawk-to-superhawk spectrum that characterized the Bush administration, General Powell actually represented the slightly less hawkish, slightly more multilateralist approach than that of others, who would ultimately prove more influential than Powell himself. There was broad political agreement over the legitimacy of US global domination, but a serious strategic divide existed over just how that US domination could best be imposed. The split between Powell at the State Department and Donald Rumsfeld and his deputy, the neo-conservative leader Paul Wolfowitz, at the Pentagon, could perhaps be characterized as one between choosing US-dominated multilateralism (ordained by the US and militarized when needed) on the one hand, and an assertion of unilateral military power as the first-choice option on the other.

Powell envisioned a US-dominated international "consensus," however artificial or coerced it might be, in whose name US policies could be imposed on the world. On the other side was the "Wolfowitz cabal," grouped around the deputy secretary and the semi-official Defense Policy Board of hard-line Pentagon hawks. Joined by the Cold War left-over nationalist militarists like Rumsfeld, Wolfowitz and his minions viewed the US as an unchallengeable superpower that needs to pay little attention to the interests of or pressures facing its allies.

In his confirmation hearings, the centerpiece of Powell's approach was the continuation of sanctions against Iraq. He outlined a spin-driven "smart sanctions" proposal designed to deflect growing domestic and especially international concern over the deadly impact of economic sanctions on Iraqi civilians, and that put a high premium on maintaining some semblance of an allied, especially allied Arab, coalition to support the US position. Protection of the Gulf War "coalition," already in tatters after the decade-long humanitarian crisis raging in Iraq, was Powell's chief strategic goal.

Wolfowitz, during the same period, emerged strongly as the voice of the administration's hard-core military unilateralists. Their policy was overtly aimed at overthrowing Saddam Hussein in what was primly called "regime change," and they cared little for the niceties of coalition politics. They had spent the Clinton years in the private sector, using their out-of-office positions of influence to urge ever-more reckless military escalation, particularly against Iraq, on what they perceived as a hopelessly soft administration.

It appeared for a while that Vice President Dick Cheney was a staunch backer of the Wolfowitz side—but questions remained because of his stance during the 1990s as CEO of Halliburton Oil Industries. In that role (while his company signed multi-million dollar contracts with Iraq for oil equipment repair), Cheney had backed an anti-sanctions and almost pro-normalization approach to Iran, and many observers at first anticipated expansion of that approach to Iraq.[10] Once they came into office, the Bush hawks toned down their rhetoric somewhat from the overheated language they had used during the Clinton years. Cheney, despite his role in arming the Iraqi opposition during his 1990s years in the private oil sector, told CNN on March 4, 2001, "I don't believe [Saddam Hussein] is a significant military threat today... we want to make sure he does not become one in the future."

Even Wolfowitz, long identified as the most committed to arming the Iraqi opposition, told his Senate confirmation hearing that while he supports US military backing for an opposition force inside Iraq, "I haven't yet seen a plausible plan" for doing so. At the time many thought his statement indicated a more nuanced view of Iraq, that perhaps Wolfowitz was not committed to military action. Only later it became unmistakably clear that Wolfowitz's hesitation was only in regard to the capacity of the Iraqi "opposition"—his solution was simply to rely directly on a US invasion force instead.

Anger grew as governments around the world recognized the recklessness and potential dangers inherent in the powerful ideologues at the center of the Bush administration. Many embraced Powell, relieved that some voice of what appeared to be reason had a place within the White House. In fact, the perception of Powell as a "moderate" force within an extremist administration played a key role in undermining what might have been a stronger, more active resistance among governments than what ultimately took place. With Colin Powell as the public face of the US at the UN and among the world leaders, it was far easier for the Bush administration to undermine opposition and even convince doubters that statements regarding Iraq's alleged weapons programs or its alleged purchases of weapons components were true. If Cheney, Rumsfeld, Wolfowitz, or even Bush himself had been the public face, governmental opposition would have come more readily.

But even with Powell as diplomat-in-chief, the unilateralist and militarist thrust of the Bush administration was inescapable. So perhaps it should not have been surprising that another significant difference with their predecessors became visible very early in the Bush administration. By the spring of 2001, with international anger toward US arrogance on the rise, there appeared some reason to hope that a global challenge—of whatever sort—might take shape to defy the policies that were emerging as exemplars of untrammeled US domination and control. Around the world anger was brewing. It was in July of this year that *New York Times* columnist Tom Friedman wrote the column about the US being called a "rogue state" in Europe.[11] A Boston University scholar described how the United States at the end of 2000 was an unrivaled superpower presiding over a Pax Americana. But the new White House team seems determined to alienate and possibly lose America's friends abroad, while antagonizing other nations (notably China and Russia) so they turn into foes rather than partners. During last year's campaign, candidate George W. Bush admonished the United States to practice humility. Now, as president, he insists others bow to whatever new rules are devised by his administration. He ignores understandings and consensus built up among many parties over many years.[12]

Right-wing US pundits answered, cheering on the "New Unilateralism."[13] But for the first time it began to look as though a collaborative multilateral challenge to post-Cold War US power might be taking shape as something more than a pipedream. The clearest indication of a new international mood, in which governments were willing to follow the lead of their angry populations, popped up on May 3, 2001, at the United Nations, when nations from around the world, led by Western Europe, voted to boot the US off the Human Rights Commission. The move surprised those who had not followed developments carefully, and astounded US officials who had come to take for granted their "right" to an unofficially permanent seat. That same day, Washington also lost its seat on the International Narcotics Control Board. (See Chapter 4 for more details.)

The US continued to hold itself above the very international law to which it demanded others adhere. The angry buzz became louder, not only in the United Nations but in individual capitals around the world. It was perhaps unsurprising that the global South was furious over Washington's high-handed behavior. Given the vast disparity of economic, political, and military power, it was also unsurprising that despite widespread public outrage, governments in the South were muted, often silent. But it was noticed when even longstanding European allies—at the governmental as well as public levels—began to complain.

In late March 2001 the *New York Times* editorialized a warning.

Europe may seem like familiar territory to Bush administration officials, many of whom dealt with the continent during the cold war years when European leaders were more deferential to Washington's wishes than they are now. Administration policy makers must adjust their thinking to Europe's new mood or risk conflicts over the environment, arms control, NATO and trade.[14]

"Cheer up, ugly Americans," wrote one national columnist, assuring them that Europe really didn't hate the US quite as much as it seemed. He agreed that "powerful American influence at the outset of the 21st century will rile some nations, be perceived as threatening to some, and spur envy among others. But Europe has not become a fortress of anti-American hatred."[15]

Not yet, perhaps. But when Bush travelled to Europe for his first outing as leader of the Atlantic alliance, Europe remained unimpressed. The Swedish Prime Minister Goran Persson, then president of the European Union, praised the EU as "one of the few institutions we can develop as a balance to US world domination."[16] European leaders may have been relieved that the malaprop-prone president pronounced all their names right, but Secretary of State Powell, serving as fire marshal of the Bush administration, stomping out brushfires of international hostility as they cropped up, was still busy. Just before Bush's trip, Powell had to assure NATO allies that the administration's pro forma discussions in Europe, to demand acceptance of its no-compromise commitment to missile defense, should not be dismissed as "phony consultations."[17] Few seemed convinced. In fact, when the NATO foreign ministers gathered in Budapest at the end of May, Powell could not even win agreement that there was a "common threat" of missile attack. His team had tried to ratchet up language that would be stronger than the same body's 2000 reference to a "potential threat." But they failed, and the only compromise they could achieve was an agreement to continue assessing the threat level.

Given the European rejection of the US missile threat assessment, it was no surprise that the NATO ministers had no interest in the Star Wars-style "missile shield" defense plan the US was trying to impose. The NATO meeting was less than four weeks after the UN Human Rights Commission debacle, and clearly Bush and his team still didn't get it. The *New York Times* editors lectured again:

Wisely, the Bush administration has stepped back from early rhetoric that suggested its missile defense plans were set and the world would simply have to adapt to them. But consultation must involve more than showcasing American proposals... During the cold war, Washington could simply impose its will on NATO when it came to missiles and nuclear weapons policies. Those days are over.[18]

But while the *New York Times* is assumed to speak for the mainstream of US ruling circles, it was clear that the Bush administration didn't see things that way. November 2001 was the target for adopting a new protocol aimed to strengthen enforcement of the 1972 Biological Weapons Convention—the germ warfare treaty. As originally drafted, the treaty prohibits possession, development, and production of biological weapons. More than 140 countries ratified it, including the US. But the terms of the treaty never dealt with verification and compliance. Negotiations had been underway throughout the 1990s to change that situation and put some teeth into the treaty. It was understood that international inspections would have to be at the heart of any verification mechanism; the debate was over the nature, scope, and authority of those inspections. But for the US officials negotiating in Geneva, unannounced inspections were viewed as an infringement on the commercial, industrial, and patent rights of the US laboratories, pharmaceutical manufacturers, and other potential targets of international observers concerned about possible "dual use" dangers by some US biological production facilities.

The 2001 draft, at US insistence, had already seriously compromised the power of international inspectors. Arms control experts disagreed on whether it would be better to endorse a weakened protocol or to continue working to strengthen the proposal. But in the run-up to the planned November conference, Bush administration negotiators in Geneva made clear that they did not want either one. They had no intention of acquiescing to international inspections of US commercial or governmental production facilities, and they made no effort to help craft a new protocol. In May, Bush's inter-agency review team dismissed the terms of the compromise proposal, and made clear the administration's intention to reject the protocol decision in November. One member of the Federation of American Scientists' working group on biological weapons verification, while recognizing that the proposed protocol was less than perfect, said that Bush's rejection of it would nevertheless "reinforce the perception that his administration is controlled by those who never saw an arms control treaty that they liked, and that his administration is only willing to give lip service rather than leadership to multilateral security efforts."[19]

By July, the Bush team made it official: the US would not accept the new protocol. Europeans, in particular, were outraged. Sarcastic writers at London's *Independent* noted that

> For six years everybody talks of the importance of verification. And then, America discovers that its facilities, too, would have to be verified. The brazen nerve! America might be treated as though it were just another country! Mr. Bush's America seems in danger of convincing itself that it can force everybody to make concessions, while itself remaining impervious to change."[20]

Again, that rising resistance was visible in the pre-September 11 environment. The US remained the leading producer of germ weapons seed stock in the world. Officially the only weapons-related germ research had to do with creating a defense against others' biological weapons—but of course that requires a stock of offensive material against which to craft such a defense. (Not many in the US took note of the irony of Washington's continuing sanctions and bombing of Iraq's so-called "no-fly zones" ostensibly because of Baghdad's very similar resistance to international inspections of biological facilities.)

After September 11, when the international disarmament conference opened in Geneva mid-November, everything changed. The US put forward its own set of proposals: it ignored the fundamental issue of inspections and left out creation of an international implementation agency, focusing instead on the responsibility of signatories to monitor their countries' own biological production. Further, led by US Undersecretary of State for Arms Control and longtime UN-basher John Bolton, who would contentiously become Washington's ambassador to the UN several years later, the Bush administration insisted that its own weak package of substitute proposals must be accepted as part of the conference's final document (though not as a legally binding component of the treaty). On December 7, as the *Washington Post* noted, the meeting "disbanded in chaos and anger."[21] The conference decided to suspend its work for at least a year, rather than accept the US-orchestrated collapse and a permanent end to the negotiations.

European diplomats, in particular, were furious. But this was soon after September 11, after all, and Europe's anger remained muted.

Earlier in the year, European and broader international animosity was growing, and public. In August, only a few weeks before the September 11 attacks, polls commissioned by the Council on Foreign Relations and the *International Herald Tribune* proved what pundits and international travelers were already reporting: Europe, in particular, was very angry at the United States. The poll examined public opinion in Europe's four largest countries, and the view of the Bush administration in Britain, Italy, Germany, and France was not pretty.

On missile defense and US withdrawal from the ABM treaty, opposition was at 66 percent in Britain, 65 percent in Italy, 75 percent in France and a whopping 83 percent in Germany. When it came to US abandonment of the Kyoto Protocol on global warming, opposition soared to 80 percent in Italy, 83 percent in Britain, 85 percent in France and 87 percent in Germany. Asked for an overall assessment of Bush's handling of international policy, the "disapprove" levels were somewhat smaller—46 percent in Italy up to 65 percent Germany. But it was perhaps even more telling that Bush's confidence ranking among Europeans was barely on a par with that of Russian President Vladimir Putin. In France, 77 percent had little or no confidence in Putin, but 75 percent had little or none in Bush. Among both Italians and Britons asked who was likely to do the right thing in world affairs, Bush ranked even lower than Putin.[22]

Growing international anger was not lost on US opinion- and policy-makers. After all, unilateralism, even isolationism might be fine for us, but being isolated *by* others was certainly not acceptable. US punditry took up the challenge, and headlines like "There's a Point to Going It Alone: Unilateralism Has Often Served US Well,"[23] and "Empire or Not? A Quiet Debate Over US Role"[24] began to pop up with greater frequency. The latter article sympathetically reported that "a handful of conservative defense intellectuals have begun to argue that the United States is indeed acting in an 'imperialist' fashion—and that it should embrace the role." The former piece went on the offensive, claiming that "Unilateralism has always been a centerpiece of American foreign policymaking, and the world is the better for it."

The debate within US intellectual and policy circles continued to simmer, largely without taking on or even acknowledging the much deeper European and other allied concerns—let alone those in the global South—regarding growing US unilateralism. Even some mainstream Democrats, including Senate Majority leader Tom Daschle and House Minority leader Dick Gephardt took the White House to task for its go-it-alone attitude.

The World Conference Against Racism

The next conflict between the US and the international community would take place in Durban, South Africa, at the World Conference Against Racism, Racial Discrimination, Xenophobia, and Related Intolerances, the UN's third effort in a quarter of a century to confront national problems of racism with international solutions.

The August 2001 conference, in planning for over five years, followed earlier anti-racism conferences in 1978 and 1983. The US boycotted both of those earlier efforts. This time around, throughout the early preparatory process during the Clinton era, there were indications that things would be different. High-level official participation from the US seemed a much more realistic goal, although it was clear early on that Washington's agenda was already clashing with the organizers' goals.

Like other global conferences the UN sponsored beginning in the early 1990s (the 1992 Rio Earth Summit, the 1993 Human Rights Conference in Vienna, the 1994 Population Conference in Cairo, the 1995 Social Development Summit in Copenhagen, the 1995 Fourth World Conference on Women in Beijing, and others), the World Conference Against Racism (WCAR) combined an official diplomatic meeting with a parallel conference of non-governmental organizations (NGOs) and national and global social movements focusing on anti-racist and other kinds of anti-discrimination campaigns.

Inevitably, the conflict between the interests of the official and the NGO sectors was sharp. The UN institutionally was committed to a serious and ambitious anti-racist agenda. But a number of governments devoted enormous efforts to excluding issues relevant to their own countries and marginalizing activists and organizations most committed to targeting their own governments' responsibility for longstanding and continuing racist policies. Activists were present from myriad groups, including the lower-caste Dalits in India, the Roma in a number of European countries, Australia's aboriginals, Palestinian refugees and those living under Israeli occupation, Tibetans challenging China, advocates for asylum seekers and refugees across the wealthy world, and African-Americans and other people of color in the US. Participation of all those groups, both as advocates and lobbyists within or against official national delegations, and as independent participants in the NGO Forum, insured a kaleidoscopic picture of the diversity and energy of the world's peoples.

But in the run-up to Durban, US policymakers and the media quickly put aside most of the broad range of demands to hone in on the two issues that would continue to shape—and limit—how Americans saw the WCAR. Those issues were the criticism of Israel's treatment of Palestinians, and the demand for reparations for victims of the transatlantic slave trade and their descendants. On the question of Israel, its longstanding and well-documented history of violations of international law, the Geneva Conventions, and numerous UN resolutions were the root of the problem for the US. The reparations debate reflected a years-long effort, primarily in the US, to force official acknowledgement of responsibility for the horrors of slavery, and serious engagement on the question of what kind of reparations to former slaves, their descendants, and their countries of origin should be paid.

Diplomatic negotiations over the language of the final intergovernmental communiqué, underway long before the meeting began, were bitter. By the time conference participants arrived in Durban in the last week of August, battle lines had long been drawn. Colin Powell, the first African-American secretary of state, had decided ("regretfully," he said on one occasion) not to attend himself and to send only a low-level delegation to the conference. The official reason was the US claim that Israel was being "singled out" for criticism. Many US activists believe that resistance to the reparations effort was actually an equal, or even more significant, ground for official US opposition to WCAR than concern about Israel.

The criticism of Israel continued to shape US public understanding of the entire conference. The US media was filled with outraged pundits claiming WCAR was going to resurrect the "Zionism equals racism" language of a 1970s-era UN resolution that was overturned in 1991. In fact, at the time of the May 2001 preparatory committee meeting in Geneva, a few governments, largely in response to the rapidly escalating Israel violence in the occupied territories, had indeed proposed similar language. The US delegates threatened to stay away from WCAR altogether, much as the US had done during similar UN anti-racism conferences in 1978 and 1983, if language they found unacceptable was even on the agenda for discussion in Durban. Reaction to Washington's heavy-handed approach was swift, and the May talks stalled.

New talks among 21 of the countries involved in WCAR were set for June. When they failed as well to reach consensus on a text, a final preparatory session was convened on July 31, only a month before the conference was to begin, in a last chance to agree on the language. When that session opened, the European Parliament described the WCAR conference as "facing the threat of failure even before it opens," largely due to the high-profile US boycott threat. The threat was magnified by events only a week before, when the US delegates had stunned international arms control negotiators in Geneva by announcing they were walking out of the negotiations to strengthen the biological weapons treaty.

So eleventh hour fears that the US would make good on its threat, as well as UN and European pressure to ensure a successful conference with the US on board, finally trumped the earlier fights. While debates over language continued even as the conference convened in Durban, the final text of the Declaration contained no references to Zionism at all and none of the other references US officials had claimed to find so offensive.

One clause in the final text stated simply that "the Holocaust must never be forgotten." A separate clause "recogniz[ed] with deep concern the increase in anti-Semitism and Islamophobia in various parts of the world, as well as the emergence of racial and violent movements based on racism and discriminatory ideas against Jewish, Muslim, and Arab communities."

In the only two paragraphs specifically referring to the Israel–Palestine conflict, the Declaration stated that

We are concerned about the plight of the Palestinian people under foreign occupation. We recognize the inalienable right of the Palestinian people to self-determination and to the establishment of an independent State and we recognize the right to security for all States in the region, including Israel, and call upon all States to support the peace process and bring it to an early conclusion;

We call for a just, comprehensive and lasting peace in the region in which all peoples shall co-exist and enjoy equality, justice and internationally recognized human rights, and security.

In the only reference to Israel and Palestine in its entire Program of Action, the Conference called for

the end of violence and the swift resumption of negotiations, respect for international human rights and humanitarian law, respect for the principle of self-determination and the end of all suffering, thus allowing Israel and the Palestinians to resume the peace process, and to develop and prosper in security and freedom.

Hardly an example of "hateful language," as Colin Powell had dubbed it. Democratic Congressman Tom Lantos, a Holocaust survivor, a well-known champion of uncritical US military and economic support for Israel, and a member of the US delegation in Durban, condemned those he said were "hijacking the conference for propaganda purposes."

It appeared, however, that the actual language was not Washington's real concern. Certainly the Bush administration, like others before it, took a hostile view toward any attempt to address Israel's occupation of Palestine in a UN or other global arena, viewing such effort as a step onto the slippery slope of internationalizing the conflict. But in this insistence, US concern was equally, or perhaps even much more, focused on paragraph 166 of the WCAR document's section on "Remedies, Reparations, and Compensation." In that clause the conference

urges States to adopt the necessary measures, as provided by national law, to ensure the right of victims to seek just and adequate reparation and satisfaction to redress acts of racism, racial discrimination, xenophobia and related intolerance, and to design effective measures to prevent the repetition of such acts.

That commitment represented a step on a slippery slope of an entirely different type: providing international legitimacy to demands for reparations for the victims of slavery and their descendants (whether to individuals, countries, or institutions), from the countries who profited so enormously from the slave trade of the last half a millennium.

Though Europe had challenged the US on the Israel–Palestine language, those governments were equally uneasy with the reparations language, particularly because other parts of the document equated the damage wrought by colonialism with that of slavery. Europe had no intention of paying reparations for ravaging much of the world during its colonial conquests. But unlike the US delegation, which refused even to engage in serious debate over the question, Europe was willing to finesse the issue. It ultimately accepted the language of the resolution, while responding in obtuse language of its own— simultaneously recognizing its own historical responsibility for colonialism and slavery in the abstract, while deflecting actual contemporary responsibility for reparations. In a document issued two weeks before the WCAR convened in Durban, the European Commission stated that it "regrets" slavery and the slave trade, and states that "some effects of colonialism" also caused suffering and that any such act must be condemned. The EC then describes its "determination to honour this obligation and to accept its responsibility," but limited any actual accountability to the level of individuals' responsibility to remember the past.[25]

The US was not prepared to accept even such a diplomatic dodge. On September 3, both the US and Israeli delegations to the conference packed up and left Durban in a high-profile fit of diplomatic pique.

The contrast between Europe's determination (however cynical) to keep the Durban process alive, and Washington's insistence on not only pulling out but attempting to discredit the entire process, was stark. One administration official in

Washington, hoping for some kind of international cover, said they had anticipated that Australia, Canada, and Britain would follow suit, but copycat walk-outs did not occur.[26] The Bush administration won kudos for its walk-out among mainstream US media and the majority of powerbrokers and policymakers at home, but condemnation for its actions abroad.

Writing several months later, after September 11 had largely pushed the drama of the World Conference Against Racism off the agenda, African scholar Mahmood Mamdani provided some historical context for the US move:

> Official America has a habit of not taking responsibility for its own actions. Instead, it habitually looks for a high moral pretext for inaction. I was in Durban at the World Congress Against Racism (WCAR) when the US walked out of it. The Durban conference was about major crimes of the past, about racism, and xenophobia, and related crimes. I returned from Durban to listen to [then-National Security Adviser] Condoleezza Rice talk about the need to forget slavery because, she said, the pursuit of civilized life requires that we forget the past. It is true that, unless we learn to forget, life will turn into revenge-seeking. Each of us will have nothing but a catalogue of wrongs done to a long line of ancestors. But civilization cannot be built on just forgetting. We must not only learn to forget, we must also not forget to learn. We must also memorialize, particularly monumental crimes. America was built on two monumental crimes: the genocide of the Native American and the enslavement of the African American. The tendency of official America is to memorialize other people's crimes and to forget its own, to seek a high moral ground as a pretext to ignore real issues.[27]

The UN High Commissioner for Human Rights, former Irish President Mary Robinson, said she regretted the walk-out but insisted the conference would go forward. "We must persist in our endeavors," she said. "The victims of racism, racial discrimination, xenophobia and related intolerance demand this of us."[28]

The South African government, hosts of the Durban conference, deplored the walk-out as "unfortunate and unnecessary." As Palestinian Ambassador to South Africa, Suleiman al-Herfi described the US decision, "It's a pretext: the Middle East is five percent of the document; they don't want to give reparations for slavery, or condemn it... It's a great pity. They themselves are confirming their isolation. They weren't able to impose their point of view... so they quit."[29]

Palestine, South Africa, and the United Nations were not the only international critics of the US walk-out. Sharp critiques came from Europe, Asia, and elsewhere as well. Australia's former foreign minister, Gareth Evans, criticized the US for its potential walk-out even before Washington had made good on its threat, saying that the conference "should not be derailed."[30] The international human rights organization Amnesty International said that "by walking out in the middle of the conference, the US is letting down the victims of racism on all sides."[31] Among most critics, the unifying thread remained the US disdain for global opinion and the go-it-alone unilateralism that had become so prevalent in US power centers.

But a week later came September 11, and immediately the global criticism stopped.

After September 11

Many more people would die before hints of international criticism of the US would re-emerge. When the planes hit the World Trade Center and the Pentagon on September 11, there was a massive outpouring of both popular and governmental sympathy for the US and for its people. The criticisms that had been rising internationally against US arrogance came to an abrupt halt. Even when Bush identified the attacks as "acts of war" and announced that his response would be a global war, a war that would be "a monumental struggle between good and evil"[32] the rest of the world's governments did not object. Indeed, most governments cheered and much of the world stood by as the US asserted the rights of empire.

Within days NATO had, for the first time in its history, invoked Article Five of its Charter, identifying the September 11 attacks as attacks against all its members.

What emerged from September 11 was the largest, most powerful mobilization of US force—military as well as political— in history. President Bush announced the following January that US military capacity would be built up to wage his new war, "whatever it takes, whatever it costs."[33] In fact, the strategic military gap between the US and the rest of the world that became so conspicuous in Washington's response to September 11 was so vast that no immediate emergency spending alone could have created it—it was clear it must already have been under way. The $48 billion addition to the Pentagon budget requested by the Bush administration in January 2002 and quickly passed by the Congress was, by itself, more money than any other country spent on its military—and that was on top of the Pentagon's existing $379 billion military budget.[34]

The expansion of Washington's "global war on terror" beyond the war in Afghanistan and the shadowy mini-wars in countries from South Asia to the Philippines to Colombia, to the invasion and years of occupation of Iraq, led directly to vast increases in global military spending. According to the Stockholm International Peace Research Institute (SIPRI), in 2002, before the Iraq war, world military spending totaled $795 billion. With the skyrocketing costs of the war in Iraq, worldwide military spending soared to an estimated $956 billion in 2003, and remained over $900 billion in 2004.[35] The United States accounts for nearly three-fourths of the worldwide growth in the uneven arms race, but according to SIPRI, most countries in the Middle East have also increased military spending, responding to the increased militarization of the region in the context of the US occupation of Iraq and the escalations of the Israeli occupation of the Palestinian territories. Also responding to the US escalations have been the major military spenders; governments including those in China, Japan, and Russia significantly increased their expenditures between 1999 and 2003, and are projected to continue to do so through 2008.[36]

No other government or group of governments could compete with the Pentagon. The US military build-up set in motion what the influential editor of *Newsweek International*, Fareed Zakaria, called "a new era of American hegemony."[37] It was a thoroughly militarized unilateralism, one that legitimized, even glorified, the use of US military force anywhere in the world, with the unchallengeable expectation that the world would join the crusade. And it was not a situation in which governments were unaware of what the US was doing. It was, in fact, immediately clear around the world that the Bush administration was responding to the terror attacks by heading into what European Security Chief Chris Patten would later call "unilateralist overdrive."[38]

Other governments made no moves to challenge that US overdrive. To the contrary, they rushed to join the US crusade even before it was clear exactly what they were joining. In the days and weeks after September 11, 76 governments granted landing rights in their countries for US military operations in Afghanistan. Twenty-three governments offered bases for US forces involved in offensive operations. Most of these governments got something in return for joining the US anti-terrorism coalition. Russia expected and got a free hand in Chechnya; China in its restive Muslim border regions; both Pakistan and India in and around Kashmir (at least until their regional conflict threatened to spill out of control); Turkey, even greater impunity for repression in its Kurdish southeast; and Uzbekistan throughout its territory. In capitals around the world, allied spin-doctors justified their governments' human rights violations by denying the basis for international finger-pointing—after all, they would intone, don't we have the same right to self-defense that the US is using in Afghanistan?

From the beginning of the crisis Bush had divided the world along Manichean terms: "either you are with us or you are with the terrorists." *New York Times* veteran hawk and wordsmith William Safire provided one means of determining who stood where on that global divide, citing a passage from a Sherlock Holmes story:

> "Is there any point," asked the Inspector, "to which you would like to draw my attention?"
> "To the curious incident of the dog in the nighttime."
> "The dog did nothing in the nighttime."
> "That was the curious incident," remarked Sherlock Holmes.

For Safire, the fact that "diplomatic dogs are not barking all over the world" was evidence not only of the lack of serious challenge, but of active international acquiescence to Bush's power-driven unilateralism. And Safire wasn't wrong. "This welcome silence is a form of grudging assent, and is the first major achievement of George W. Bush's first year as president."[39]

That silence of the diplomatic dogs, audible from the first hours after the attacks, was certainly true for the first months after

September 11. No one was quite sure what Bush's war "between good and evil" would look like, where it would be fought, who would be on the other side. But no government wanted to risk being tarred by Bush's "you're with the terrorists" brush.

China provided a good example. In contrast to its tough, uncompromising rhetoric in the 2001 spy-plane conflict, in a new crisis in 2002 China took a far more conciliatory posture. At that time news emerged that the US-made Boeing 767 plane China had purchased for use by President Jiang Zemin had been built with spy gadgets throughout its luxury fittings. The story broke on the front page of US newspapers, but, on the record, the Chinese government refused even to confirm or deny the report—and maintained a tight-lipped refusal to challenge Washington's espionage.

It was an unsurprising response, perhaps, even from Washington's emerging competitor in Beijing, to the new aggressiveness in US policy. Bush had made it very clear that the US would tolerate no defiance from governments. In his speech to Congress and the nation less than ten days after the September 11 attacks, Bush had described the coming war. It would be, he said,

> a lengthy campaign unlike any other we have ever seen. It may include dramatic strikes visible on TV and covert operations, secret even in success. We will starve terrorists of funding, turn them one against another, drive them from place to place until there is no refuge or no rest. And we will pursue nations that provide aid or safe haven to terrorism.... From this day forward, any nation that continues to harbor or support terrorism will be regarded by the United States as a hostile regime.[40]

There was no call to engage other nations in the planning or the strategizing—only a threat that any country that did not come on board Washington's coalition, on Washington's terms, would be treated as a hostile regime, presumably risking the same punishment as that meted out to the terrorists themselves. The speech made references to other governments, but only to "ask every nation to join us. We will ask and we will need the help of police forces, intelligence services, and banking systems around the world." Nowhere did we hear of asking for ideas or for collaboration; we heard only Bush's demand for uncritical acceptance of our plan, our strategy.

The sidelining of other countries was no accident. It was a decision based on an ideologically consistent agenda reflecting the Bush administration's decision of how to achieve worldwide dominion. "This was not just America's fight. And what is at stake is not just America's freedom," Bush said. But the discussion did not then turn to the essential internationalism that would have made possible a serious response to the horrific crime against humanity that occurred on September 11, and would have begun the process of changing the conditions that would continue to give rise to terrorism. Bush turned, instead, to his absolutist division of the world, claiming that "this is civilization's fight... the civilized world is rallying to America's side." Those who are not with "us," by the Bush administration's logic, are not simply "with the terrorists," but outside the bounds of civilization.

For the first months following the invasion of Afghanistan, there was little criticism from governments around the world. A few hesitantly expressed hopes for a break to allow food supplies to be sent in; there was an occasional wish for a Ramadan pause in the bombing. But certainly no government stood ready to challenge the US strategy of full-scale military assault on Afghanistan as an answer to the attacks of September 11.

The call for an international "coalition" reflected the still-unresolved debate within the administration over the best way of maintaining US global hegemony. Colin Powell supported operating through US-imposed "coalitions of the willing." The neo-cons and militarists led by Cheney, Wolfowitz, and Rumsfeld acted on the view that the US should simply use unilateral military force with the assumption that the rest of the world would fall into line. Bush's September 19 speech demonstrated a remarkably agile negotiation between the two positions: on the one hand, the aggressive join-us-on-our-terms-or-face-our-wrath approach was designed to satisfy the fiercest unilateral instincts of the most hawkish elements of the administration. On the other hand, the reassuring rhetoric that "the civilized world is rallying to America's side" provided at least a symbolic concession to those pragmatists in and out of the administration concerned about the consequences of going it alone. It was a balance that would continue throughout the early months of the Afghan war: the most extreme assertion of raw unbridled power would be softened by iconic references to global participation and the images of international cooperation. But neither the multilateral rhetoric nor the actions on the ground took seriously the possibility that other governments might have legitimate opinions and independent strategic approaches of their own—or that nations might have the right to diverge from or even oppose US war moves.

When Bush came to answering his own "why do they hate us?" query in his post-September 11 speech, things got even more interesting. The fundamental basis of his answer focused on the question of democracy—and the lack of democracy among some relevant governments. Maintaining his "us" and "them" dichotomy, Bush told members of Congress that they

> hate what they see right here in this chamber, a democratically elected government. Their leaders are self-appointed... They want to overthrow existing governments in many Muslim countries, such as Egypt, Saudi Arabia, and Jordan.

But somehow Bush's speechwriters managed to miss the irony of blaming "self-appointed" terrorists for their US-backed governments' self-appointed leaders. The three Arab governments he later mentioned, approvingly dubbing them the "moderate" Arab states, are classic examples not only of Washington's key junior partners in the Arab world, but of completely undemocratic, self-perpetuating regimes. US-armed Saudi Arabia and US-financed Jordan are two of the world's last old-fashioned absolute monarchies. US-supported Egypt's president Hosni Mubarak has remained in office for more than twenty years, "elected" over and over again in what Human Rights Watch called "no-choice" balloting.[41] Mubarak's much-heralded 2004 announcement of his intention to allow opposition candidates to run for president in 2005 was quickly exposed as a fraud, as many political parties were disenfranchised and opposition protests attacked by government-supported mobs. Mubarak's overwhelming victory in the September 2005 "multi-party election" only highlighted the false claims of democratization of the Nile.

There is little doubt that public opinion throughout the Arab world was outraged by the US choice of war in Afghanistan. But the legacy of Washington's long years of backing repressive and corrupt absolute monarchies and false democracies throughout the Arab Middle East effectively ensures that no government in the region would be willing to follow the lead of its population and challenge the US. Despite Bush's belated claims that the Afghanistan and Iraq wars were waged to spread democracy across the region, it was and remained common knowledge that US backing for the absolute monarchies was a permanent feature of US policy, despite occasional rhetorical criticisms. Saudi Arabia has for years been the top purchaser of US military equipment and hardware. In 2001, the UAE, that tiny collection of Gulf sheikdoms with a total population significantly less than that of Chicago, was the first country to be allowed to purchase 80 of what were then one of most advanced fighter jets in the US arsenal, the F-16 Block 60s, at a cost of $6.4 billion.

It was widely known, and deeply resented, that the call for democratization that shapes US policy toward so many other governments is virtually absent regarding the royal families of Saudi Arabia, Kuwait, the United Arab Emirates, and most other Gulf states. When Secretary of State Condoleezza Rice visited the Middle East in June 2005, she unexpectedly exposed key fault lines and failures in US policy in the region. Her speech on "democracy" in Cairo was particularly significant in her acknowledgement of past and present failures. "The United States pursued stability at the expense of democracy in this region, here in the Middle East, and we achieved neither," she said. Her statement was significant—but there was still no evidence that the Bush administration was prepared to take seriously what real support for democracy in the region would require. A genuine US commitment to democracy would mean conditioning aid to Egypt on substantive moves toward ending government repression and curbing Mubarak's unofficial dynasty of power; stopping the massive export of US arms to Saudi Arabia; enforcing the Arms Export Control Act equally throughout the region, including as it relates to Israel; and holding Israel accountable for its massive violations of international law and human rights instruments. But Rice's speech heralded no such commitment.

During the decade since the end of the 1991 Gulf War, the US has installed troops, bases, warships, fighter jets, and more in virtually every country in the area, helping to keep in power the repressive regimes, abjuring criticism in favor of pragmatic diplomacy and joint military training exercises. Osama bin Laden was hardly the first to call for getting US troops out of Saudi Arabia; democratic opponents of the Saudi monarchy in and outside the kingdom had long raised just such a demand with a very different goal in mind. Maximizing the monarchy's ability to withstand popular demands for democratic reform was probably not Washington's primary goal in making the kingdom a forward military base and crucial oil provider. No one in Washington would have complained if the royal family had suddenly decided to cede power to a newly-elected parliament, to enfranchise women, to stop abusing non-citizen workers. But the kings and their brothers and sons made no such offers, and the repressive discrimination (albeit partly assuaged by oil wealth for Saudi citizens) remained in place, and the US was happy to accept that, too. While US policy, especially Washington's newest wars in the region, continued to stoke popular anti-US sentiment, challenging that policy, on which their power depended, would not be the task of the Middle East's despots.

From Regional to Global
Beyond the specifics of US strategy in the Middle East and surrounding regions, there is a particularity to US foreign policy that engenders antagonism around the world, from Washington's closest European and Canadian allies to the poorest countries of the impoverished global South. More than any single policy or even set of policies, it is the arrogance with which US policy is imposed that is so infuriating—international law dismissed, UN requirements ignored, and internationally supported treaties abandoned. While the US demands that other governments strictly abide by UN resolutions, treaties, and international law, and threatens or imposes sanctions or even military assault in response to violations, it holds itself accountable only to its own separate law of empire.

Every empire in history has created its own set of laws for managing its far-flung possessions and colonies. As mentioned earlier, Athens had separate laws for its colony Mylos than for itself. The Roman empire had one set of laws for Rome itself, another for its far-flung possessions. The Ottoman, Russian,

British empires did much the same thing. Finally, toward the end of the 20th century, having scaled once unimaginable heights of military, economic, and political power, it was Washington's turn.

This American law of empire exuded extraordinary arrogance, the arrogance of absolute power unchallenged by any other global force. The arrogance was evident in Washington's rejection of the International Criminal Court in 1998, its refusal to sign the 1997 Convention against anti-personnel land mines, its failures on the Convention on the Rights of the Child, the Law of the Sea, the Comprehensive Test Ban Treaty, and more. It was also sharply apparent in the dramatic abandonment, by the late 1990s, of Washington's 1990–91 Gulf War assertion (however cynical or tactical) of the need for United Nations endorsement to confer legitimacy on fundamentally unilateral interventions.

In the context of September 11, US arrogance took on a particularly hypocritical cast. The US purported to champion democracy as the linchpin of US foreign policy, while continuing to prop up governments infamous for denying any democratic opening to their own peoples. So when Bush claimed the September 11 attackers were motivated by hatred for American democracy, it was difficult for anyone around the world to take it seriously. Far more likely was the possibility that the fury of those who cheered on the September 11 attacks (if not that of the attackers themselves) in Saudi Arabia, in Indonesia, in Gaza, in Uzbekistan, was fueled less by hatred of American democracy than by American support for governments denying their people that same democracy.

Those governments were among the clearest beneficiaries of the US response to September 11. But they were by far not the only ones to sign on. As the tentative but growing pre-September 11 resistance to Bush-style US hegemony screeched to a halt that Tuesday morning, presidents, prime ministers, parliaments, and kings, ignoring their peoples' widespread opposition, went into overdrive, competing to see who could be the first ally, the strongest supporter, the most reliable partner, to board Washington's war train. What would soon pass for "coalition"-building was in the air.

On to Iraq

As the war in Afghanistan ground on, and war plans for Iraq ratcheted up, the Bush administration moved boldly to conscript allies, agreeable or not, to its so-called coalition of the willing. The move attempted to follow the successful script implemented by the first President Bush in the 1990 when, as the great Pakistani scholar-activist Eqbal Ahmad wrote, "the US has used a multilateral mechanism to start a unilateral war."[42]

Although Bush administration officials announced publicly in 2002 that they would not attempt to bully other nations into supporting their Iraq policy, there was already ample precedent for the United States doing just that. In 1990, the US government under the senior Bush bribed China with post-Tiananmen Square diplomatic rehabilitation and renewal of long-term development aid to prevent Beijing's threatened veto of the UN resolution authorizing the 1991 Gulf War. The votes of several poor countries then on the Security Council, including Ethiopia, Colombia, and Zaire (now the Democratic Republic of Congo) were guaranteed with cheap Saudi oil, new military aid, and enhanced economic assistance. And when Yemen, the sole Arab country on the Council, voted against the resolution authorizing war against Iraq, a US diplomat told the Yemeni ambassador, "that will be the most expensive 'no' vote you ever cast." Three days later the US cut its entire aid budget to Yemen.[43]

The second Bush administration would try the same thing. But this time around Bush would find it impossible to duplicate his father's diplomatic success. The 2002–03 effort to enroll other governments into Bush's "coalition of the willing" relied, as did the approaches in the run-up to the 1990–91 Gulf War, on a diverse arsenal of sticks and carrots. George W. Bush relied far more on sticks, often leaving the diplomatic carrots behind.

With its economy accounting for a quarter of all economic activity in the world, the US had a wide range of economic pressures to bring to bear against any countries, particularly the poorest—the most important being in the realms of trade and investment. During the fall 2002 run-up to the Iraq war the US was negotiating new "free" trade agreements with several nations; threats were made, sometimes hinted, sometimes openly, that failure to support the Iraq war could jeopardize these negotiations. Serious tariff negotiations were underway with several nations, including Security Council member Mexico (with whom the US was also negotiating immigration policies), and there was a constant threat that the US might withdraw tariff concessions from Mexico or other countries opposing the war. And of course the United States already had a long history of using trade sanctions against nations that have invoked its ire. The strongest examples included the crippling US-led economic and trade sanctions against Iraq in the twelve years since the first Gulf crisis of 1990. Iran and Cuba, for more than a generation, as well as Venezuela more recently, continue to face punishing trade sanctions.

Economic aid was also a powerful lever. The US spends a lower percentage of its GDP on economic and development assistance than any of the 22 wealthiest nations. Those aid levels have been falling even further in recent years, but US aid remains very important to recipient governments, especially to the poorest nations. The US has long used its aid programs as a political instrument to reward allies and punish countries that stray from Washington's approved path. When it comes to rewards, most Americans, who generally believe foreign aid goes to the poorest countries, likely have little idea that about one-quarter of the US foreign aid budget (including both economic and military aid) goes to Israel, the seventeenth wealthiest country in the world. If one adds the amount the US sends to Egypt, a much poorer country with ten times the population of Israel, whose aid allocation is by Congressional mandate set at percentage of that to Israel, the total comes to about one-third of the entire foreign aid budget. Rewards in the form of increased aid allocations to other countries have been miserly indeed.

As to punishments, the clearest example was the 1990 penalty imposed on Yemen when its government had the temerity to vote against the US war in Iraq and lost its entire US aid allocation as a result. This time the US effort to enforce acquiescence with its war strategy would be the same—but the results, at least in the short term, would be quite different.

A Resolution—But Not Permission for War
In November 2002, after eight weeks of negotiations, the US and UK managed to force the Security Council to pass a

resolution giving Iraq "one last chance" to comply with earlier UN disarmament demands. (In fact, Iraq was by that time already in compliance, having allowed UN weapons inspectors back into the country and already being in the process of preparing the "full accounting" of their weapons programs they had agreed to earlier.)

Despite Washington's capacity for pressuring other nations, the resolution's passage was not assured or automatic; in its earliest versions the proposed language had come very close to officially endorsing war against Iraq. During the negotiations, virtually every country on the Council insisted that the US and Britain soften the language so that the resolution not authorize the use of force. France, China, and Russia each said their governments had supported the resolution only because of US assurances that Washington would return to the Security Council before launching a military attack on Iraq. The resolution in its final compromise form, they argued, did not provide the US with a UN authorization for the use of military force.

The two European members, Norway and Ireland, were expected to support the US–British position. A third Council member, Syria, was almost certain to oppose. As a result, the most extensive pressure campaigns were waged against those seven members, all from the global South countries most dependent on US largesse and military or political support— Bulgaria, Cameroon, Colombia, Guinea, Mauritius, Mexico, and Singapore—and thus most vulnerable to US pressure.

The impoverished African island nation of Mauritius soon became the poster country for US pressure. The government actually temporarily recalled its ambassador, Jagdish Koonjul, in late October because in Security Council debates he continued to express what was perceived as diplomatic ambiguity regarding his country's support for the US resolution. Mauritius' vulnerability was rooted in the country's desperate poverty and its government's eagerness to join the globalized economy even on Washington's harsh terms. The Mauritian government was generally more conservative and more open to privatization, deregulation, and other aspects of globalization than many African countries, and was trying to attract new foreign investment in its fledgling information technology sector.[44] Mauritius was a recipient of the Africa Growth and

Opportunity Act (AGOA), passed in 2000, which granted preferential access to US markets to select sub-Saharan African countries that met a list of eligibility criteria. But alongside the economic and governance criteria, AGOA included the requirement that recipient countries "not engage in activities that undermine United States national security or foreign policy interests."

The language received little notice until the fall 2002 Security Council negotiations over the US–British resolution on Iraq. Nothing in AGOA defined what would constitute "activities that undermine United States national security or foreign policy interests," but it was a pretty good bet that voting against a hard-sought US-sponsored resolution in the UN Security Council, with the stakes as high as the Iraq war, was pretty certain to qualify. When Koonjul appeared insufficiently enthusiastic about an early version of the resolution, his foreign minister recalled the ambassador for a tongue-lashing and orders to make clear Mauritius' full support for the US position. Perhaps remembering the Yemen precedent from the 1990 Gulf crisis, the government was worried that even hesitation, let alone opposition, to the US war could result in the loss of AGOA preferences.

With the new Council members taking office in the new year, African members of the Council, Guinea and Cameroon, both also recipients of AGOA preferences, no doubt took notice. Guinea's repressive government had received $3 million in direct US military in grants in 2002 and was anticipating an increase to $20.7 million in development assistance in 2003. Cameroon, along with its AGOA trade deal, was given access to surplus US weapons without charge and also qualified for about $2.5 million annually for military education and training.

The US-backed regime in Colombia, an impoverished South American country languishing under Washington's lethal "Plan Colombia" militarization schemes, ostensibly designed to limit coca growing and cocaine production, received about $380 million in US grants under the International Narcotics Control and Law Enforcement (INCLE) program in 2002; the proposed amount earmarked for 2003 was $439 million. Exactly twelve years earlier, Colombia had also been an elected member of the Security Council, when the Council was again the focus of the senior Bush's campaign of bribes, threats, and punishments to win UN support for war in Iraq, Colombia's support had been assured with a pre-vote commitment to an increase in US economic aid and a new military assistance package. In 2002, Colombia's latest government no doubt remembered just how lucrative support for an important US resolution could be.

Mexico received about $12 million in 2002, also under the INCLE anti-narcotics program, along with about $28.2 million for general financial assistance from the US Economic Support Funds (ESF) program. Perhaps more significantly, Mexico was engaged in difficult negotiations with the Bush administration over immigration policies, with the Mexican government under heavy domestic pressure to win at least some concessions from Washington regarding the rights of Mexican workers in the US.

Bulgaria had already received $13.5 million in US military grants in 2001 (though like military aid to all countries other than Israel, virtually all of those funds had to be used to purchase US-manufactured weapons or other military goods), and an additional $8.5 million in 2002; $9.5 million in military aid was in the works for 2003. The US already saw Bulgaria, which was hoping to enter both NATO and the European Union, as a key long-term ally in Europe, so Sofia had also received $69 million from Washington's Support for East European Democracy (SEED) program; the proposed 2003 grant was set at $28 million.

Aside from Syria (which was already under political as well as economic pressure from the US and was assumed to be a strong opponent of the resolution), Singapore was the only country among the Security Council's Southern members that did not receive economic or military aid from the United States. But Washington was still able to arm-twist wealthy but tiny Singapore because the US remained the Asian nation's biggest single arms supplier. In 2001 the US sold Singapore weapons worth $656.3 million, and the 2002 purchases totaled an estimated $370 million more. Ensuring continued access to US weapons purchases kept Singapore on a short leash.[45]

Given the multitude of pressure points Washington could push on Council members, particularly those from the global South, it would have been astonishing if the US–British resolution did not pass. Many observers, particularly those who perhaps had not paid sufficient attention to the US threat and pressure campaigns underway in the capitals of affected nations (where one could find higher ranking officials than those available at UN headquarters in New York), were puzzled at the unanimity of the final vote. But given the disparity of power between the US and the rest of the Council, the acquiescence was hardly a surprise. What was more significant was that the tentative resistance taken up by some of the Council members, in the form of fighting hard over the language of Resolution 1441 and refusing to include an authorization for war within it, succeeded.

The language of 1441 focused on returning United Nations arms inspectors to Iraq to complete their unfinished work of confirming that no weapons of mass destruction existed. Baghdad had already announced its willingness to allow the inspectors to return, and the UN's nuclear (International Atomic Energy Agency) and biological/chemical weapons (UN Monitoring, Verification and Inspection Commission) inspectors soon were back on the ground.

Ironically, in many ways the text of the resolution reflected the rising strength of the global anti-war movement, governmental and popular. Despite enormous US and British pressure, Resolution 1441 did not, ultimately, endorse the use of force against Iraq, and it reasserted, defying intense US efforts, that the solution to the Iraq crisis, at least in the international arena, was disarmament, not overthrow.

Every Council ambassador, speaking after the unanimous vote, emphasized clearly that the resolution provided no authorization for war. Even the ambassador of the United Kingdom, Sir Jeremy Greenstock, acknowledged that the resolution has no "automaticity," a diplomatic term referring to an automatic result, in this case going to war against Iraq, without requiring any additional decision. He repeated that in the event of a further Iraqi breach, the matter would return to the Council.

French Ambassador Jean-David Levitte hailed the fact that the resolution ensured that the Security Council maintained control over the future course of action, and said explicitly that a Council meeting would be required to determine any action in the event of future Iraqi non-compliance. "France welcomes the elimination from the resolution of all ambiguity on this point," he said, "and the elimination of all automaticity."

Mexico's ambassador, Adolfo Aguilar Zinser, challenged the US most directly. The use of military force could only be valid, he said, "with the prior, explicit authorization of the Security Council." In the case of Iraq's failure to comply, the Council itself would determine the existence of a threat to international peace and security. "The decision of the Security Council confers the legitimacy, the effectiveness, and the relevance of this body. It strengthens the Security Council, the United Nations, multilateralism and the construction of an international system of norms and principles," he said, noting that Council decisions must themselves comply with international law on the basis of objectively verifiable facts.

The ambassador from Cameroon, Martin Belinga-Eboutou, welcomed the fact that the sponsors, the US and UK, had affirmed that the resolution contained no hidden triggers or automaticity, and that they would work to preserve the Council's central role in maintaining international peace and security. Colombian Ambassador Alfonso Valdivieso stressed his country's insistence on preserving the Security Council's core role in dealing with the matter. "This resolution is not, nor could [it] be, a resolution authorizing the use of force," he said.

And Irish Ambassador Richard Ryan welcomed what he said were assurances given by the US and the UK that the resolution's text aims achieving disarmament through inspections, and not to establish a basis for the use of force. "This is a resolution about disarmament, not war," he stressed. "It is about removing all threat of war."[46]

In fact, even Secretary of State Colin Powell, a few days after the resolution was passed, said that

> If [Saddam Hussein] does not comply this time, that lack of compliance goes right to the Security Council for it to convene immediately and consider what should be done, and serious consequences are held out within this current resolution. I can assure you that if he doesn't comply this time we are going to ask the UN to give authorization for all necessary means.[47]

Of course he immediately followed that statement with the threat that "If the UN is not willing to do that, the United States with like-minded nations will go and disarm him forcefully." But the unanimity of Council opposition to a unilateral US decision to go to war forced the Bush administration to at least pay lip service to the UN Charter and multilateral obligations. And that Council opposition set the terms for Washington's failure to win international support for its war in Iraq, and ensured the clarity of the war's illegality.

It was clear that for virtually every country on the Council (except perhaps the UK), the vote was less about constraining Iraq than it was about constraining the US.

It certainly was not the case that key Security Council governments opposing the war were acting out of humanitarian or even consistently anti-hegemonic or anti-empire goals. French President Jacques Chirac had not become a sudden protector of Iraqi children, nor had the Russian leader Vladimir Putin taken up the cause of human rights. German Chancellor Gerhard Schroeder was not courageously risking re-election by saying no to Bush's war.

What was undeniable was that those powerful governments, operating within a joint framework of opportunistic political goals and a set of broader international concerns about the consequences of a militaristic unilateral superpower driving toward empire, made the choice to challenge that drive and stand up to George Bush. In all of those cases, sitting governments gained political support from populations already ahead of their governments, outraged by the war and the military thrust of Bush policies. What turned governments around the world into opponents of the war was the combination of citizen campaigners demanding that their own governments defy the war drive and the governments' recognition of the dangers posed to their own positions and power by Bush's unilateral global agenda. The result of that combination was a changed dynamic, in which the domestic political costs of giving in to US demands (something most governments, rhetoric and posturing aside, are usually eager to do) were much higher than the domestic political costs of standing against Washington.

The question remains as to what degree the popular support for anti-war positions created, extended, or strengthened governments' willingness to maintain their defiance of Washington. Perhaps Chirac, for example, first said no to the

Bush plan for war out of a combination of historic French antipathy toward the US, some specific economic concerns (read: French oil investments in Iraq), and personal distaste for the unilateralist style of leadership. Chirac may have planned a short-term, politically useful but ultimately rhetorical 'non' campaign—but when public opinion all over France, from all political parties, embraced his defiance, he rose to the occasion and emerged at the head of a growing coalition of governments opposing empire. In Germany, the governing Red–Green coalition of Social Democrats and Greens faced serious challenges because of their economic policies. But public opinion was massively anti-war, and taking his place as a leader of the German as well as European resistance to the US war brought Chancellor Schroeder much-needed political support.

At the end of the day the powerful governments long allied to the United States came to oppose the Iraq war based on a wide assortment of motives, from venal to principled. But they did the right thing, even if sometimes for the wrong reasons. And in so doing, they empowered smaller, weaker, poorer countries that alone could never have gone head to head with the world's "hyper-power."

One of the most significant consequences of the successful fight to change the final language of 1441 was that at least in the short term, the informal collaboration among often-squabbling Security Council member states held, and those disparate governments acting together were able to resist the US pressure to endorse war. In doing so, they put the world on notice that the US (and its junior partner, Britain) must be held accountable to international law and the UN Charter. And finally, after eight weeks of hard negotiations, the US was forced to back down on its language and soften the text. Only then did the Council vote unanimously to support the resolution, thus denying Washington any pretext for punishing recalcitrant members. None of the threats regarding aid, trade, military assistance, or other earlier blandishments were realized.

On the Other Hand...

There were, however, other examples in which US pressure triumphed and governments collapsed. One day before the December 8 deadline set for provision of its arms declaration,

Iraq submitted to the Security Council a massive inventory of its chemical, biological, and nuclear facilities, including all civilian production. Its presentation quickly fueled major controversies between the US and the governments serving on the Council.

Under the terms of the resolution, Iraq was obliged to provide a "full and accurate" accounting of its WMD programs and materials to the Council. The huge compilation of records the Iraqi government presented totaled 12,000 pages and five CD-ROMs. But in an extraordinary hijacking of UN authority, only the US, of all the Council members, unquestionably received the full text.

The Iraqis provided two complete sets of the documents, one for the UN arms inspectors (the nuclear section destined for the International Atomic Energy Agency or IAEA in Vienna, and the chemical and biological sections for UNMOVIC at UN headquarters) and one for the Security Council. The Council had agreed, unwillingly and under enormous US pressure, that the five permanent members, all nuclear weapons states, would get the entire document, while the ten elected members of the Council would receive edited versions, with the "how to build a nuclear bomb" material excised. Several countries, including Norway and Syria, expressed sharp disagreement to this two-tier approach to Council members, but accepted it.

However, what happened when the document was actually handed over to the ambassador of Colombia, the Council's rotating president, had little to do with UN decisions and everything to do with US power. During December Colombia was president of the Security Council. Just before Iraq was due to submit its declaration, Colin Powell visited Bogota, offering a huge increase, reportedly of $700 million, in long-promised military aid. Two days later, when the UN inspectors presented Colombia's ambassador, on behalf of the Council, with the enormous pile of documents and CD-ROMs at UN headquarters in New York, he immediately turned them over to a waiting US diplomat. The entire dossier was whisked off to a waiting helicopter, and ferried to Washington, DC "for copying" before the other four permanent members were able to see it. As a result, the US had sole and secret access to the document for an entire day.

Twenty-four hours later, Russia, France, China, and the UK,

the other four permanent members and other four nuclear weapons states, received what the US told them were exact copies of the dossier. More than a week later, the ten elected Council members received their versions of the documents—now edited down from 12,000 pages to just over 3,000. It seemed unlikely that almost 9,000 pages could have been devoted to bomb-building, ostensibly the only material to be deleted. A leak in the German press of some of the thousands of pages that Washington deleted from Iraq's arms declaration provided some clarification.

The sections the US had deleted documented 24 US corporations, 55 US subsidiaries of foreign corporations, as well as several US government agencies, all of which had provided parts, material, training, and other support to Iraq's chemical, biological, missile, and nuclear weapons programs throughout the 1970s and 80s. Some had continued till the end of 1990. The US corporations include Honeywell, Rockwell, Hewlett Packard, Dupont, Eastman Kodak, Bechtel, and more. (A year later, when the those same corporations were winning multi-million dollar Pentagon contracts for "reconstructing" Iraq, few remembered the role Bechtel, Honeywell, and so many others had played in arming and equipping Saddam Hussein's Iraq for years before the 2003 US invasion.) US government Departments of Energy, Commerce, Defense and Agriculture; federal laboratories at Sandia, Los Alamos, and Lawrence Livermore were also involved. The US "editors" had deleted extensive documentation of European involvement, particularly German and British, as well as Chinese and others.[48]

UN Secretary-General Kofi Annan called the US seizure of the document "unfortunate" and "wrong." Council ambassadors were said—off the record—to be furious. It was a clear example of how US pressure so often works to force governments to their knees—making the brief moments of resistance all the more surprising.

A Second Resolution?

At the end of 2002, five elected members of the Council rotated off, and Mauritius, Colombia, Ireland, Norway, and Singapore were replaced by Angola, Chile, Germany, Pakistan, and Spain. They joined the five remaining elected members (Bulgaria,

Cameroon, Guinea, Mexico, and Syria) as well as the five permanent members (US, Britain, France, China, Russia). Even before the Downing Street memo surfaced more than two years later,[49] governments and social movements around the world already understood that war was on Washington's agenda. The UN arms inspections then underway in Iraq would not determine anything regarding US policy.

But into the winter of 2003 the Bush administration still claimed that it preferred a diplomatic solution to the Iraq crisis, and hoped that the UN would "enforce its own resolutions." At the UN in January the US could count on support for the Iraq war only from Britain and two of the new Security Council members, Spain and Bulgaria. Washington and London were still talking about winning support for a second Council resolution, which would provide the explicit endorsement of war—but this time it was becoming more difficult to find the votes.

The pressure was on. The ideologues in the Bush administration, led by Cheney, Wolfowitz, and Rumsfeld, were getting desperate to finalize their plans for war, and Colin Powell's diplomatic wrangling in the UN was proving a major headache. They began to prepare a new diplomatic approach, explicitly sidelining the United Nations and replacing it with what they would call a "coalition of the willing." That meant the administration needed a campaign to persuade, bribe, threaten, and otherwise force other countries, outside the Security Council, to join Washington's crusade.

The United States campaign at first played out most visibly in Europe. On January 22 Secretary of Defense Rumsfeld set the stage with his division of new and old Europe.[50] France and Germany, of course, already at the center of the international front of anti-war governments, were dismissed as "old Europe" (read: irrelevant, anachronistic, insignificant). On the other side was Rumsfeld's vision of "new Europe" (read: vibrant, energetic, 21st-century), which included war-supporting Italy and Spain (then still under the pro-Bush government of Jose Maria Aznar), but primarily focused on the central and eastern European countries.

Rumsfeld's statement actually went beyond the new and old characterizations to encourage the greater division of Europe. As he put it, "Germany has been a problem, and France has been a problem... But you look at vast numbers of other countries in

Europe. They're not with France and Germany on this, they're with the United States." Not surprisingly, many of Washington's backers in "new Europe" were former Warsaw Pact countries, whose government officials had viewed the US as their key international protector since the days of the Cold War. Virtually all of them aspired to membership in the European Union, but they maintained a largely tactical approach to the alliance. Many appeared to view the EU primarily as a kind of cash cow for their strapped economies, while continuing to rely on the US as their most important backer. With their strategic eggs remaining in Washington's basket, it might have been expected that those governments would resist any view of Europe as a potential counterweight to US global dominance. There was no indication that the America-First approach of these countries would change even after joining the EU. So US promises to sponsor favored allies through the EU process (as the US was already doing with Turkey) became a powerful inducement to jump publicly onto Washington's war wagon. And *sotto voce* threats that such support could be withdrawn provided an even stronger incentive for "new Europe" to toe the US line.

On the military side, because the US maintains an effective veto on new members of the North Atlantic Treaty Organization, several aspiring NATO members were among the countries that signed on to the looming US war in Iraq. Military bribes were hinted at—including the possibility that allies in "new Europe" might become the sites for new US military bases. That hint was expanded when the US threatened to close key US bases in Germany, ostensibly for military efficiency but understood as direct retaliation for Berlin's opposition to the war. The closing of US bases in Germany, however, never happened, nor did the Pentagon announce new base construction in Latvia, Bulgaria, Moldova, or elsewhere in eastern or central Europe.

Standing Fast
Well into January 2003, still only four Council members (the US, Britain, Spain, and Bulgaria) were prepared to support a second resolution explicitly endorsing the use of force against Iraq. Five others had already staked out early opposition to the war: veto-wielding permanent members France, Russia, and

(with some ambivalence) China, along with Germany and Syria, the sole Arab country on the Council.

Iraq's next-door neighbor Syria had long been on the US list of "states supporting terrorism." But in the run-up to the war Syria had not yet reached, as it did by 2004, its place at the top of the list of governments the Bush administration was targeting for destabilization or overthrow. Although Washington's arm-twisters largely ignored Syria in their search for Security Council support, President Bashar al-Assad faced the near-certainty that refusing to support a US war in Iraq would quash any possibility of being removed from the list, with all of the sanctions and isolation it entailed. It was almost certainly that same fear back in the fall of 2002 that had resulted in Syria's decision to vote with the unanimous majority in support of Resolution 1441. While existing US sanctions and the "anti-terrorism" list meant there were few diplomatic or economic US–Syrian ties, no country, especially one so close to both Iraq and Israel–Palestine could risk antagonizing the US. It was Syria's same Ba'athist government, after all, then led by Bashar al-Assad's father Hafez, that agreed to join the first Bush's war against Iraq in 1991, lending the appearance of Arab legitimacy to the US war. So while no one expected Syria to support a US call for war against Iraq in 2003, neither was there any expectation that Damascus would play a vocal mobilizing role to build the anti-war front.

Contrasting to their dismissive attitude toward Syria, Washington used intense pressure to try to shake the resolve of Germany and France. The campaigns were signaled by Rumsfeld's earlier attack on the two countries as "old Europe," while he embraced the "new Europe" of former Warsaw Pact and NATO aspirants in Central and Eastern Europe.

In general, the close strategic, military, and economic relations between the US, Germany, and France, both bilateral and also through the NATO-based and other multilateral and transatlantic links, as well as the independent economic clout of the two European giants, limited Washington's options. The kind of dire threats Washington could throw against smaller, weaker countries were not a serious likelihood in Paris and Berlin. But that did not mean that France and Germany could defy the US with impunity. Both countries faced the possibility of repercussions in the form of lost US contracts for defense-related goods and services. *Defense News* described how German and French defense manufacturers' recent efforts to obtain more lucrative Pentagon contracts might fail. An early indication of such consequences was seen in a bill in the US Congress that would have banned US firms from attending the Paris air show in June 2003.[51]

The attack was most intense and most visible against France, which, as a permanent veto-wielding power on the Security Council, was viewed in Washington as the most powerful force within the anti-war camp, and thus was publicly excoriated as the symbol of defiance of US policy. There were other, more solid reasons for identifying France as the center of the multilateral anti-war mobilization. They included, of course, a long history of French opposition to US foreign policy, most notably in NATO where France for decades fought for a Eurocentric concentration of power as opposed to the US primacy asserted by Britain and other partisans of Washington's favored transatlantic focus. And among French intellectuals old-fashioned anti-Americanism remained popular. So unlike the US pressures imposed relatively quietly on the potential swing governments in the Council, the anti-French campaign was waged publicly and with harshly vitriolic rhetoric. Some US lawmakers, including the Republican majority leader Dennis Hastert, threatened to propose trade sanctions on French wine and water. Other lawmakers resorted to crude insults. Rep. John McCain likened France to an aging starlet from the 1940s who is "still trying to dine out on her looks, but doesn't have the face for it anymore."[52] Perhaps most memorably, Congressman Walter Jones (who three years later, in June 2005, would join a bipartisan group of congresspeople to demand that President Bush present a plan for withdrawing troops from Iraq) called for the French fries in the House cafeteria to be renamed "freedom fries." President Bush announced he would stay in Switzerland during the summit of the Group of Eight industrial nations to avoid having to sleep in France.

Germany faced less public, but in many ways more serious, pressures. Unlike France, Germany was only an elected, non-permanent member of the Security Council, and Berlin had been engaged for years in a high-profile campaign to win US support for a permanent seat in an expanded Council. Chancellor Gerhard Schroeder and his Red–Green (Social Democratic and Green Party) coalition faced the likelihood that US support would be denied if Germany kept up its high-profile opposition to war. (In May 2005, Secretary of State Condoleezza Rice announced to members of Congress, in a statement leaked to the *Washington Post*, that the US would not support Germany's bid for a permanent Council seat.[53] Given the administration's continuing support for expanding the Council to include a permanent seat for Japan, there could be little doubt that the US opposition to Germany's bid was based on Berlin's opposition to the Iraq war.

More immediately, the Bush administration threatened publicly to remove, or at least scale down, US military bases from Germany, linking the threat to a highly publicized consideration of moving some European bases to more deserving countries in "new Europe." Such a move would have a seriously damaging impact on Germany's struggling economy. Before the war began in 2003, the Pentagon maintained about 71,000 US troops in Germany, and that number would rise once the US invaded Iraq. Although their presence was increasingly controversial, the bases played a key role in the economies of the local communities where they were located. The Pentagon estimated at that time that the US bases brought as much as $4.5 billion per year into Germany's economy, primarily through purchases of goods and services, direct and indirect hires of foreign nationals, and other expenditures.[54]

In both France and Germany, the political stance of the governments and their willingness to risk US ire by publicly leading the global governmental resistance, were bolstered by sky-high public opposition to the looming war in Iraq. Schroeder's coalition was reelected in the fall of 2002 after a victorious campaign focused on only one issue: that Schroeder was stronger against war in Iraq than his opponent. In Paris, it was massive public opposition to the war that transformed what likely began as tactical opposition by the right-wing Jacques Chirac into the French president's staunchly defiant stance from which it would be virtually impossible to back down.

China and Russia, both powerful countries with long histories of acting independently, were from the beginning deemed unlikely converts for the US–British search for support. While no country can leave the US out of its economic equation and US–Russian trade was significant, Russia was far more dependent on European than US markets for its exports, mostly natural gas and oil products. China had already showed, by winning US approval of its bid for membership in the World Trade Organization, that it held substantial power in its relations with the US due to its huge market and the widely coveted investment opportunities within its borders. On the other hand, both Beijing and Moscow needed good relations with the United States. China was the US's fourth largest trading partner, with $125 billion in exports to the US in 2002, about 40 percent of China's total exports.[55] In Russia, a major concern was the $8 billion owed by Iraq, as well as the multi-billion dollar contracts then held by Russian companies to develop Iraqi oil wells. Bush's early claimed commitment to honor those contracts after an anticipated US-led military victory was viewed with some skepticism, and Russian officials presumably saw that their chances of getting Bush to keep his word would have been weakened further if they refused to back the US in the Security Council.

As a result, though either China or Russia could have vetoed any US resolution in the Council authorizing war in Iraq, neither was a likely candidate to do so. From the beginning of Washington's campaign to round up Council votes, the most likely outcome always centered on Russian and Chinese abstentions, not vetoes—though that would still make the US goal harder to reach.

Seeking the Uncommitted

The US would need a minimum of nine votes and no veto to get a Council resolution passed endorsing war. With only four votes in favor and five likely-to-certain opponents, the key players soon became known as the "Uncommitted Six"—insultingly dubbed the "six-pack" by some US pundits. Those countries, all from the global South, were Angola, Cameroon, Chile, Guinea, Mexico, and Pakistan. They were all relatively or profoundly poor, none were major players on the world stage, and they were all dependent on the US for a variety of economic and strategic backing. They would each take enormous risks to antagonize Washington with a "no" vote.

Winning support from these nations became Washington's

strategic priority. In all six countries, public opinion was strongly against war in Iraq. In only two, Chile and Mexico, were the governments mostly democratic and mostly accountable to popular opinion, but these countries were also in the midst of difficult negotiations with the US over trade and immigration policies. Impoverished Angola and Cameroon struggled with problems of governance and corruption, and especially with the legacies of colonialism and more recently the impact of failed "structural adjustment policies" (forced privatization, ending regulatory protections, and so forth) imposed by the IMF and the World Bank. Guinea faced all of those problems as well as a history of brutal domestic repression. Pakistan was run by General Pervez Musharraf, who came to power in a military coup, who refused to yield power, whose government continued to squander scarce money away from desperate social needs to fund a massive military and nuclear weapons program—yet Islamabad remained a virtual US protectorate in return for backing the US war in Afghanistan.

None of the six, on their own, were likely candidates to challenge US demands. None, alone, were capable of going head-to-head with Washington. But somehow the collaborative power of opposition, backed in the Council by wealthy and powerful (and not incidentally close US allies) members France and Germany, made possible an unprecedented collective resistance.

Despite public support at home, it was not easy for the governments to maintain their opposition, and right up until the US and Britain abandoned their effort to win a second resolution, it was unclear whether the six would stand firm. Dependence on US economic aid, trade deals, and military aid raised the stakes for each government assessing the US demand to support war.

Throughout February, France, with long-standing ties to both Cameroon and Guinea, tried to trump Washington's offers of new economic and military aid. Guinea, Cameroon, and Angola indicated their support for France's position on the war in a Paris summit of African leaders on February 21, but all three African nations remained vulnerable to US pressure.[56] But the overarching reach of US influence, in the diplomatic, military, and economic areas, made it more difficult for Paris to outbid the United States.

Angola, the poorest of the three African Council members,

remained devastated by the 27-year civil war, long exacerbated by Cold War rivalries, that had ended only in 2002. The US government had refused to grant Angola trade preferences through AGOA, officially because of concerns over corruption, labor standards, and human rights. Still, the US was critically involved in Angola's economy, and other government pressure existed as well. USAID was the largest bilateral donor to Angola at the time ($14 million in 2002), followed by Spain and Italy, both of which supported US military action in Iraq. The US was also by far the country's biggest source of foreign direct investment. According to the US trade representative, Angola ranked second after South Africa in sub-Saharan Africa in the value of US investment in the country ($1.32 billion at year-end 2000).[57] Much of this investment was facilitated and backed by US government agencies. Since the late 1990s, the US Export-Import Bank and the Overseas Private Investment Corporation had financed hundreds of millions of dollars in contracts for US oil companies in Angola, including a $200 million contract for Halliburton to provide oil field services and a $146 million oil pump contract for a Chevron subsidiary.[58] In 2001, almost half of Angola's total exports, dominated by oil, went to the United States. So despite the lack of accountability to AGOA's specific language prohibiting actions "that undermine United States national security or foreign policy interests," Angola faced the possibility of dire consequences for their defiance.

In Mexico, of course, the US is extraordinarily dominant; more than 80 percent of Mexico's exports are to the US. To frighten President Vicente Fox into continued support of the Bush administration, officials warned that a failure to back the war would likely spark an anti-Mexico backlash in the US Congress. The *Washington Post* reported that US Ambassador to Mexico Tony Garza warned that Congress might block any legislation related to Mexico as revenge for a "no" vote in the Security Council.[59] There was particular concern over the fate of negotiations underway regarding US treatment of undocumented Mexicans in the United States.

Fox was also particularly vulnerable because he was counting on the Bush administration to continue allowing Mexico to delay lifting tariffs on sensitive farm products. In January 2003, tens of thousands of Mexican peasants had threatened to close key border points if tariffs were reduced on US chicken and other products, as required under the North American Free Trade Agreement (NAFTA). The US government had agreed to a delay, but Mexico faced the possibility that Washington could change its position at any time if Mexico refused to back the war in Iraq. But like many other leaders, Fox faced massive public opposition to the US war drive; that public pressure significantly strengthened Fox's willingness to remain firmly in the "Inspections Not War" camp despite his country's intense vulnerability to US economic pressure.

Chile's socialist government had been in power since the end of the Pinochet military dictatorship in 1990. In 1994, the US, Mexico, Canada, and Chile announced a plan to become the "four amigos" through a quick expansion of NAFTA to Chile. When the process slowed, Canada and Mexico negotiated separate bilateral deals with Chile on the same basis as NAFTA, but in 2003, as the crisis in the Security Council escalated, Chile was still waiting for the promised free trade agreement with the United States. In late 2002, Chile and the US had finally completed negotiations, an accomplishment received with much fanfare in the Chilean business community. (Anti-corporate globalization activists in Chile and the NAFTA countries had fought against the deal from the beginning.) But with the high level of business support, the Bush administration would be expected to move quickly to enact the long-awaited deal; all that was left was ratification. Instead, while war pressure mounted, Bush's trade officials dragged their feet in seeking needed congressional approval. In mid-December 2002 the US trade representative had announced that he expected to give Congress the required 90-day notification of the administration's intent to sign the agreement "early next year,"[60] but by the time the war began there was no motion from the White House. The refusal to finalize the accord was widely understood to be Washington's key pressure point to demand that Chile back the US war in Iraq. But Santiago refused to buckle.

In Mexico 80 percent of the population was against the war.[61] Chilean opposition to military action stood at 76 percent.[62] But caught between US economic threats on the one hand, and popular pressure at home, much of which was reflected in the Security Council in speeches by Santiago's and Mexico City's ambassadors, neither government was prepared to take a direct stance. A week after the giant demonstrations of February 15, the Associated Press reported that Chile and Mexico had agreed that both would abstain if the pro-war US–UK and anti-war France–Russia–China blocs failed to reach a compromise in the Security Council. "We're just not going to be used or bought off by either side," a Chilean diplomat said.[63] Despite the neutral-sounding language, what was significant was the refusal of both governments to give in to US pressure.

In Pakistan in the aftermath of September 11, General Musharraf's swift support for the US "war on terror" in neighboring Afghanistan reaped considerable benefits for the government of the impoverished and debt-strapped nation. In exchange for Pakistan's support in the offensive against the Taliban, Bush dropped economic sanctions related to Pakistan's 1998 nuclear tests and 1999 military coup, whose generals remained in power. The administration also committed more than a billion dollars in US assistance and several billion dollars from international organizations,[64] and Bush made promises about lifting quotas on textile imports from Pakistan.[65]

However, as the push for Security Council backing for war heated up, Bush's support for Musharraf began to face some challenges at home, as Pakistan's image in the United States took a turn for the worse. Reports that Musharraf had manipulated Pakistan's fall 2002 elections led some members of the US Congress to begin efforts to renew aid restrictions against the country.[66] In January 2003, press reports emerged that Pakistan had provided North Korea's covert nuclear weapons program with uranium enrichment centrifuges and data on building uranium-triggered nuclear weapons. Such allegations could have triggered cut-offs of all but essential humanitarian assistance, unless Bush certified that continuing the aid to a nuclear-exporting Pakistan was necessary for US national security.

As for Musharraf, like so many other world leaders, particularly in Islamic countries, he faced powerful and angry opposition from his population to the US war in Afghanistan, the possibility of war in Iraq, and Islamabad's own close ties to the US. The generals faced a decision between a vote aimed at pacifying Washington to prevent an aid cut-off, and the recognition that such a vote might well trigger massive anti-government protests that could destabilize or even overthrow the military regime. They also recognized the vital role Pakistan continued to play in support of the US war in Afghanistan. Without access to bases, assistance in their lethal anti-Taliban campaign in the rugged territory on the Afghan–Pakistan border, the US war would face serious military setbacks. At the end of the day, despite the US pressure and the generals' overall lack of concern with their own public opinion, Islamabad appeared to recognize just how powerful the geographic card they held was, and refused to sign on to the US war.

Throughout the first months of 2003, as highly specific pressures were being brought to bear on each Security Council member, and right up until the US military invaded Iraq beginning on March 19, the UN weapons inspectors continued their work inside the country. They found no evidence of biological or chemical weapons, production facilities, or viable systems; they found no evidence that long-demolished nuclear weapons program had been restarted. But then-Secretary of State Powell continued to spearhead the Bush administration's high-visibility global propaganda campaign, within and outside the United Nations, to convince a deeply anti-war and skeptical world that the US "knew" there were WMDs, that the US "knew" that Iraq had purchased uranium yellow cake in Niger for its nuclear weapons program, and that Colin Powell himself "knew" that the aluminum tubes Baghdad had purchased for ordinary rockets "could only" be used for nuclear weapons—and that therefore a US-led war was not only right and just but necessary. The world, however, wasn't buying it. And even before each of those (and all the myriad other) individual lies was proven to be false, legions of voices from people, from social movements, and even from some officials in some countries (including the US), were saying no to Washington's claims.

Increasing the Pressure

Even after February 15, when the resistance seemed to pay off and Washington and London gave up their quest for a resolution specifically authorizing war, the US continued to bring pressure to bear on other governments, outside of the

Council, individually and in the context of broader UN participation. Bush cancelled a long-planned meeting with the Canadian prime minister, announcing he was too busy to go to Ottawa. The threats expanded to virtually every member state of the United Nations. In the General Assembly, where constant debate and even discussion of passing a resolution opposing war had emerged, no such resolution was put on the table. Washington intended to keep it that way. On the very eve of the invasion of Iraq, US ambassadors and other diplomats in virtually every capital of the world sent letters to officials, warning of dire consequences if that particular government dared to support taking up the question of the Iraq war in the General Assembly. In the Assembly, a far more democratic organ of the UN than the Security Council, the US had no veto power, and opposition to a US war was overwhelming.

The letter sent on March 18, 2003, to South Africa's deputy foreign minister, for example, demanded that South Africa "oppose such a session, and either to vote against or abstain if the matter is brought to a vote." The language was harshly threatening. "Given the current highly charged atmosphere," the letter went on, "the United States would regard a General Assembly session on Iraq as unhelpful and as directed against the United States. Please know that this question, as well as your position on it, is important to the US."[67] While individual governments continued to express varying degrees of opposition and dissent, no anti-war resolution was passed in the Assembly.

Coalition of the Coerced[68]
Around the world governmental resistance remained high. Washington recognized its inability to win support for an official resolution authorizing war, and so shifted its emphasis to recruiting, cajoling, bribing, and threatening governments to "join" its "coalition of the willing." Like the "coalition" that the senior Bush took to war against Iraq in 1991, the job for this aggregate of willing and weak governments would be to provide a multilateral political gloss on a thoroughly unilateral military action. Only Britain sent enough troops to be of much use to the Pentagon in Iraq, and the coalition's real role was understood to be that of substitute for the missing United Nations authority.

As the *Washington Post* described it,

> the symbolic importance of international participation has
> been at least as vital for the Bush administration as the often-
> limited military role the troops have played. And while
> administration officials have stressed the number of countries
> that have sent troops, others have noted the small size of many
> military contingents and the continued absence of some major
> powers. Several participating countries sent fewer than 100
> troops. In other cases, forces diminished significantly over
> time. By the middle of 2004, Moldova's contingent was the
> smallest—down to 12 from 42 [until in February 2005 the last
> 12 were withdrawn.[69]]

Singapore quietly reduced its presence from 191 to 33.[70] On
December 17, 2004, the Kingdom of Tonga brought home its
entire contingent of 40 soldiers.[71]

The credibility was bad enough that some coalition
"members" would not even agree to be publicly named. As of a
month before its invasion of Iraq, the US could include only
three other members of the Security Council as participants in
its highly touted coalition—the same small coven of Britain,
Spain, and Bulgaria. Washington claimed numerous countries
were somehow part of the coalition, but a full list of
"participants" was never made available. Unlike in 1991, in 2003
few governments were prepared to publicly support the overtly
illegal US war. It was a phantom coalition—though even fewer
governments were prepared to publicly defy the US.

According to the Pentagon's Marc Grossman, undersecretary for political affairs,

> Twenty-six countries are providing US with access, basing or
> overflight rights, or some combination of the three. Another 18
> countries have granted US access, basing or overflight rights
> based on our contingency request for those rights, or have come
> forward voluntarily to offer such rights to us, should we wish to
> make use of them. Nineteen countries have offered US military
> assets or other resources. This number includes many countries
> that have granted US access, basing and overflight rights, but
> also a number of additional countries.[72]

He didn't name the countries.

Of those that were public, other than European heavyweights

Britain, Spain, and Italy, the most visible and vocal members were from Rumsfeld's "new Europe." Most were NATO aspirants, and eager to maintain a strategic relationship with the US even after joining the EU. On February 5, ten European governments issued a statement expressing support for US policy on Iraq, stating "we are prepared to contribute to an international coalition to enforce its [UN Resolution 1441's] provisions and the disarmament of Iraq."[73] The signatories included Albania, Bulgaria, Croatia, Estonia, Latvia, Lithuania, Macedonia, Romania, Slovakia, and Slovenia. All except Croatia were in line for NATO membership, and each would have to gain approval from all current NATO members, giving Bush easy leverage by threatening to block or delay approval. In addition to Bulgaria, Romania also gave the Pentagon authority to use its military bases for any operations against Iraq.[74] Albania, Latvia, Lithuania, Macedonia, and Slovakia granted requests for US military use of their airspace.[75]

A month later, on the night before the invasion began, Secretary of State Powell released a list of 30 countries that he claimed had agreed to be publicly identified as members of the US-led coalition. But even that claim could not stand up. According to the *Washington Post*, officials of at least one of these countries, Colombia, were apparently completely unaware that they had been designated as a coalition partner. Similarly, according to the *New Zealand Herald*, the prime minister of the Solomon Islands (whose population approximates that of Washington, DC)

> said "thanks but no thanks" after hearing his nation had been shanghaied [sic] into the US-led Coalition of the Willing. "The Government is completely unaware of such statements being made, therefore wishes to disassociate itself from the report," said Sir Allan Kemakeza.

As the *Herald* noted, "Sorry, President Bush, but if you are counting on the Solomon Islands National Reconnaissance and Surveillance Force to watch your back in Iraq, you're out of luck."[76]

It is not clear how many other governments may have first learned of their "membership" in Washington's coalition through media reports. At the same time the State Department claimed that an additional fifteen countries had joined the coalition, but were unwilling to be publicly identified. Other nations, including Hungary and the Netherlands, allowed their names to be placed on the coalition list, but at the same time reassured their citizens that they would not actually support the military action in any substantive way.

In the Middle East, key petro-states Bahrain, Kuwait, Oman, Qatar, Saudi Arabia, and the United Arab Emirates, plus the oil-deprived Jordan, were stuck. The absolute monarchies of these countries depended on the US for help to keep them in power, primarily through arms sales, military training, and the presence of US bases. Jordan also relied on the US for economic backing, and was the only Arab country with a direct free trade agreement with the US. Every instinct told those royals to jump on Washington's war train.

But those same Arab countries were also closest to Iraq, and their populations were angrily and vociferously opposed to the US war plans. In mid-February, responding to that popular anger (at least while in public) each of those governments voted in what would be a unanimous Arab League decision to oppose any Arab country providing military assistance to any war on Iraq. But their dependence on the US was strong enough that the Gulf royals cast their votes while already providing bases, overflight rights, and direct staging areas for the Pentagon's Iraq build-up right on their territory. Jordan, for example, was already hosting US special forces and collaborating with US intelligence agents. In exchange, they hoped to seal a deal for an additional $1 billion in US aid.[77] Saudi Arabia's Prince Sultan Airbase, since the 1990–91 Gulf crisis, had been home to the main component of US troops in the Middle East. In the run-up to the 2003 invasion of Iraq, as the US grew more concerned about rising antipathy and violence aimed at US troops, the Pentagon created an entirely new regional command center in Qatar, a tiny thumb-shaped peninsular country jutting out from the Saudi coast. It seemed Washington's favored Arab "allies" were not so reliable.

Israel, of course, remained Washington's most stalwart partner in the region, sharing military intelligence, use of the naval port on Israel's Mediterranean coast, and more. Israel's loyalty on this issue was never a question; to the contrary, although still more consumed with "containing" Iran, Tel Aviv had acted as Washington's surrogate cheerleader for war in Iraq for years. But in the months immediately before the war, when the US was scrambling to round up enough supporters to credibly claim it was leading a coalition, rather than having to acknowledge it was simply invading Iraq unilaterally with Britain trailing along, a significant public role for Israel could only complicate matters. The situation was particularly bad because since April 2002, when Israel had reoccupied cities and towns across the West Bank and had dramatically escalated its assassination of Palestinian militants along with dozens of civilians in "collateral damage," international anger at Israel had risen equally dramatically. While the Pentagon had already asked Israel for help in training how to occupy an Arab country on the basis of Israel's lethal April assault on Jenin, in the West Bank, as a tactical decision Israel was largely avoiding a major role in Washington's Iraq "coalition."

But other countries in Iraq's neighborhood presented much more serious problems for Washington's war. The government of Turkey, a NATO member and longtime US ally in imposing wars, sanctions, and bombings against Iraq, faced 95 percent public opposition to a new US invasion of its neighbor.[79] The US already had thousands of troops in Turkey, and for more than a decade had relied on the Incirlik airbase to carry out bombings of the so-called no-fly zone the US and Britain had unilaterally imposed in northern Iraq in 1991. But the massive anti-war sentiment soon coalesced around a demand that the government in Ankara reject Washington's demands to use Incirlik and other Turkish bases as staging grounds for a second front of the planned invasion of Iraq.

Turkey was determined to play hardball. The government's Islamic-oriented ruling party asked for vast sums of new US aid money to sweeten what was sure to be a widely hated deal. By mid-February, there were reports that Washington had offered Turkey a package of $5 billion in grants and $10 billion in loans to soften the arrangement. But Turkey's parliament had to approve the deal, and while the ruling party anticipated grudging consent, the parliament took public outrage into account, and refused to give permission for Washington to use the bases. It was an extraordinary moment, because unlike almost all of the other symbolic "partners," Turkey had something the Pentagon actually needed—military bases bordering Iraq, indispensable if the US and Britain hoped to open a second front against Baghdad. It was also significant because the resistance came from a close, though qualitatively dependent, US ally—and it was particularly galling because the Bush administration had repeatedly heralded Turkey's political system as a model "Islamic democracy." If this was what Washington could expect from its "democratic Islamic" allies, the US was indeed facing some serious problems.

Given the variety, intensity, and specificity of US bribes, threats, and other blandishments used to coerce governments into joining the war coalition, what was amazing was the number and variety of governments that still refused to sign on, even besides those who signed on secretly or signed on with a public commitment at home not to really help the US military. An African–French summit on February 19 issued a unanimous statement opposing war except as a last resort. While Chirac claimed it as a sign of support for France's leadership against the US (the summit was held in Paris), the unified commitment of the 52 African nations to opposing war in Iraq and defending the centrality of the United Nations in the crisis remained intact in its own right. The language was unequivocal, and the heads of state agreed to

> Reassert that the disarmament of Iraq is the shared goal of the international community, and that the only legitimate framework for handling this issue is the United Nations; ...
> Reiterate their entire confidence in [UN arms inspectors] Messrs Blix and El Baradeï;
> Consider that the use of force, which entails serious risks of destabilisation for the region, for Africa and for the world, should only be a last resort.
> There is an alternative to war.[79]

Less than a week later, on February 25, leaders of the 116 nations that make up the Non-Aligned Movement, the major political representative of the countries of the global South who together represent two-thirds of the member states of the United Nations, passed a resolution opposing war at their summit in Kuala Lumpur.

Much closer to home, the United States' number-one trading partner and neighbor, Canada, refused to back the Bush administration on Iraq. Canada's then-Prime Minister Jean Chretien told Parliament on February 18 that he would not contribute forces to an attack that was not authorized by the UN Security Council.[80]

And from the vantage point of Washington's lack of success at winning over the world's most important economic players, it was significant that the country with the highest GDP in Europe, South America, Africa, and Asia each opposed the US war in Iraq: Germany, Brazil, South Africa, and China.

The Coalition of the Killing Goes to War

In the first years of the Iraq war and occupation, it became clear that the vast majority of countries participating in the "coalition" were there to provide political cover for the US. The 8,000 or so British troops took major responsibility for military action against the Iraqi resistance in and around Basra in southern Iraq, and Italian, Polish and South Korean contingents were occasionally heard from. But by and large the war was carried out by US troops, aided by the largest single component of foreign soldiers among the occupation forces: the international mercenaries (often identified as "military contractors") whose contingent numbered about 25,000.

Many of that number were made up of low-paid cooks, laborers, drivers, and others who provided basic services to the US and other military forces. Many were lured to Iraq from impoverished countries such as the Philippines or India despite the grim danger, by salaries that, however low relative to those paid to US or other western contractors, were sky-high by Philippines standards. But key sectors of the mercenary army were highly paid, if unevenly and unaccountably trained, for work in sensitive positions such as prison translators and interrogators, and providing protection details for visiting dignitaries as well as top ranking military officials. Many of the mercenaries were Americans—and many others were South Africans, veterans of the brutal apartheid-era security services who once served to protect South Africa's white privileges.

As the war heated up, demands mounted in coalition countries to bring the troops home. Hostage-taking and execution of nationals of countries with military troops in Iraq had continued, with the seizures of citizens of Japan, Poland, Bulgaria, South Korea, Italy, the UK, and the Philippines, as well as the US. A few of the hostages were longtime humanitarian activists whose work in Iraq pre-dated the 2003 invasion to years of efforts to help Iraqis combat the impact of economic sanctions. The resulting pressures on the coalition governments rose even higher. The cost of loyalty to Washington was rising, counted in the rapid decline of political support at home.

For those governments who resisted the public demands, the domestic political costs were high. One example was Prime Minister Silvio Berlusconi, who refused to withdraw Italian troops from Iraq despite wide and deep anti-war mobilization across party lines in his country. The pressure on Berlusconi mounted with the kidnapping of Simona Pari and Simona Torretta, "the two Simonas," who were kidnapped in September 2004. The two young Italian aid workers, both with years of experience in Iraq working against sanctions on behalf of one of the leading Italian anti-war organizations, were held for almost a month; their release, widely rumored to have included a ransom paid by the Italian government, did not end the demand for a withdrawal of troops, and Berlusconi remained politically weakened.

As a further result, Italians remained at risk. During the next Italian kidnapping crisis in Iraq, Berlusconi's government, if not Berlusconi himself, had to move further to pacify public opinion. In February 2005, Giuliana Sgrena, a journalist with the leftist *Il Manifesto* newspaper was kidnapped while returning from interviewing refugees from the US offensive in Fallujah. The Italian government sent one of its top intelligence officials, Nicola Calipari, to negotiate her release, which he managed to arrange by March 4. After picking up Sgrena upon her release from her kidnappers, Calipari and another agent were driving her to the airport. On the airport road, their car was attacked by US soldiers. Calipari protected Sgrena with his own body and was himself shot and killed in the burst of machine gun fire. Sgrena suffered serious injuries. In the subsequent investigation, Italian officials said not only Sgrena herself but the surviving intelligence operative confirmed that the US occupation authorities had been notified that the released hostage and her protectors were on their way, but US officials refused to take responsibility for killing Calipari and shooting Sgrena. The incident led to further escalation of anti-war and anti-American mobilization in Italy; Calipari's state funeral became a rallying point for massive anti-war participation.

Berlusconi repeated his claim that Italy's "alliance with the United States is not up for debate, likewise our military commitment to Iraq."[81] But his own deputy prime minister, Marco Follini, noted that "All Italy demands that the United States give an account of what happened. It demands, and I underline the word, *clear* answers, and will not content itself with vague responses."[82] Rome soon announced it was not accepting the US version of what happened on the airport road.

Following a similar trajectory, in June 2005 an Italian judge issued arrest warrants for thirteen CIA agents for their responsibility for kidnapping a Muslim cleric in Italy, holding him incommunicado, and then turning him over to Egyptian authorities in Cairo, where he faced lengthy torture.[83] The move reflected a growing level of increasingly active discontent among governments, including US allies, with Washington's unilateral actions not only in Iraq but more broadly in the so-called war on terror.

That discontent was also evident in the countries that refused to sign Article 98 agreements with the US. Those reciprocal agreements, named for the relevant article in the Rome Treaty establishing the International Criminal Court, would exempt US personnel—military and civilian—from ICC jurisdiction. The US had always opposed the court, fought hard to prevent its birth, and then worked to weaken it when it was created. In fact the ICC's jurisdiction is significantly limited anyway, largely because of US pressure during the negotiations to create the Court, but Washington demanded absolute impunity for the crimes included in the Court's jurisdiction—war crimes, crimes against humanity, or genocide. Demanding that other governments sign Article 98 agreements became the Bush administration's mantra.

Moving even further to exempt Americans from ICC jurisdiction, of particular concern because of actions in the wars in Afghanistan and Iraq, less than six months after the US invaded Iraq, right-wing unilateralist Republicans succeeded in getting Congress to pass the "American Servicemembers Protection Act." The Act prevents the US from cooperating with the Court (prohibiting, for example, extradition of an indicted war criminal) and forbids US involvement in peacekeeping unless full immunity from ICC jurisdiction is guaranteed to all American citizens involved. It also includes an authorization for the president to "use all means necessary and appropriate" to free US personnel (and certain allied personnel) detained or imprisoned by the ICC, leading some to nickname the law the "Invade the Hague" Act. While such sections tend to mean the Act is not taken seriously, it does include serious other requirements. Significantly, the Act mandates punishing countries that do not ratify the Article 98 agreements by denying them military aid. By May 2004, 89 governments, threatened with such sanctions, had signed the Article 98 agreements.[84]

Given the level of pressure, what was most surprising was the number of governments who refused to sign on to US immunity agreements. Even before the Act was passed, on July 1, 2003, the US began cutting military aid to 35 recipient governments who refused to sign Article 98 agreements.[85] The countries affected did not include the worst human rights offenders among US allies, such as Pakistan, Uzbekistan, and Egypt; those countries were not signatories of the ICC and were presumably eager to gain immunity for their own military forces. And the Act gave the president authority to exempt any country he deemed important for US national interests. As a result, the military aid sanctions targeted a number of important democratic countries, especially in the global South, such as South Africa, Peru, and Mali. The fervor of the Bush administration's antagonism to the ICC was visible in the US decision to withdraw military aid even from Bulgaria, their key eastern European ally on the Security Council in the run-up to the Iraq war, because as a candidate member of the EU Sofia was obligated to follow the EU decision to reject any Article 98 agreements.[86]

Certainly it is true that each country, and the world as a whole, would be better off without military assistance (not to mention the obligations that aid entails when it comes from the US). But governments do not often share that view. So what is significant is that the governments of those 35 countries, along with others who did not face immediate sanctions, were willing to defy the US pressure to grant immunity to potential American war criminals.

The Coalition Erodes

As the war ground on, military casualties mounted (though Iraqi civilian casualty figures remained far higher) and the possibility of a triumphal US "victory" appeared more and more remote. Increasingly, governments with troops in Iraq either withdrew their forces altogether before their deployments were to have ended, or figured out ways of drawing down the numbers so fewer vulnerable troops would be left in Iraq. By the spring of 2005, only 25 of the original 40-plus members of the "coalition" still had troops in Iraq.[87]

The unraveling of the military coalition began with the withdrawal of Spain's 1,300 troops immediately following the spring 2004 defeat of the pro-war Aznar government. The defeat of Jose Maria Aznar came just days after the horrific terror attack on the Madrid subways. The Spanish people's response to the bombing, and especially their response to the Aznar government's lies in response to the bombing, provided a new model for countries around the world where governments backed Bush's war against massive public opposition. Immediately after the subway bombings, the government announced that the perpetrators were "almost certainly" from the Basque separatist group ETA (a claim that later proved false). That cast the blame on earlier governments who had failed to end the sometimes violent Basque separatist movement, and deflected blame away from the Aznar government's own culpability for sending troops to Iraq to join the illegal US invasion in defiance of the overwhelming majority of Spaniards. But the people of Spain rejected the government's claims. Instead, refusing to respond to the bombings with paralyzing fear, they focused on Aznar's lies and answered with a resounding defeat of his right-wing government. The new government, led by José Luis Rodriguez Zapatero, swept into office committed to bringing home Spain's troops.

Spain's early pull-out of troops led Honduras and the Dominican Republic to recall their small contingents soon after. The next large-scale premature withdrawal, that of the entire Philippines contingent to prevent the execution of a captured Filipino contract worker, was among the most visible.

In Italy, Australia, even the UK itself, Bush's allies found their approval ratings dropping precipitously as they struggled to justify their unpopular—and increasingly deadly—decisions to deploy troops. Following Zapatero's announced commitment to withdraw Spanish troops, Norway and Kazakhstan announced they would pull out as well. South Korea, Bulgaria, and Poland suspended all military operations by their troops and pulled their contingents back to their bases, while staunchly pro-Bush Bulgaria then demanded that the US provide military protection for its troops. Japan announced it would not send any additional troops.

Increasingly unnerved by the rapidly eroding "coalition," in June 2004 Bush met a series of top leaders from countries with troops in Iraq, urging them to stay to provide vital credibility. He told Australian Prime Minister John Howard that a withdrawal of coalition troops would be "disastrous."[88]

But withdrawals continued nonetheless, and the analysts at GlobalSecurity.org documented the erosion. As of March 15, 2005, eleven countries had pulled out all their troops: Nicaragua, Spain, Dominican Republic, Honduras, Philippines, Thailand, New Zealand, Tonga, Hungary, Portugal, and Moldova. Five more planned to withdraw by October 2005, including Poland and Italy, two of the largest troop contributors, along with the Netherlands, Bulgaria, and Ukraine. Norway reduced its 150 soldiers to 10 in late June 2004.[89]

Backing Bush from Across the Pond

It was clear that the governmental opposition to Bush's drive toward war and empire, even when backed by a far more grounded global movement, was not, ultimately, enough to prevent the war. The US was too committed, long before the global opposition took shape, to invading Iraq and seizing dominion of that vital center of the Middle East. And indeed, the UN-based resistance within which individual governments said no to war largely collapsed by two months or so into the war, with the passage of a new Council resolution acknowledging, if not actually endorsing, the US occupation of Iraq as an international reality. The model of governmental resistance, though, driven by a global mobilization of opposition forces in virtually every country on earth, remained.

That the Bush administration's plans for war in Iraq were rooted in a thoroughly unilateral process, unaccountable to international public, governmental, or United Nations opposition, was widely known among people around the world almost from the time of September 11. But that reality was largely ignored or denied by governments, as even the strongest challengers to the Bush policy, such as Germany and France, operated diplomatically, as if they took seriously Bush's statements that he had not made any decisions regarding military action.

It took the release of what came to be called the "Downing Street Memo" in the spring of 2005 to "prove" Bush's longstanding unilateral intentions. The memo's importance had to do less with its substance than with its authors: it described the report of Richard Dearlove, then the head of Britain's MI6 intelligence agency, as he was briefing Prime Minister Tony Blair. The memo was from July 23, 2002, and reflected Dearlove's assessment of his just-completed trip to Washington. He told Blair that Bush wanted to go to war against Iraq, that "Bush wanted to remove Saddam, through military action, justified by the conjunction of terrorism and WMD [weapons of mass destruction]." Dearlove recognized that Bush's plan was now in operation, that "military action was now seen as inevitable." This was seven months before the war, months during which Bush administration officials repeatedly stressed their claim that no decision had been taken.

Dearlove had identified a particular problem to Bush's close friend Tony Blair. Rather than the decision to go to war being driven by good information and a solid analysis, he said, things were upside down in Washington. "The case was thin," the memo reported Dearlove saying. "Saddam was not threatening his neighbours and his WMD capability was less than that of Libya, North Korea, or Iran."

Ultimately, Dearlove concluded, "the intelligence and facts were being fixed around the policy."[90]

The memo provided the first documentary evidence that the head of Britain's intelligence services believed at that time that Bush had already decided to go to war, and that he believed his US counterparts were making claims about Iraqi threats that were not supported by actual facts. It paralleled reports from Britain's investigating committee, the Butler Commission, which had concluded that the Blair government's justifications for war in Iraq exaggerated claims of Iraqi threats beyond what intelligence showed. That commission also provided its own version of the July 23 meeting, describing it as a venue for Blair to call for issuing an ultimatum to Iraq regarding the return of the weapons inspectors. The goal was not to actually get the inspectors in, since the memo indicated the British officials knew that that the US National Security Council "had no patience with the UN route." Rather, the goal was to use the expected Iraqi rejection of the ultimatum to provide legal and political justification for war. "The prime minister said that it would make a big difference politically and legally if Saddam refused to allow in the UN inspectors," the memo says.[91]

At the same time, the memo provides new evidence that the US war against Iraq had essentially already begun. In the spring and summer of 2002, observers had already noted a significant increase in US bombings inside, and also more widely outside, the "no-fly zones" in Iraq. Now it was clear that those strikes were the first of a coming war. According to Britain's defense secretary, Geoff Hoon, in the Downing Street memo, the "US has already begun 'spikes of activity' to put pressure on the regime."[92]

The Downing Street notes also confirmed that Bush's top international partner, Britain's Tony Blair, was well aware that the US had no viable plan for the occupation of Iraq. Again, anti-war forces around the world knew that the powerful ideologues among the top Bush leadership had been shaping their plans based on the assessment of exiles like Ahmad Chalabi, the longtime Pentagon favorite, convicted criminal and Iraqi presidential hopeful, who insisted that no post-war strategy was necessary because invading US troops would be greeted in the streets with rice and flowers, everyone would be thrilled and the next day everyone would go back to work, pump a lot of oil, and get on with rebuilding Iraq as a Norman Rockwell-esque utopia. Already people around the world knew that was nonsense. The memo confirmed that Tony Blair knew it too. "There was little discussion in Washington of the aftermath after military action," the memo said.

Tony Blair's government remained very much at the core of Bush's coalition.

Future Resistance

But the model of governmental resistance remained intact, even as it failed to stop the war. A key component of the next phase of governments standing up to empire emerged with the recognition that virtually none of the most important threats made against countries around the world had actually been implemented. However nervous the governments of Cameroon and Guinea were about losing their AGOA trade privileges, however desperate Chile was to protect its long-fought-for free trade agreement, however frightened Mexico was about risking the still-shaky negotiations over immigration rights—none of those threats materialized. They stood up to the first superpower and got away with it.

That is not to say, of course, that no one paid any price. Germany may have faced the highest price, losing the possibility (already uncertain at best) of US support for its campaign for a permanent seat on the UN Security Council. But no bases have been shut down in Germany; the huge US military hospital in Reinstahl remains the preeminent venue for US casualties from Iraq; and diplomatic relations between Berlin and Washington are at least cordial, if not quite as warm as Germany would like.

Among the Council's "Uncommitted Six," the smaller countries who refused to back Washington's war, the major threats were never realized. The only ones who paid the price directly were the UN ambassadors of Chile and Mexico during the time of those governments' resistance in the Council. Both Mexico City and Santiago replaced their ambassadors; Adolfo Aguilar Zinzer of Mexico, who had played a particularly vocal and powerful role in mobilizing Council opposition to the US war, returned to academic life. (He died in a Mexico City car accident in June 2005.) Chile's Juan Gabriel Valdes was transferred to become ambassador to Argentina. It is likely Chilean president Ricardo Lagos hoped that Valdes would serve as the fall guy for Chile's tension with the Bush administration. To replace Valdes at the UN, Lagos dispatched Heraldo Munoz, who, perhaps not coincidentally, was a former classmate of National Security Advisor Condoleeza Rice. But Chile's trade agreement was finalized after the war began (in June 2003); Mexico continued its negotiations over immigration; AGOA trade privileges remained in effect.

The lesson was understood differently by different countries and groups of countries. For the most powerful of the anti-war camp, not coincidentally the closest allies of the US, the response was an eagerness to "put the past behind us," to move on to consolidating the next stage of a fruitful new relationship. As early as the fall 2003, the Bush administration responded, believing it was possible to win over, or at least neutralize, some of its staunchest opponents to the Iraq war. Powell praised both Germany and Russia for ostensibly trying to develop a compromise in the UN that would provide greater international legitimacy for the US occupation in Iraq. Part of the plan involved offering Russia, at least, a share of reconstruction contracts in Iraq. The plan was to "talk to the Germans, buy off the Russians, and isolate the French." One administration aide was less diplomatic, quoting Condoleezza Rice as calling the US approach "ignore, reward, and punish."[93]

Germany in particular tried a more conciliatory approach, assuring Washington that while it would not send troops to Iraq (public opinion was overwhelmingly opposed to such a move), they were prepared to help with reconstruction. Some tensions remained however, as Germany backed France's insistence that any new resolution authorize the United Nations to play a "central role" in Iraq; the Bush administration refused to budge from a "vital role" for the UN that would leave the US military occupation in charge. And despite clear indications that the Bush administration had no intention of supporting Germany's bid, Berlin continued its campaign to win US support for a permanent seat on the Security Council right through the summer of 2005.

The Bush administration was still angry with France. Some in the administration advocated trying to isolate France. "There are just a lot of bad feelings toward the French," one US official said. "Every time they talk about multilateralism, we know that it's nothing more than a euphemism for constraining the United States."[94]

There was little the US could actually do to punish France. French wine remained at the top of the list of US imports, and other than a few much-publicized scenes of outraged Americans pouring—hopefully cheap—French wine into the streets, the threats to cut wine imports were never realized. Later in the fall of 2003, France took the initiative to make a much more direct bid for reconciliation with the US, signaling it had no strategic problem with the US continuing its occupation of Iraq. One official announced that France does not enjoy being "the bad kid on the block," and that it is simply trying to make the occupation of Iraq more acceptable to Iraqis and to the other nations being asked to supply troops and support. "We are not demanding," said a French official. "We are advising. We aren't saying that the United States has to give all the keys to all the ministries to Iraqis tomorrow. But you have to send a political signal that Iraqis represent the sovereignty of their country."[95]

More significant, though not unexpected, were France's moves to restore its close ties with Washington. In early spring 2004, when the crisis in Haiti ratcheted up, France and the US teamed up to impose a "solution" based on forcing the expulsion of President Jean-Bertrand Aristide and replacing him with a government more accountable to Washington and Paris agendas and willing to do anything to prevent a refugee crisis for Washington. As the *New York Times* described it:

> It took a crisis over the Caribbean country of Haiti to get French–American relations back on track. There is nothing romantic about the reconciliation. The United States and France are motivated by their own histories, national interests and domestic politics in deciding to work together to send troops to restore order to Haiti after the departure of Jean-Bertrand Aristide.[96]

The reconciliation was all the more dramatic because the two protagonists, the foreign ministers, were the same representatives of their respective governments who had squared off against each other only a year before. During the run-up to the US invasion of Iraq, French Foreign Minister Dominique de Villepin

> turned a Security Council meeting into a forum to severely criticize Washington and declare that nothing justified envisaging military action in Iraq. American officials who were with Mr. Powell that day said at the time that they had never seen him so angry. In turn, Mr. de Villepin said he felt betrayed by Mr. Powell's assurances that the goal of American policy was not to overthrow Saddam Hussein but to disarm Iraq.[97]

A month later, on February 14, de Villepin went on to denounce the looming war again, telling the Council that "the United Nations must be an instrument for peace, and not a tool for war." But, as the *Times* reminded us, "that was then." For the US and France, concerned about protecting their alliance of power, this was now.

As for the future, the question remains whether Europe will consolidate as a strategic challenger to the US drive toward empire. In the short-term, the exigencies of joining the European Union will likely lead to at least grudging support for EU positions by new aspirants in central and eastern Europe, even if they contradict Washington. That will strengthen the EU numerically, but not fully strategically, since all sides understand that the stronger, long-term loyalties of many of those central and eastern European countries remain with Washington. And their urgent economic needs will remain a huge drain on EU funds.

Also in the short-term, the 2005 collapse of the ratification campaign for the European Constitution significantly weakened at least the sense of unified power among Europe's elites. With the overwhelming "no" votes in Germany and the Netherlands, the stumbling process of referendum and parliamentary polls scheduled to take place in each European country came to a discordant halt. In both countries, opposition from social activists concerned about the constitution entrenching the moves toward neoliberalism and escalated militarism (as well as from xenophobic anti-immigrant forces on the right) led to the defeat of the constitution and perhaps the beginning of a reconsideration of the entire basis of the European project.

But the constitution process and governmental-level negotiations were not the only venues for Europe's challenge to the US. Europe's Inter-Parliamentary Assembly, representing the separate national parliaments of all EU member states, intervened as well. Following the unofficial precedent of the UN General Assembly in acting when the Security Council is unwilling or unable, the Assembly rejected the war in Iraq far more strongly than the EU as a whole could.

Three weeks after the war began, the Parliamentary Assembly passed a resolution unequivocally condemning the war.

The Assembly remains convinced that the use of force at this stage to disarm Iraq is not justified, and that there is as yet no evidence that this country posed a threat to the states which attacked it. In the absence of an explicit decision by the United Nations Security Council, it considers this attack unlawful and contrary to the principles of international law, which prohibits the use and threat of force except in cases provided for in the United Nations Charter. The Assembly considers that the military intervention in Iraq can find no justification in the United Nations' earlier decisions. It condemns this intervention firmly and asks the governments of the states involved to put an end to it.[98]

The parliamentarians went on to call on the UN Security Council to stop the war and restore international peace and security, and then noted that "Should it be unable to do this, an extraordinary session of the United Nations General Assembly must be convened as a matter of urgency." And significantly, while reaffirming the importance of Europe's relationship with the US, the Assembly

observe[d] with satisfaction the impressive mobilisation of many people around the world for peace, which should neither be misinterpreted nor exploited as anti-American demonstrations. It also notes the opposition to the war within the United States and United Kingdom themselves.

Like the General Assembly at the United Nations, Europe's parliamentary agencies (the Parliamentary Assembly and the European Parliament itself) have little legal power of enforcement. But because they are far more democratic and representative than the Council of Europe (heads of state) and the European Commission (the EU's collective executive, also representing ruling governments), they hold sway in the court of public opinion and legitimacy. Europe's parliamentary opponents to US unilateralism and militarism may turn out to be key players in consolidating otherwise ephemeral resistance to war and empire.

Europe and the US Go Head to Head over Iran
Europe's challenge to the US was also ultimately weakened in the realignment over policy toward Iran's nuclear program in 2004–05. In the early stages of the conflict Britain, France, and

Germany began negotiating with Iran over a solution to the US claims that Iran had become a potential nuclear threat. In November 2004, Iran had agreed to freeze its production of enriched uranium, used in nuclear power production but also a potential precursor component for nuclear weapons, while negotiations went forward about the long-term future of Iran's program. As required by the Non-Proliferation Treaty, Tehran had also agreed to intrusive snap inspections by the UN's International Atomic Energy Agency (IAEA). The diplomatic process, though slow, was moving forward steadily. Then, when Bush began his second term in January 2005, he suddenly upped the ante, identified Iran as an active threat to the US, and pledged to defend the US and its allies "by force of arms if necessary."[99] Then the administration, utilizing its trademark message discipline, took to the airwaves. Bush explicitly refused to rule out military action against Iran, while his secretary of state nominee, Condoleezza Rice, refused during her confirmation hearings to deny that the goal of the US was "regime change" in Iran. Then Vice President Cheney weighed in, claiming that Iran was "top of the list" of international problem states; he went on to suggest that Israel "might" attack Iran to get rid of its nuclear facilities. The statement, however facile, could not be dismissed out of hand; memories were still sharp of the 1981 Israeli raid on the Osirak nuclear power reactor in Iraq, a move that actually elicited sharp condemnation from the Reagan administration at the time as a violation of international law.

For a while it looked like the "E-3" European negotiators would take up the challenge to the US. In late January French Foreign Minister Michel Barnier said, "I cannot explain American policy to you. That would be French arrogance and I am not someone who is arrogant. But I think that the Americans must get used to the fact that Europe is going to act." German Chancellor Gerhard Schroeder added that "the last thing we need is a military conflict in that region. I'm very explicit and outspoken about this because I want everybody to know where Germany stands." Even the British, who had abandoned their tight alliance with Washington to rejoin their European partners on the Iran issue, criticized the US warmongering, with Foreign Secretary Jack Straw calling a military attack on Iran "inconceivable." And EU foreign policy chief Javier Solana told the *New York Times* that the European-led diplomatic track was "the only game in town, no doubt about that."[100]

Unfortunately there were other players waiting in the wings. By March 2005, the US had significantly ratcheted up the pressure on Iran and, derivatively, on the E-3. The US position was that despite the legality of Iran's uranium production under the terms of the Non-Proliferation Treaty, Washington simply "didn't trust" Iran not to hide a secret weapons program and because of that lack of trust the US had the right to impose sanctions, go to war, or overthrow the government in Tehran.

Within weeks, the Europeans began to waver, and by the end of March their resolve had largely collapsed. When the ensuing US–EU "agreement" was announced, it became clear that despite the Bush administration's and media spin that the US and Europe both compromised to create a unified policy toward Iran, the reality was far more unbalanced. The E-3 collapsed under US pressure and accepted Washington's demands to ratchet up the pressure on Iran. To be sure, the European surrender included a thin veneer of political cover for London, Paris, and Berlin. But the new "unified" transatlantic approach to Iran was thoroughly rooted in the US preference for military threats over diplomatic engagement. In this round there was little question the empire had beat back the competition.

Washington never abandoned its earlier rejection of Europe's strategy to engage Iran. The US, with great fanfare, "accepted" Europe's approach of offering small economic carrots to Iran, but stipulated that such carrots would be made available only *after* Tehran implemented a permanent halt to its nuclear production program, something Iran's government had said it would never do. And the carrots themselves were of limited value. Access to imported spare parts for civilian aircraft, useful but hardly a match for the symbolic importance Tehran placed on its nuclear program, would be made available only on a case-by-case basis. Allowing Iran to apply for membership in the WTO only begins a process that takes years or decades to complete and would require such massive shifts in Iran's domestic economy that it remained unclear whether Iran even intended such a move.

What Washington did not give up was its continuing threat of military force—whether bombing, allowing Israel to bomb alleged nuclear facilities, or full-scale "regime change"—against Iran. In what was called a compromise but was in fact a major abandonment of the European Union's longstanding commitment to diplomatic engagement, the E-3 not only accepted Washington's militarized threat approach but agreed to join it. In so doing Europe essentially abandoned the Non-Proliferation Treaty. The E-3's letter to the president of Luxembourg, then presiding over the European Union, described a situation of no progress, despite Iran's continuing, internationally verified halt in enrichment activities. The E-3 letter also supported the US intention to hand the issue over to the UN Security Council (which would then be pressured to authorize harsh multilateral sanctions or even military force against Iran) if Tehran did not accept the demand it had already rejected to make its current nuclear pause permanent.

Essentially the US–E-3 agreement brought European acquiescence to, and willingness to provide international legitimacy for, Washington's unilateral claim of the right to impose its will around the world. Europe agreed to toss international law out the window. As the *New York Times* acknowledged, without a hint of outrage or even unease, "the statements made clear that the West would not tolerate Iran's enriching uranium for civilian nuclear energy, despite international accords that allow it."

Europe, not the US, made all the serious concessions. Along with accepting the US-mandated referral to the Security Council if Iran rejects an imposed permanent halt of enrichment activities and/or an imposed timetable, Europe gave up two important positions. First, it agreed to drop its longstanding rejection of selectivity in enforcing nuclear non-proliferation. Specifically, Europe had long recognized that imposing demands for ending nuclear production on one country while allowing other non-nuclear states to carry out exactly the same production simply doesn't work. So since other non-nuclear signatories to the NPT, such as South Korea, Brazil, South Africa, and others were carrying out identical NPT-authorized nuclear enrichment programs without challenge, confronting Iran alone over the same program would likely fail. Second, it appeared that Europe—or at least the E-3—supported Washington's assertion that even with instruments of multilateral arms control like those in the NPT, Iran's nuclear power could never be reliably surveilled or prevented from misuse. What this may have signaled was that key European powers were themselves prepared to abandon rather than reinforce the NPT, a long-sought goal of the unilateralists central to the Bush administration.

Further, the White House rejected the idea of a US–Iran non-aggression pact, something that might reduce Iran's ambition for nuclear weapons. Nor was there mention of even considering an end to the punitive unilateral sanctions the US had imposed on Iran since 1979. To the contrary, in an aggressive move largely unreported in the US press, on the night before the high-profile announcements of a new "US–European unity" regarding Iran, President Bush announced he was extending the existing sanctions regime against Iran. On the night of March 10, Bush renewed the executive order first imposed by Bill Clinton in March 1995. In his order Bush called Iran a "significant and unusual threat" and accused Iran of supporting international terrorism, undermining the Middle East peace process, and attempting to obtain weapons of mass destruction. Bush's renewed executive order went even further, claiming that "the actions and policies of the Government of Iran continue to pose an unusual and extraordinary threat to the national security, foreign policy, and economy of the United States."[101]

On March 13 Bush's new national security adviser, Stephen Hedley, told CNN that Europe also supported Washington's claims regarding Iran's violations of human rights and alleged support of terrorism. This marked a major reversal of the earlier European stance that the negotiations with Iran should focus solely on the nuclear threat. Europe's nascent challenge to Bush's drive toward domination of Iran was reversed as well.

The Cancún Challenge

For the poorer, less powerful countries, the lessons of 2002–03—standing up to the US and getting away with it—were different. Less than six months after the US invaded Iraq, the World Trade Organization (WTO) ministerial meeting was held in Cancún,

Mexico. The WTO had since its inception remained a venue for negotiating the harsh rich–poor, North–South divides among the world's most powerful and least powerful states. The WTO's goals of "eliminating trade barriers" virtually always translate into massive advantages for huge western-based multinational corporations, and concomitant disadvantages for impoverished southern countries whose traditional agriculture and fledging industries, if any, cannot compete against the giants.

So when foreign ministers and trade representatives gathered in the resort city of Cancún in September 2003, tensions were already high. The ostensible goal of the meeting was to expand the WTO's power and control over more sectors of global trade. Such a move was sure to hurt the poorest countries the most. Further, the US occupation of Iraq was widely seen as having been waged in direct defiance of the opinions of the people of the world, most governments, and the United Nations. Anger was palpable. Longstanding anti-American sentiments had stiffened, bolstered by thousands of global protesters demanding an end to the ravages WTO-orchestrated economic arrangements had brought to poor and disenfranchised people around the world. Tensions heightened when one member of the large contingent of South Korean demonstrators committed suicide to protest the impact of the WTO's decisions.

Inside the conference hall, even though participants were kept sheltered from contact with the protesters outside, a new diplomatic grouping took shape. Quickly dubbed the "Group of 20," or G-20, its leading government participants included Brazil, India, Argentina, China and South Africa. Led largely by the relatively wealthier and more powerful Southern governments, the G-20 immediately staked out a powerful rejection of the US–European plan to expand WTO power. With the G-20 to back them up, a much larger group of poor countries soon emerged, emboldened by their collective strength to resist the EU and the US with more determination than any of them would have been able to muster alone.

This reliance on other countries from the South, albeit the strongest and wealthiest among them, was important. In the Security Council context the six governments of the South (Angola, Cameroon, Chile, Guinea, Mexico, Pakistan) had wealthy and powerful European allies of the US to back them up. However influential they might be as regional powers, there was no way Brazil, India, South Africa, or even China could match Germany and France as protectors of the smaller states. This time it was the US and the EU together, the coalition of the rich and powerful, that stood against the South's resistance. (Proving, if anyone doubted it, the tactical nature of European opposition to US empire.) But nonetheless the resistance held. Within just a few days, the agenda of the meeting completely stalled, and the ministerial summit collapsed. Delegates returned home uncertain whether or how the once seemingly unstoppable trajectory of WTO expansion could ever get back on track.

There can be little doubt that at least part of the assessment of the governments of the poor countries, particularly those like the G-20 leaders who were the most visible and outspoken in representing their positions, was grounded in an understanding of what had—and what had not—happened to those governments who defied the US in Iraq. If the major threats that Washington had issued against the "Uncommitted Six," for example, had been realized, it is unlikely that even in a collective fashion vulnerable governments would have risked antagonizing the US.

Another key example of governments—in this case Latin American governments—standing defiant of US pressure came in March 2005, when the Organization of American States, a Cold War-era creation long dominated by the United States, held new elections. The OAS includes every Latin American government with the exception of Cuba, excluded by relentless US pressure. In the past the OAS was a compliant tool for implementing US policy in the region, and other than an occasional rhetorical salvo, there was little challenge to Washington's demands.

But things are changing. And one of the biggest sets of changes is underway in Latin America, where progressive governments committed to empowering their poor are coming to power— governments democratic in practice, rather than merely in form. Led by regional powerhouse Brazil's President Luis Ignacio Lula da Silva, widely known as Lula, and oil-rich Venezuela's Hugo Chavez, Argentina, Uruguay, and Ecuador have joined the ranks and Bolivia stands on a precarious but potential-filled brink.

The US choice for a secretary-general of the OAS, who could be counted on to implement Washington's agenda, was a former president of El Salvador, Francisco Flores. The other candidate, backed by Venezuela's Chavez and Cuban President Fidel Castro (lobbying from outside the OAS itself), was Chilean socialist and former interior minister Jose Miguel Insulza. Washington couldn't mobilize any support for Flores, so it switched its endorsement to Mexican Foreign Minister Luis Ernesto Derbez. The Mexican candidate wasn't quite as marginalized, but still Washington couldn't get majority support for him, and Brazil, Venezuela, and other key countries continued to back Insulza. In what *Washington Post* political satirist Al Kamen called a "stunning vote," the OAS deadlocked over the two candidates 17 to 17.

Chile's government accused Washington of pressuring some of the small US-dependent Caribbean island states to support Derbez, but it didn't seem to be working. Then word came that a couple of countries that the US had counted on were considering changing their vote to support Insulza. That would have won the election for the Chilean candidate. To head off such an embarrassment to the Bush administration, Condoleezza Rice stepped in to save face. She pressed Insulza to agree to at least go through the motions of criticizing Venezuela and Cuba, promising US support if he did so. The result was a unanimous vote for Insulza, with Washington's first and second choices abandoned by their patron.

Then the OAS refused to pass Washington's proposed statement on democracy, a thinly veiled attack on Venezuela and Cuba. Bush's Latin America team was not happy. As the *Washington Post*'s Kamen put it:

> now someone might look at this and say it appeared as though all this was pretty much a defeat for US efforts. The folks they supported lost. The guy they opposed won. Ah, but that would be, as Assistant Secretary of State for Latin America Roger Noriega explained in an April 30 e-mail to State Department officials, absolutely, completely, wrong.[102]

Other challenges to US domination followed the WTO collapse in Cancún. A month after the WTO summit, Miami hosted a similar high-level meeting, this one to move forward the creation of a Free Trade Area of the Americas, which would in theory encompass the entire western hemisphere from Canada's Northern Territories south to Tierra del Fuego. While the 1994 campaign to expand NAFTA to Chile had collapsed, replaced by bilateral trade deals with each of the three original NAFTA members, other efforts had long been underway to expand the North American Free Trade Agreement. The most ambitious was the campaign for the FTAA, and negotiations had been underway for years, challenged every step of the way by determined continental-wide coalitions such as the Hemispheric Social Alliance, committed to fighting the privatization, anti-regulation, and pro-corporate policies that the FTAA would impose. The plan called for final FTAA negotiations to be completed by January of 2005. But the November 2003 meeting in Miami had also collapsed in failure. It did not feature the visible blow-up of the WTO summit in Cancún, but the meeting (also surrounded by international protesters) ended early with no real agreement reached. Ten years after negotiations began, the FTAA stalled as Latin America's growing cohort of emboldened progressive governments refused to accept Washington's dominion.

The Governments and the People

The Iraq war of 2003 was certainly not the first time in history that the US went to war unilaterally, without UN authorization, without justifiable self-defense claims, without any legitimacy in international law. But this was the first time the US had openly asserted the right to do so, based solely on the vast disparity of power between the US and every other country or group of countries in the world. As a result, most nations around the world rejected this US doctrine of preventive war (except for a very few, like Israel and Russia, which saw it as a convenient blueprint for justifying their own aggressive wars), believing that such a policy would actually increase insecurity around the world and heighten the global power-gap. So a wide range of governments, along with intergovernmental organizations themselves, were pulled into an alliance with popular movements to create the "second superpower."

The peace and justice movements—nationally and internationally—face a difficult task of sorting out relationships with governments when we find ourselves suddenly on the same side. Certainly we must rigorously abolish any illusions about the strategic character of those relationships; not a government in power can be counted on to defend the whole panoply of human rights—economic, social, cultural, political, and civil— for which people around the world struggle. But given the over-arching power—economic, social, cultural, political, and civil—that the US empire controls today, there will frequently be occasions when one or two or a group or maybe even the majority of governments around the world will find themselves standing defiant of the US use and abuse of those powers.

In most cases that will be precisely because the global social movements, operating internationally and within the borders of every country, were powerful enough to force governments to respond. They will also have been strong enough to raise the political price of refusing to do the right thing (even if for the wrong reasons)—so that it becomes more costly for a government to give in to US pressure than to side with its people and the people's movements and to resist.

Even understanding the tactical nature of such alliances, though, there will continue to be challenges based on the nature of such governments. The relationship between the social movements and the emerging bloc of progressive governments in Latin America or South Africa will look very different than the links that may emerge with non-aligned, anti-occupation, but repressive governments like Malaysia. The links will be quite distinct depending on whether the government in question supports popular positions on an explicitly international issue such as the war in Iraq or the occupation of Palestine, or on the other hand takes a solid critical position against neo-liberal policies both at home and abroad. Certainly the relationships will differ whether the governments represent impoverished countries of the South, middle-economy emerging nations, or strategic allies and sometime-competitors with the US imperial project.

The social movements' relations with governments during the run-up to the Iraq war required far different strategies for dealing with anti-war governments in Cameroon and Guinea, in Mexico or Chile or South Africa, and perhaps trickiest of all in Germany and France. Sometimes there will be clarity on the limits of what a tactical alliance looks like, other times there may be broader possibilities and more long-term planning. Sometimes it might be as clear-cut as having one group of global activists operating within international arenas (within the United Nations institutional structures, in the media, in capitals of the most powerful countries) play one role vis-à-vis representatives of those potentially allied governments, while their counterparts in the country involved continue their long-term work of pressuring their usually recalcitrant government from within. Other sets of relations might be more complicated, with varying levels of "inside-outside" tactics.

In all cases, crafting "inside-outside" strategies requires flexibility and breadth of vision. Internationalism involves primarily building bonds of solidarity between people and peoples around the world; but relations between governments are involved as well. The "second superpower" that rose on February 15, 2003, only became a superpower because the global social movements at the heart of that power were strong enough to bring at least some governments to their side—at least for the moment. The challenge for those social movements is precisely how to make that happen again.

4

THE UNITED NATIONS

Of the three components of the "second superpower," people, governments and the UN, it is certainly the United Nations that is least able to play a consistent role in the global challenge to US war and empire. This is ironic because its Charter and its Universal Declaration of Human Rights represent the cornerstone of international law and the greatest prohibition against war and oppression; however, the UN still remains dependent on governments, and ultimately people, to build the strength sufficient to carry out its mission. Left to its own devices the United Nations relapses into what it has often—though crucially, not always—been used as throughout its 60-year history, what Washington's then-UN Ambassador Madeleine Albright once called "a tool of American foreign policy."[1]

From August 2002 until May of 2003, as people poured into the streets and governments stood up to say no to US war, the world also saw a clear moment of strengthened UN resistance—within the Security Council, among General Assembly members, and including the UN secretariat itself. The "Uncommitted Six" joined France, Germany, Russia, and China in the Council to prevent a UN authorization of war. The secretary-general and heads of both UN arms inspection agencies rebuffed US pressure to endorse its Iraq war or to provide false intelligence information designed to make its war look good.

Then in May 2003, two months after the US invasion and only weeks after Bush's specious declaration of "mission accomplished" in Iraq, the UN's resistance foundered as governments' defiance collapsed and the Security Council, however bitter and reluctant, passed Resolution 1483, "recognizing" the US and Britain as the occupying powers in Iraq.

Looking at the UN after the collapse of its resistance (along with that of many governments) it is hard to see how the global organization remains a part of the multifaceted global front defying US power. There were and remain serious concerns that even the short periods of UN defiance and challenge were in danger, that the intensity of US attacks on the UN as "irrelevant" was leading too many around the world—including some supportive of or even working within the United Nations—to accept Washington's view of the world's organization. Too many were prepared to dismiss the UN as unimportant in the global struggle for peace and justice. Some central to that struggle were even prepared to casually condemn the UN as nothing but "imperialism with a global face." That dismissive attitude was perhaps understandable—ironically, my own book, *Calling the Shots*, subtitled "How Washington Dominates Today's UN" may have played some role in popularizing that assessment. What was too often missing was any nuance in the analysis of the complicated role of the United Nations, any understanding that the United Nations could play a key role as a partner within the international mobilization for peace and against empire, but only if it were part of a grand international coalition anchored by engaged, critical, and supportive social movements. Ultimately the model of a three-part internationalist superpower, which came to such vivid life during the run-up to the Iraq war, remains important, and the potential for the UN as both venue and player in that challenge remains central.

There can be little doubt that at present, at all levels, the US dominates the UN. When it chooses, the US largely controls the actions and inactions, determines the successes and the failures of the United Nations. But not all the time. So despite Washington's overarching dominion, at the end of the day internationalism requires a bold defense of the UN. No other global institution holds even the possibility of representing the broad diversity of the world's countries, and no other multilateral institution maintains even a pretense of democratic governance. If there is ever to be a successful multilateral and internationalist challenge to the US drive for empire—a challenge that to succeed must also involve both governments

and especially international civil society and social movements—
it will require organization and mobilization within such a
global institution.

The US and the UN: Power vs. Democracy

Right from its origins in the last years of World War II, the
United Nations embodied the conflict between democracy and
power. When the war ended, the Allied powers that had won the
war clearly viewed the nascent United Nations as a means to
rule the post-war peace. And from the beginning, Washington
viewed the UN as an instrument to orchestrate its own power
and dominion in—and over—the rest of the world.

Years before the San Francisco conference that brought the
United Nations to life, the limitations of the League of Nations
and the need for a truly empowered global organization were
already clear. Throughout the horrifying years of World War II,
efforts toward creating a new multilateral body were underway.
The 1941 Inter-Allied Declaration issued a resounding, if vague,
call for international cooperation after the war. Roosevelt's and
Churchill's Atlantic Charter, that same year, provided the first
sign of US–British intentions to establish a replacement to the
failed League. The Washington Declaration of January 1, 1942
first used the term "united nations" and included 26 countries as
signatories. Allied conferences in Moscow and Tehran, in late
1943, actually began to lay the political foundations for a new
organization, and the Dumbarton Oaks conference in mid-1944
was finally assigned the task of crafting a structure.

It was in Dumbarton Oaks, in Washington, DC, that the
Proposals for the Establishment of a General International
Organization were adopted by four of what became the
permanent five members of the Security Council: the US, the
Soviet Union, Britain, and China. A few months later, in
February 1945, after the end-of-the-war Yalta Conference, de
Gaulle's Free French government joined in and the Five worked
out a conflict-resolution formula; it was the first step toward the
creation of the Security Council. Weeks later, the San Francisco
conference was convened.

Even within the US delegation to the early negotiations and
founding convention of the United Nations, of course, there was
tension between State Department officials who controlled the

decision-making and brilliant internationalists, mainly from civil society—academics and activists, as well as prominent people such as Eleanor Roosevelt. It was, for example, a Columbia University professor named Virginia Gildersleeve, the only woman in the US delegation in San Francisco, who took the original proposed draft of the inter-governmental treaty being discussed, a dry diplomatic instrument beginning with "the high contracting parties…", and rewrote it in the soaring terms that begin the Charter of the United Nations, in which "we the peoples of the United Nations" pledge to succeeding generations to "prevent the scourge of war." More importantly, it was Gildersleeve who fought successfully to include within the Charter a commitment "to reaffirm faith in fundamental human rights, in the dignity and worth of the human person, in the equal rights of men and women, and of nations large and small… to promote social progress and better standards of life in larger freedom," and to create within the new organization an Economic and Social Council to implement those goals.[2]

But the US delegation's officials were not prepared to turn the new UN organization over to activists and academics. The US government controlled the bottom line, and its representatives, headed by Secretary of State Edward R. Stettinius, had not settled into Dumbarton Oaks for the negotiations, and later traveled to San Francisco for the founding convention, only to talk about peace and justice and internationalism. Washington's agenda was power.

The San Francisco meeting brought together representatives of the governments of 50 countries—primarily the wealthy countries of the North, mostly European and North American. The cornerstone was the five-power alliance of the US, the Soviets, the French, the British, and the Chinese—the victors of the war, with their allies. There were a few US-dominated Latin American states, plus still-colonized India, Egypt, Iran, French-controlled Lebanon, Saudi Arabia, Turkey, and the US-dependent Philippines. (Poland was a signatory, bringing the number of original signers to 51, but did not have a representative to the San Francisco conference.) The overall balance was at least 35 countries closely accountable to the US, five close to the Soviet Union, and only ten non-aligned. The vast majority of the countries of the world were not represented; the majority of the global South was still locked in colonial or semi-colonial bondage and had no representation. And this was a multilateral, not truly international, undertaking, so people, ultimately, were nowhere to be seen. Only governments had the vote.

The drafting of the Charter in San Francisco posed numerous vexing questions for the delegations, most of them shaped by the constant tension between democracy and power. How could an organization be designed that would end war, protect the smaller and weaker countries, encourage egalitarian access to resources and development, improve human rights and standards of living—all while quietly insuring that the richest and most powerful countries remained in control?

For the US, there was no question whether power or democracy would carry the day. And there would be no taking chances on decision-making. Intelligence documents clearly demonstrate that for months prior to, as well as during, the San Francisco founding conference, US intelligence agencies were bugging the offices and rooms of the other delegations, and intercepting and breaking coded diplomatic messages—including those of Washington's closest allies—in what was known as "Operation Ultra." The intercepts allowed the US team to know ahead of time what were the positions, special concerns, potential pressure points, and vulnerabilities of competitors and allies alike. The spying worked. By the end of the conference, the US delegation had won support for structural, economic, and mandate decisions that effectively guaranteed Washington's domination of the UN for years to come.

At the structural level, that meant appointing the five powerful Allies as permanent members of the Security Council with the right to veto any decision. The five, who would later become, as the US already was, the recognized nuclear powers in the world, held on to that privilege throughout all future changes—the claim of the People's Republic of China to take over Taiwan's seat, the emergence of the new government of Russia to claim the Soviet seat after the USSR collapsed in 1991, and most of all the shifts in overall power in the world away from the five-power alliance of 1945.

As Australia's former Foreign Minister Gareth Evans described it, the veto was justified largely on the grounds that it saved the Security Council from voting for commitments it was incapable of fulfilling, namely enforcement action against one of the five permanent members or the imposition of sanctions against the will of one of those states. In other words, to convince the permanent members that they should adhere to the Charter and the collective security framework embodied therein, a deliberate decision was taken to establish a collective security system which could not be applied to the permanent members themselves.[3]

The veto, then, consolidated the imbalance of power within the global order.

The Ultra documents also expose some of Washington's approach to the future of its colonial allies in the beginning of what was becoming the era of decolonization. France, committed to retaining its African and Southeast Asian colonies, worried about the US effort to establish the Trusteeship Council within the UN, couched as the proposed language was in rhetorical commitments to the colonies' evolution toward autonomy or even independence. The British government, which hoped to rely on its own colonies' resources for a return to economic power after the devastation of the war, initially shared those concerns. The US quickly reassured London that continuing its colonial control was not a problem. Then, seeking to persuade the French that Washington had no serious anti-colonial intentions, British Foreign Secretary Anthony Eden reminded France's provisional foreign minister, Georges Bidault, that although the trusteeship plan was an American one, it was not really designed to challenge colonialism at all. It was, Eden told Bidault, actually designed by the new rising power in Washington to "permit the United States to lay hands chastely on the Japanese islands in the Pacific. The system is not to be applied to any region in Europe nor to any colonies belonging to the Allied countries."[4]

The United Nations would, like any international organization, reflect, rather than challenge, existing disparities of economic, military, diplomatic, strategic, and other arenas of power in the world of 1945.

"A Tool of American Foreign Policy"

When then-Ambassador Madeleine Albright made her infamous statement in 1995, it was very much a dog-bites-man story; there was nothing new or different about the United Nations being "a tool of American foreign policy." What is far more surprising is that throughout its history, the UN has seen moments when it actually did resist the drive toward war and empire, most often orchestrated by the United States.

The United Nations could never be, on its own, capable of a consistent, strategic challenge to its most powerful member states. But what the UN provides is an instrument—actually a wide range of political, social, economic, and strategic instruments—which can be seized as tools by people's movements and, on occasions, worried governments, in campaigns to hold even the most powerful governments accountable to international law and the commitments of its own Charter.

As the noted UN scholar, the late Erskine Childers, described it,

> Taken together, the constitutions of the [UN] System gave humanity a comprehensive international social contract for the first time. The constitution of the new Food and Agriculture Organization of the United Nations (FAO) committed governments "to contribute to the expansion of the world economy and to liberate humanity from hunger." That of the World Health Organization (WHO) declared that "the health of all peoples is fundamental to the attainment of peace and security." Approaching the same web of problems with another causal insight, the constitution of the UN Educational, Scientific and Cultural Organization (UNESCO) avowed that "since wars begin in the minds of men it is in the minds of men that the defenses of peace must be constructed.

(Childers went on to note that the UNESCO reference is "one occasion in a UN document when the word men is entirely apposite.")[5]

So perhaps it was not surprising that when George W. Bush came into office pledging an assertion of unilateralism and militarism, global governmental unease and opposition emerged quickly in the venue of the United Nations. In the first months of his first term, by the spring of 2001, international anger toward US arrogance was on the rise. There appeared some reason to hope that a global challenge—of whatever sort—might take shape to defy the policies that were emerging as exemplars of untrammeled US domination and control.

The first organizational challenge to the new US administration came in the UN in early May, when some of Washington's closest European allies took the lead in rejecting the US as a member of the UN Human Rights Commission, denying the US a seat for the first time since the Commission was created. The vote choosing the new Commission members took place in the General Assembly, but nominees were chosen first by the regional groups—and in WEOG (the Cold War-era Western Europe and Others [the US, Canada, and Australia] Group) the US simply didn't get the votes.

The US response was angry and combative. Noting that Sudan had just been voted in to one of Africa's rotating seats on the Human Rights Commission, US officials and pundits alike excoriated the 56 member states of the Commission for allegedly replacing the US with the human rights pariah Sudan. In fact, the US was replaced by Sweden—a country against whom Washington would fair quite poorly on almost any human rights standard. The Sudan reference was simply convenient for spin-control. As is the practice in most UN agencies, regional groups determine nominees for Commission membership. The Western Group, which includes the US and Europe, was allotted three open seats for this election cycle, but fielded four candidates—France, Austria, Sweden, and the US. Withdrawal by any one of those European allies would have guaranteed the US another term. Instead, Sweden won the third highest votes among the Group's candidates, beating out the US, which polled the lowest.

Certainly Africa might have nominated a country less egregiously symbolic of human rights violations than Sudan. But the Africa Group is far more democratic than the Western European and Others Group, and rotates virtually all its countries onto the Commission in turn, rather than choosing to exclude those who might actually learn something or even be pressured to improve their practices while functioning as a Commission member. South Africa, Senegal, and Cameroon were among the other African members when Sudan was voted in.

So the US setback was not the result of some back-room

campaign orchestrated by human rights violators or enemies of the US. It was an expression of growing frustration by Washington's friends and allies, especially in western Europe, at what they saw as increasing US rejection of the United Nations and other international commitments. As Harold Hongju Koh, human rights chief in the Clinton administration, described it, "the world was trying to teach us a lesson."[6]

US human rights violations were certainly part of the problem, but that issue sharpened international anger on a host of other examples of US unilateralism and hypocrisy. European diplomats explaining the Human Rights Commission vote pointed to the US imposition of the death penalty; its refusal to sign or ratify numerous treaties and conventions including those guaranteeing the rights of women and children (the CTBT, land mine prohibitions, the International Criminal Court, the Kyoto protocol on global warming, and threats to the ABM treaty), and Washington's rejection of international protection for the Palestinians. Secretary of State Powell described his Security Council veto of that resolution, which called for unarmed international observers in the Occupied Territories, as one where the US "left a little blood on the floor."[7]

That blood on the floor of the Security Council chamber was a big part of why the US lost its seat on the Human Rights Commission. But Bush's then-National Security Adviser Condoleezza Rice called it an outrage, and claimed the loss of the Commission seat was because other countries resent US support for human rights. In the House of Representatives, the response was a decision to withhold the partial payment of back dues to the UN they had voted on a few months earlier. As former US Ambassador Dennis Jett put it, the congressional tantrum "cemented the claim that the US is now the world's only super-pouter."[8] Bush was still complaining about it more than four years later, in September 2005, when, in his remarks to the General Assembly at the start of the UN's 60th session, he said, "When this great institution's member states choose notorious abusers of human rights to sit on the UN Human Rights Commission, they discredit a noble effort and undermine the credibility of the whole organization."[9]

The willingness of countries to stand up to the US on UN

agency seats (on the International Narcotics Control board as well) gave some additional hope to the idea that the United Nations could serve as a venue of challenge. Even if full-scale global insurrection against US unilateral domination was not yet on the agenda, it was starting to look as though the UN could at least become a center for collective efforts to hold Washington accountable to the basics of international norms.

The UN conference on racism, held in Durban, South Africa, was the next opportunity. Washington failed to win support for its effort to orchestrate a global walk-out (see Governments chapter), and ended up only isolating itself further.

But then, only days later, came September 11 and the collapse of the growing global opposition.

September 11 and After

In the immediate crisis following the attack on the Pentagon and the World Trade Center, the UN itself was deemed a potential target. Restrictive security measures were imposed, and UN headquarters in New York was largely quarantined from ordinary people. The secretariat staff faced the same traumatic reality as every other person living in New York—many had friends, family, loved ones who lived, worked, or went to school in and around Ground Zero. The smoldering wreckage of the World Trade Center, after all, was only a few dozen blocks south of the United Nations.

But the UN itself did not close down, was not prevented from functioning. And in the context of the Charter-imposed limitations on responding to an attack, that ability to continue functioning and the fact that the Security Council was able to meet only 24 hours after the attacks would turn out to be of critical importance in determining the illegality of the US response.

The US called the UN Security Council into special session on the morning of September 12. Many thought the convening of the Council foretold a US decision to work collaboratively, collectively, with the rest of the world, hoping that the shock of the terrorist attacks had brought about a new decision to abjure earlier Bush tendencies toward unilateralism and automatic military responses. Those hopes, however, proved groundless.

Article 51 of the UN Charter seemed precisely drafted to

deal with just such a scenario. It recognizes the inherent right of a nation under attack to use force to defend itself against an armed attack—but only "until" the Council itself could take the necessary steps to deal with the conflict, and to maintain or restore peace and security. Convening the Council so quickly after the attacks seemed to portend a US plan to engage the United Nations, to engage the international community as a whole to respond to this massive crime against humanity. In light of the outpouring of popular and official sympathy and solidarity in the wake of the attacks, there was certainly no fear that anything the US proposed might be rejected. Whether it was a US request for creation of a new anti-terrorism tribunal backed by a new international police enforcement unit whose first mandate would be the identification and capture of the perpetrators of the attacks or anything else, all would have been supported with enthusiasm. Significantly, given the immediate collapse of the global governmental opposition to US hegemonic power in the wake of the 9/11 attacks, it is certain that even a US request for UN authorization for a coalition-based or even unilateral military strike would have been accepted.

But the US-drafted resolution did none of those things. It turned out the September 11 attacks had not moved the Bush administration away from its commitment to unilateral action. Washington had no intention of collaborating with the United Nations, or indeed any intention of allowing the UN to play any decisive role in its response. Resolution 1368, passed on September 12, recognized the right of self-defense in an introductory clause, but authorized no use of force, whether by UN Blue Helmets or by anyone else. It was not passed under the auspices of Chapter VII of the UN Charter, a prerequisite for authorizing military force. The resolution called on all states "to work together urgently to bring to justice the perpetrators, organizers and sponsors of these terrorist attacks and stresse[d] that those responsible for aiding, supporting or harbouring the perpetrators, organizers and sponsors of these acts will be held accountable." It went on to call on "the international community to redouble their efforts to prevent and suppress terrorist acts including by increased cooperation."

The Council discussion leading up to the passage of 1368 was characterized by unanimity of condemnation of the attacks, and unanimity of support for creating precisely the kind of cooperation needed for what the French ambassador called a "global strategy" to deal with terrorism. Jamaica's Ambassador Patricia Durrant, in words similar to other Council ambassadors, called on the Council to insure that "the masterminds, and those in collusion with them, must be brought to justice, and the global community must demonstrate a solid front to defeat terrorism."[10] Bringing perpetrators to justice, and using global cooperation to do so, were the consistent themes of the discussion; launching a war half a world away from the ruins of the World Trade Center was not on the UN agenda.

In less than an hour, Resolution 1368 was passed unanimously and with enormous emotional fervor; in an unprecedented show of solidarity, the fifteen Council ambassadors stood to cast their votes in favor of the resolution, rather than simply raising their hands.

The Council resolution concludes by expressing "its readiness to take all necessary steps to respond to the terrorist attacks of 11 September 2001, and to combat all forms of terrorism, in accordance with its responsibilities under the Charter of the United Nations." And finally, the Council decided "to remain seized of the matter."

What the resolution did not do was authorize military force. Expressing "readiness to take all necessary steps" is a far cry from actually taking any specific step, including the authorization of force. The resolution did not identify what the Council believed to be "necessary steps." The limits of the resolution were clarified further by the crucial concluding language that the Council "remains seized" of the issue. In UN diplo-speak, that means the subject remains on the Council's agenda, and under the jurisdiction solely of the Council, to be revisited as necessary.

It was ironic that eighteen months later, on the eve of its invasion of Baghdad when Washington was engaged in a high-stakes pressure campaign to quash UN opposition to war in Iraq, the US relied specifically on Council prerogatives based on exactly that same language. Numerous governments in the General Assembly were considering taking up the issue of Iraq based on a UN precedent that allows the Assembly to address issues ordinarily limited to Council consideration, if the Council is for any reason unable to act. But in highly threatening letters sent to many Assembly members aimed at preventing the Assembly from even considering the issue of the looming Iraq war, the Bush administration said "We deeply regret that the Council was unable to agree on a new resolution to enforce UNSCR 1441. However, the Council remains seized of this matter. For this reason alone, the GA must refrain from taking up the matter."[11]

Washington's refusal to put before the Council a resolution explicitly authorizing military force reflected a very conscious strategy of unilateral power assertion. The Bush administration's problem was not that Council support would have been difficult to obtain. Unanimity of endorsement for anything the US asked for on September 12, 2001, was a virtual certainty. Rather, the challenge for Washington was to craft a resolution that would put the UN and the Council governments on record supporting the US, without seeming to acknowledge the Security Council's right to confer or withhold the legal authority granted to it by the UN Charter to wage the war that Washington was already planning. From that vantage point, Resolution 1368 fit Washington's bill admirably.

But without such an explicit Council mandate, when the Council had indeed met and endorsed a response, the US war in Afghanistan lacked international authority. Launched weeks after the New York and Washington attacks were over, launched across the world against targets of unproven responsibility for the attacks, with inevitable and disastrous civilian consequences, Bush's war remained a serious violation of international law and the UN Charter.

Relying on Resolution 1368 to claim UN legitimacy for the US war simply didn't work. The Charter language describes the right of unilateral self-defense only until the Council can take over. In this instance, there was no problem of the Council being unable to meet, or of an unacceptably long delay between the armed attack and the relevant meeting. There was not even a problem of the Council deciding it was unable to accede to the US request for action or authority. To the contrary, this meeting was held only 24 hours after the attack, with the full participation of every member state, and the US-proposed resolution was voted unanimously, without any amendments, in less than one hour.

As soon-to-be Ambassador Negroponte later described it, "this was no instance where the United States had to lobby for votes. Among all the issues and problems the UN confronts, global terrorism clearly was the new priority. Humanity was appalled; solidarity was complete."[12] If the US chose not to ask for authorization for its response of choice when the Council met as required by the Charter, it could not then rely for authority on what Article 51 allows a country to do only before the Council acts. The unilateral US military attack, following a Council meeting that could have authorized such a response but did not do so because the country under attack did not request it, would not constitute lawful self-defense and would simply be outside the bounds of the UN Charter.

The US violation of the UN Charter was in two parts. First, and most important, the Charter-granted right of unilateral self-defense is not unlimited. If, for instance, the US had scrambled a fighter jet to shoot down the second hijacked plane before it hit the World Trade Center, that would have been a legal use (however horrific) of unilateral military self-defense. Launching a full-scale war, defined as one without an identifiable end point, across the globe against speculative targets, with the inevitable result of economic and human devastation for civilian populations, is retaliation, not self-defense. (Even if one accepts the claim that invading and overthrowing the Taliban government in Afghanistan would somehow make Americans safer, that is still an illegal preventive war—not an act of national self-defense.)

Secondly, the Charter language in Article 51 is very explicit regarding the responsibility of any country asserting the right of self-defense to consult and involve the Security Council in responding to an armed attack. In an October 2001 analysis of the international law factors involved in the US response to the September 11 attacks, the legal director of the British human rights organization Interights described how

> self-defense under the Charter… is clearly permissible only as a temporary measure pending Security Council engagement. If measures of force are initially justified, as necessary and proportionate self defense, they may still fall foul of the law if they are coupled with a subsequent failure to engage the Security Council.[13]

In other words, even if an immediate military attack in the name of self-defense was later deemed lawful, the US would be in violation if it later refused to return to the Council for discussion, involvement, and approval.

What was so important about the Charter, and the limits of Article 51 was not, as we know, that they stopped the US war. What was important was the tools they provided to people in the US and around the world to identify and challenge—and attempt to force governments around the world to challenge—US unilateralism. Similarly, in the later run-up to the war in Iraq, the fact that the war was being waged in direct violation of international law, specifically the UN Charter, played a key role in broadening the anti-war mobilizations. It was not only people who consciously recognized and opposed the US drive toward empire that the Iraq war represented who became part of that movement. The US violations meant that people around the world and most significantly people within the United States, who did not necessarily recognize the dangers of the broad trajectory of US policies, but who could not support their own government's defying the United Nations Charter, would join the anti-war movement as well.

By the beginning of the 21st century the United Nations remained mostly a player on the margins, a largely dependent actor in world affairs, whose ability or impotence to fight to "end the scourge of war" remained contingent on the scraps of power and dregs of resources bestowed on or denied it by Washington and its Security Council allies. In most cases the Charter, and decisions of the United Nations, are only relevant and empowered when they are taken up by people's movements and by governments prepared to use them to isolate, expose, and challenge the unilateral power of imperial centers. But there were key moments when that reality was reversed, when the United Nations stood defiant of US and British pressure, and joined with civil society and a rotating set of governments prepared to challenge the US trajectory toward power and empire.

And there were times when the voice of the global organization itself becomes a direct voice in the challenge to the goals of empire. Two months after the September 11 attacks, when the belated session of the General Assembly convened,

Secretary-General Kofi Annan rose to address the delegates. "One is tempted to say that we must now focus all our energies on the struggle against terrorism, and on directly related issues," he said.

> Yet if we should do so, we will be giving the terrorists a victory of a kind. Let us remember that none of the issues that faced us on 10 September has become less urgent. The number of people living on less than one dollar a day has not decreased. The numbers dying of HIV/AIDS, malaria, tuberculosis, and other preventable diseases have not decreased. The factors that cause the desert to advance, biodiversity to be lost, and the Earth's atmosphere to warm have not decreased. And in the many parts of the world afflicted by the scourge of war, innocent people have not ceased being murdered, mutilated, or dragged or driven from their homes.[14]

Throughout his tenure, Annan, like most of his predecessors, struggled to defend the legitimacy and at least some level of partial independence for the organization, and of its Charter, against the consistent assaults and varying efforts at domination or sidelining that characterized US policy toward the UN. From its origins the US attempted to prevent the UN from emerging as an independent actor on the world stage that might, with its global reach and international legitimacy, prove a successful challenger to US domination and hegemony.

In his first term, Annan arguably saw more success in defending the UN's role in that global challenge than in his second term, which began in 2001. It was surprising in those first five years, because Annan, strongly supported by then-ambassador to the UN Madeleine Albright to succeed Boutros Boutros-Ghali (in an unprincipled effort to gain support in her campaign to become secretary of state), had been expected to automatically follow Washington's dictates. In fact he didn't. Embraced by the Clinton administration largely because he wasn't Boutros-Ghali (who, while doing most of what the US demanded, tended to talk back while he did it—and on one memorable occasion actually ignored US pressure and released a UN report critical of Israel), Annan turned out to be more independent than Washington had expected.

Soon after he took over, in January 1997, Annan found widespread support as he moved to reassert UN centrality in crises across the globe. In February 1998 Annan won international acclaim, but condemnation from the US, for traveling to Baghdad to meet with Saddam Hussein. He brokered a diplomatic end to that version of the US–Iraq crisis, which the US had rather hoped would escalate and thus provide new pretexts for full-scale war.

Some in the Clinton administration believed that replacing the prickly (though also US-accountable) Boutros-Ghali with the courtly Ghanaian Annan would make it possible to convince right-wing extremists in the US Senate to pay Washington's overdue $1.5 billion-plus unpaid dues to the UN. But diplomatic niceties failed, and the US arrears continued to mount and Annan remained under attack in Washington.

In March 1998 during a debate on paying the billion dollar-plus back dues, Rep. Gerald Solomon (R-NY) took the floor, repeating his longstanding condemnation of the UN. (The conservative Republican had co-sponsored the first legislation to prevent the US from paying its UN dues, back in 1985.) In an astonishing display of racism and chauvinism, he announced that the secretary-general "should be horsewhipped." One month later, announcing his resignation after twenty years in the House of Representatives, Solomon declared "I just don't believe in hiding your feelings... If you believe somebody ought to be horsewhipped, you should say it." Rep. Donald Payne (D-NJ), former chair of the Congressional Black Caucus and a member of the House Subcommittee on Africa, noted that "for the descendants of slaves to be told by a US congressman that an African man should be 'horsewhipped' is outrageous."

So it was. But Solomon's racist attack in many ways only reflected a cruder, more overtly offensive version of the disdain with which official Washington so often viewed the United Nations.

Despite the US

Certainly Washington's continuous effort to control the United Nations represents the most important impediment to the global organization's ability to play a more consistent role in challenging war, aggression, poverty, occupation, human rights violations, and more. But that US control was never absolute. And despite the best US efforts at domination, and even despite the sometime failures of courage or capacity by UN leadership, the United Nations continues to have an objective role in that international mobilization. The organization, whatever the intentions of the US or even its own leadership, remains the repository of international law.

Whatever the weaknesses of the UN as an independent challenger, its Charter and its resolutions remain crucial tools for those around the world who stand up far more consistently to their violations. So when the resolution passed the day after the September 11 attacks did not authorize war, the Afghan war could truly be called illegal. Whether or not official UN spokespeople or agencies could act on that illegality (given the disparity of power in the world it was never surprising that they could not), a mobilized global drive against war and empire could and did seize that illegality to strengthen its movement. By itself the fact of illegality—of the Afghan war or later, more publicly, of the Iraq war—meant little. But when held up as a banner by a movement already committed to preventing or later stopping those wars, the lack of UN approval provided a basis for participation by a much broader sector of society than those who would respond alone to the wars' immorality and inhumanity.

In the run-up to the war in Iraq the UN took its place much more visibly and actively as a central component of the huge internationalist crusade of defiance challenging Washington's drive toward empire. By joining the world's anti-war majority and refusing to pass a war resolution, the UN emerged as the key diplomatic counterweight to Washington's assertion of the legitimacy of aggressive preemptive wars. The UN's role in that "second superpower" can perhaps best be understood as providing the multilateral component of a three-part internationalism—which also depends on mobilized governments, but more than anything else on a consistent, empowered global civil society prepared to bring relentless pressure onto those governments and ultimately onto the United Nations itself.

The United Nations, made up of governments, cannot by itself represent internationalism, for even when they collaborate across borders and oceans, governments alone do not represent the people of the world. But without a multilateral component, an internationalist movement cannot effectively challenge power; people in the streets have power, challenge power, or take power only when their influence is felt within the institutions that control the power before them. That is true in every country, and it is true in the global arena as well, where a powerful superpower wages war in isolation across borders and oceans.

Hans Blix, the former director of the UN's last arms inspection team operating in Iraq before the US invasion noted that

> we learned before the invasion of Iraq that in the view of the US administration, the Security Council had the choice of voting with the US for armed action—or being irrelevant. A majority on the council did not allow itself to be pushed into supporting the action, and the invasion took place. Many saw this as a loss of prestige for the Council and as a crisis for the UN. …[But] the refusal last year of a majority of the Security Council to follow the tune that the US wished the Council to play can also be seen as the saving of the Council's authority and respectability. How would the world look at the Council today if it had endorsed an armed action to eradicate weapons of mass destruction that did not exist and whose evidence was often concocted, even forged?[15]

That the Council ultimately refused Washington's campaign of bribes and threats reflected the power of the huge social movements around the world. But another real, albeit limited, victory for anti-war forces lay in the fact that the Bush administration agreed to go to the UN at all. As recently as three months earlier, after all, the Pentagon's hawks appeared to have derailed any UN-based strategy for Iraq. The Joint Chiefs of Staff remained skeptical of war; polls showed less than a quarter of Americans supported attacking Iraq without UN approval; city councils across the US passed resolutions protesting the coming war, and hundreds of thousands of protesters filled the streets. Washington's closest allies, from Germany to Mexico to France, and even the members of Tony Blair's own Labour Party in the UK, railed against growing US unilateralism.

The fact that the Bush administration, so adamantly anti-UN, had to spend more than eight weeks in the fall of 2002 negotiating the terms of Resolution 1441 and still failed to get it to include authorization for war, reflected the enormous international and domestic opposition to Washington's planned war. The resolution put significant pressure on Washington to at least appear to be acting in concert with the international community. The Republican Party's sweep of the November 2002 midterm election further empowered the administration's most unilateralist voices, but the rapidly rising US public opposition to a solo attack, bolstered by the UN refusal to endorse war, clearly acted as a brake on that trajectory.

In his September 12, 2002, speech to the General Assembly, Bush had staked out his claim that the UN would be "irrelevant" if it did not join the war. Without a hint of irony in consideration of the huge number of resolutions routinely violated by Israel or indeed by the US itself he asked, "Are Security Council resolutions to be honored and enforced or cast aside without consequence? Will the United Nations serve the purpose of its founding or will it be irrelevant?"[16]

Bush's September speech, an effort to intimidate the world body into joining this crusade against Iraq, opened a newly strengthened period of UN resistance in parallel to the governmental and especially popular mobilizations rising around the world. As the war came closer and the global organization still refused to back the coming US–UK invasion, the US attacks on the United Nations sharpened. On February 9, 2003, Bush told a Republican audience that "it's a moment of truth for the United Nations. The United Nations gets to decide, shortly, whether or not it is going to be relevant, in terms of keeping the peace, whether or not its words mean anything."[17]

The US still wanted UN approval for war, but the administration was increasingly worried about getting it. Soon after Bush's "moment of truth" statement, as Colin Powell prepared the General Assembly testimony that would mark the Bush administration's last attempt to force the UN to endorse war in Iraq, US diplomats at the UN ordered that the tapestry reproduction of *Guernica* outside the Security Council chamber be removed from sight. Recognizing the power of Picasso's anti-war masterpiece, Bush administration spin doctors were leaving no detail of their campaign to chance. UN officials ceded to the demand and covered the tapestry. They even tried to take the heat off Washington, claiming UN public information staffers had realized (though it had been hanging since 1985) that Picasso's images were "too busy" a background for Council ambassadors' television interviews; the blue cloth was more tele-friendly. But no one was buying it. The role of the Bush administration's behind-the-scenes hands was too obvious, and it was clear that the real problem was simply that Picasso's powerful anti-war message was unacceptable as a backdrop to Washington's efforts to mobilize international support for war. The UN press corps, among many others in the UN "house," were outraged, and counter-pressures rose. Within days, as UN defiance mounted, the cover was removed and the *Guernica* continued to stand sentinel over Council deliberations.

A month later, on March 6, 2003, only two weeks before his bombers would attack Baghdad and his invasion would begin, Bush taunted the UN further, saying: "The fundamental question facing the Security Council is, will its words mean anything? When the Security Council speaks, will the words have merit and weight?... If we need to act, we will act, and we really don't need United Nations approval to do so."[18]

Bush's aides waged even sharper attacks on the United Nations. Two days after the US launched its invasion of Iraq, then-Chairman of the Defense Policy Board and powerful neo-con Richard Perle celebrated what he saw as a key accomplishment of the war in an article titled "Thank God for the Death of the UN." Perle had earlier asserted, in a debate with me, that if the US launched a first strike, without the US having been attacked, "I don't believe it does violate international law."[19] Now he cheered the prospect that the Iraq war would expose "the intellectual wreckage of the liberal conceit of safety through international law administered by international institutions."[20]

In the meantime the UN arms inspection agencies—the UN Monitoring, Verification and Inspection Commission (UNMOVIC) and the International Atomic Energy Agency (IAEA) continued their work in Iraq, and continued to report the truth, that they had found no evidence of weapons of mass destruction in Iraq. The US refused to accept the reports of the UN arms inspectors as legitimate, and put enormous pressure on Hans Blix and Mohamed el-Baradei (the UNMOVIC and IAEA directors) to issue reports that would provide new pretexts for a pre-determined war.

The US position became more desperate, but not in their war preparations—those were already proceeding apace as if there were no question about the necessity for war. The so-called Downing Street Memo, which would be leaked only in the spring of 2005, proved that even Britain's top intelligence chief understood that in Washington as early as July 2002, military action in Iraq was already a foregone conclusion, and officials were tailoring intelligence to that end.[21]

The military build-up was already underway—the memo also quoted Donald Rumsfeld saying that the US had already begun "spikes of activity" to put pressure on the Iraqi regime. All the Bush administration had to do was figure out a way to justify it.

But on the diplomatic side, serious public cracks began to show. UN resistance had continued, and an embarrassing leak in the British press revealed a massive US spying campaign against the United Nations, bugging the homes, cars, and offices of Security Council ambassadors and other envoys from key countries. Veteran US diplomats began to resign their positions in protest of having to defend an indefensible war.

Colin Powell returned to the Council in early March to disparage what the UN arms inspection agencies had accomplished, only to find his claims directly contradicted by inspection chiefs Hans Blix and Mohamed el-Baradei. The IAEA director also stated directly that President Bush's earlier claim that Iraq had attempted to buy "yellowcake" uranium oxide from Niger was not simply wrong, but was based on forged documents. (Bush's specific reference to the same alleged Iraqi effort to purchase the uranium in his January 2003 State of the Union address sparked a new set of investigations and public outrage.) Secretary-General Annan affirmed that a war launched without explicit Security Council authorization would indeed be in violation of the UN Charter.

By February 14, 2003, the day before the global demonstrations against the war, the reports to the Security Council by the two inspectors gave rise to the powerful statements by French Foreign Minister Dominique de Villepin and others rejecting Washington's efforts to force the arms inspectors to its will.

When de Villepin said "the United Nations must be an

instrument of peace, and not a tool for war," diplomats broke into a huge wave of applause that swept across the usually staid Security Council chamber. But the significance was far more than a break with diplomatic decorum; it signaled the intensity of opposition to US efforts to marginalize the UN and impose a unilateral war in defiance of international public opinion. Word of de Villepin's statement—and the ovation that greeted it—spread quickly around the world where demonstrators were beginning to gather for what would become the historic global mobilizations of February 15.

The following day, when the delegation from the New York protest met with Secretary-General Kofi Annan before the rally began outside of UN headquarters, Archbishop Desmond Tutu's words were more incantation than analysis. "We are here on behalf of the people marching today in 665 cities around the world," Tutu said. "And we're here to tell you that those people marching in those cities all around the world, we claim the United Nations as our own, we claim it as part of our global mobilization for peace."

For the vast majority of those marching around the world, that claim was certainly true. It did not, however, reflect the perspective of top UN leadership, already facing high and escalating US pressure to bring the UN's credibility to the US war. Annan did not respond to Tutu directly, expressing instead only his hope that the UN diplomats, who had left after the Security Council meeting the day before to consult their governments for final decisions on Washington's demands, would find some means of compromising to avoid war. Those diplomats, he knew, had headed home just in time to see first-hand the massive protests thronging the streets of their capital cities. The competing pressures on the secretary-general during that brief morning meeting were visible in Annan's face: ultimatums from Washington to throw his influence and the UN's credibility behind the looming Iraq war vying with desperate appeals from civil society led by his friends and fellow African statesmen and fellow Nobel laureates to stand up for UN opposition to war and defense of its Charter.

Despite the intense pressure, lucrative bribes, and frightening threats characterizing US "war diplomacy" at the United Nations, Washington's crusade for a UN endorsement failed. UN resistance held, and the Security Council never did pass a resolution authorizing war.

The UN weapons inspectors continued their work and still found no evidence of weapons of mass destruction. On March 18 the US and Britain withdrew the informal discussion draft of a war resolution they had been circulating until then. The next day the war in Iraq began, a preventive (not preemptive) war of choice waged in defiance of the UN Charter, without Security Council authority, and in violation of international law. While challenging the war as immoral, brutal, and based on deliberate lies, its incontrovertible international illegality remained an important tool for the global anti-war movement.

UN resistance would not last, ultimately, but it showed the world a potential alternative, when national governments' authority, multilateral credibility and popular power unite to say no to war and empire. It was the beginning of a new kind of internationalism, linking cross-border social movements with willing governments and the United Nations itself in a global challenge to the emerging US empire. The US had played hardball, but the UN didn't back down. And that time, at least, they got away with it. The US had threatened dire consequences, but despite Washington's rhetorical fury the sky did not fall in. The UN had done what its Charter mandates: acted as both venue and player in the global resistance to "the scourge of war." It was a breathtaking moment.

When US pressure triumphed and the period of defiance collapsed in May 2003, with the passage of a new UN resolution that provided a kind of multilateral gloss on Washington's and London's still-unilateral military invasion and occupation of Iraq, only the most important component of that internationalist triad remained: a mobilized global civil society. Still, the world had seen the possibility of a moment when the United Nations, when the world's peoples and governments together demanded it, could stand with protesters in the streets.

In his anguished speech on March 26, just after the invasion of Iraq began, Kofi Annan told the Council,

> we have all been watching hour by hour, on our television screens, the terrifying impact of modern weaponry on Iraq and its people. We not only mourn the dead. We must also feel anguish for the living, and especially for the children. We can

only imagine the physical and emotional scars that they will bear, perhaps for the rest of their lives. All of us must regret that our intense efforts to achieve a peaceful solution, through this Council, did not succeed.

He noted that "many people around the world are seriously questioning whether it was legitimate for some member states to proceed to such a fateful action now—an action that has far-reaching consequences well beyond the immediate military dimensions—without first reaching a collective decision of this Council."[22]

And then, perhaps acknowledging his friend Bishop Tutu's words, the secretary-general recognized that "in the last few months the peoples of the world have shown how much they expect of the United Nations.... Many of them are now bitterly disappointed." Whether or not his speech referred directly to what Bishop Tutu had said a month earlier, it was clear that Annan's remarks did refer to the powerful global movement against the war. In the long effort to prevent the US war those protesters had laid claim to the United Nations as a key component of the global mobilization for peace, had identified the organization as a key venue for, as well as sometimes actor in, the anti-war campaign. During the last months before the war, despite Bush's rhetoric of "irrelevance," it was the UN that reflected and projected the demands of the global opposition movements into the world of diplomacy and power, and thus helped to prevent, despite the massive death and destruction in Iraq, Bush's broader effort to claim a political triumph.

The Collapse of UN Resistance
Within the first months following the invasion of Iraq, most of the UN's defiance largely collapsed. Recognition that the war was now underway, despite all the earlier efforts, morphed into a sense of hopelessness about the UN's inability to stop it. Instead, governments, including many who had led the anti-war efforts, turned to rebuilding their now-fragile relations with Washington.

The UN collapse was not complete. Washington still never got clear UN endorsement for the war. But the collapse of resistance was evident in the passage, in May, of Security Council Resolution 1483. It did not assert official legitimacy for the US invasion of Iraq, but it did "recognize" the US and

Britain, identified as "the Authority," as occupying powers there. Much of the resolution focused on articulating the power— including control of all funds around the world from previously frozen Iraqi oil accounts. The resolution also spelled out the obligations of "the Authority" under international law to provide for the needs of the civilian population. In the context of the US search for international legitimacy, the UN resolution came perilously close to granting it.

The original draft the Bush administration had put on the table would have given the US-controlled military force "authority to take all necessary measures to contribute to the maintenance of security and stability in Iraq," though the final resolution left out those precise words. The final resolution, however, still gave the US most of what it wanted. It was carefully drafted to include the key buzzwords that many European, Arab and other governments were looking for— "sovereignty" was mentioned twelve times, and the text was sprinkled with references to the "territorial integrity of Iraq," the UN playing "a leading role," even the "end of the occupation." But its real goal remained to legitimize continuing US control of the occupation while giving the illusion of international support—"bluewashing" the unilateral Iraq war with a multilateral UN endorsement.

Most significantly, the UN resolution essentially accepted the US plan for Iraq: full US military control, an unlimited occupation, widespread privatization to be imposed on the country, an "election" scheme decreed by the US, laws to be drafted and enforced by the US occupation authority, and more.

And crucially, the resolution called for an active role by the UN itself, in providing humanitarian assistance to the population in Iraq and helping to organize "elections" even while the US occupation continued. But the resolution provided no authority and no independence of action for the UN staff. It looked like a set-up. As one UN staff member in Baghdad described it,

> it was this resolution that rang the death knell for the UN in Iraq. Having heroically resisted American pressure to authorize the war, Security Council members decided to show goodwill to the 'victors.' 'A step too far' was how an Iraqi put it to me on my second day in Baghdad. He said that even those

who had grown accustomed to the double standards the Security Council employed in punishing Iraqis for the 1990 invasion of Kuwait, while acquiescing to a quarter-century of Israeli occupation of Arab lands, were horrified that it could legitimize an unprovoked war that the entire world had clamorously opposed.[23]

The secretary-general persuaded his reluctant top aide, Sergio Vieira de Mello, a brilliant Brazilian diplomat, to lead the UN deployment. While Vieira de Mello had good relations with the US occupation authorities at first, they quickly deteriorated, and concerns grew in the UN that Iraqis increasingly saw the UN as an arm of the US.

The consequences of the lack of UN independence grew serious. According to Salim Lone, a longtime UN official who served as Vieira de Mello's communications director,

the low point came at the end of July [2003], when, astonishingly, the US blocked the creation of a fully fledged UN mission in Iraq. ... Clearly, the Bush administration had eagerly sought a UN presence in occupied Iraq as a legitimizing factor rather than as a partner that could mediate the occupation's early end, which we knew was essential to averting a major conflagration. Indeed, the UN chiefs of communication in Iraq had met that morning to hammer out a plan to counter the intensifying perception among Iraqis that our mission was simply an adjunct of the US occupation.

The UN itself—the institution and its international staff— would soon pay an enormously high price for the Security Council's decision to legitimize the US occupation.

On August 19, 2003, a huge truck bomb exploded outside the United Nations headquarters at the Canal Hotel in US-occupied Baghdad. The killing of 22 UN staff members, including Vieira de Mello, demonstrated in a visceral and human way the price the global organization would pay when US pressure forced it to submit to a role subservient to Washington's strategic control. The attack derived directly from the understanding among Iraqis that the UN was playing a role within, and supportive of, the US occupation of their country. The international and Iraqi humanitarian workers, and the UN as a whole, made an easier, more accessible target than the Pentagon's tanks and armored humvees patrolling Baghdad's streets. The United Nations and its staff that day became the latest victims of US policy.

The UN paying a price for US domination was nothing new in the organization's history, though the August 2003 attack was certainly the most horrific example. As a result of the Canal Hotel attack and another attack on the UN in October 2003, Annan decided to pull out virtually the entire UN contingent in Iraq. Future participation would be on a very small scale.

But the debate over whether and how the global organization could maintain some presence in Iraq remained. Throughout that fall the top leadership of the UN debated whether, as the *New York Times* posed the question, "any change can give it the freedom it needs to survive without being seen as either a lackey of the United States or an easily swattable gadfly." The willingness of the Germany, France, and Russia as well as the "Uncommitted Six" to stand up to the US on Iraq had destroyed the myth of international consensus on issues of peace and security, and the early September collapse of the Cancún summit of the World Trade Organization demonstrated the ability of poor countries in the global South to divide the world on trade.

But once the war began and the US occupation of Iraq was consolidated, the role of the UN in challenging the US over Iraq was replaced, for many throughout the world, by "the assumption that the United Nations is simply a stalking horse for the imperial ambitions of the United States." Similarly, in Iraq itself, as Salim Lone, the communications director of the Baghdad mission and a survivor of the August 2002 bombing, told Kofi Annan a month later, "it was clear to many of us in Baghdad that lots of ordinary Iraqis were unable to distinguish our UN operation from the overall US presence in the country."[24]

Fundamental differences remained over what role the UN should play in Iraq—and what kind of UN changes would be needed for the future. *New York Times* correspondent Felicity Barringer described how

> Europeans today view the United Nations as the embodiment of international law and world order. The United States seems to view it as a tool to be used when handy. Africans and Asians tend to have more case-specific uses for United Nations diplomacy and its general advocacy for the poor and

disadvantaged who are not much in the minds of rich nations. But for United Nations officials, many of whom have never worked anywhere else, the bottom-line question remains how to relate to the United States.[25]

But the uncertainty about the UN's future role did not prevent the continuation of UN efforts to maintain some kind of presence in Iraq. Again the secretary-general prevailed on a reluctant longtime associate, this time former Algerian Foreign Minister Lakhdar Brahimi, to become the UN special envoy in Iraq. Brahimi was approved by the Bush administration despite his longstanding criticisms of US policy in the region, precisely because Washington needed credibility from Iraqis and from the Arab world in choosing its first interim government in Baghdad. But the Bush administration kept up relentless pressure on Brahimi, who was ostensibly empowered to select the interim government. The result was a government ultimately chosen and vetted not even by the representative of the international community, however marginally legal that might have been, but rather by the occupying power itself and its own chosen minions. Brahimi described "terrible pressure" from the US occupation forces that kept him from selecting the more able and popular candidates he favored for the interim government in Iraq.[26] Ultimately, he recognized that the interim government itself lacked any legitimacy. Brahimi told the Council in April that "the absence of such a sovereign government is part of the problem in the first place."[27]

Frustrated with the level of US control of his work in Baghdad, Brahimi refused to play by the UN's normally restrictive diplomatic rules—and in doing so he probably came closer than anyone else to reclaiming at least a little of the UN's lost credibility and legitimacy in the Middle East. In April 2004 he made clear that ending the Iraq crisis was tied to the problem of the Israeli occupation of Palestine:

> There is no doubt that the great poison in the region is this Israeli policy of domination and the suffering imposed on the Palestinians, as well as the perception of all of the population in the region and beyond of the injustice of this policy and the equally unjust support... of the United States for this policy. I think that there is unanimity in the Arab world, and indeed in much of the rest of the world, that the Israeli policy is wrong,

that Israeli policy is brutal, repressive and that they are not interested in peace no matter what you seem to believe in America. What I hear [in Iraq] is that... these Americans who are occupying us are the Americans who are giving this blanket support to Israel to do whatever they like. So how can we believe that the Americans want anything good for us?[28]

"There's an obligation of all of us," Brahimi said, "to see how we can cohabit on this small planet with this superpower which is the United States. There are quite a few other people on this planet and the Americans should also make an effort to learn how to live with them."

It was a sign of Washington's desperate need to claim some kind of legitimacy in Iraq that the Bush administration did not move to oust Brahimi at that point. As the noted Middle East analyst Patrick Seale described it, "Brahimi is the man of the hour. The US and Britain are relying on him to find a way out of the catastrophic mess in which they find themselves in Iraq."[29]

But if Colin Powell was not going after Brahimi and the UN, others were. William Safire, right-wing pundit in the *New York Times*, accused Brahimi of seeking to "gain quick local support by denouncing Israel" and said he was guilty of "anti-Western Arab demagoguery."[30] Israel's ambassador to the UN, Danny Gillerman, called Brahimi "vitriolic and biased."[31]

But in the meantime Washington's new proconsul in Iraq, former UN Ambassador John Negroponte, was joining Powell to craft an entirely new concept in international law. Iraq would be "sort of" sovereign while the US occupation remained, which is a bit like being "sort of" pregnant. How could a nation be any kind of "sovereign" with 150,000 foreign troops occupying their land? According to Powell, "some of that sovereignty they are going to allow us to exercise on their behalf and with their permission."[32]

In case anyone wondered about the viability of such an arrangement, Senator Richard Lugar (R-IN) had the answer. During the Senate Foreign Relations Committee confirmation hearings for Negroponte, Lugar made clear the basis of Washington's reliance on Brahimi and, by extension, on the UN itself. "UN involvement can help us generate greater international participation, improve the political legitimacy of the interim Iraqi government and take the American face off the occupation of Iraq."[33]

Staying Outside

But the UN was not prepared to provide that kind of political cover. In September 2004, Secretary-General Kofi Annan finally said specifically and directly that the war in Iraq was "illegal" and stood in violation of the United Nations Charter.[34] His statement was late and reluctant, but nonetheless his call was important in reaffirming the UN's commitment to its Charter and to international law, even when the violator was the most powerful member state.

As the US occupation ground on, and the US-controlled political process sputtered on in Iraq, the interim "Iraqi National Council" gave way to the transitional Iraqi Interim Government. The January 2005 elections, assisted by a small UN technical team but taking place under the control of the US military occupation, brought out millions of Iraqis willing to brave serious threats of violence to cast their vote—overwhelmingly for parties that had pledged to ask the US troops to leave. Unsurprisingly, once they were placed in office under US protection, the new politicians in the assembly did no such thing, knowing that their hold on power depended on the occupation armies remaining in control.

As the occupation continued, the resistance escalated (from about 40 attacks a day before the elections to an average of 60 a day after[35]) in both numbers and lethality. Still there were far more Iraqis being killed, both ordinary civilians and those attempting to join Iraq's occupation-backed security agencies, than the better protected, better armed, better trained US and British and the few other remaining "coalition" troops. In the fall of 2004 the respected British medical journal the *Lancet* reported on a new study from Johns Hopkins School of Public Health indicating that more than 100,000 Iraqi civilians had died because of the war. The deaths were "mainly due to violence and much of it was caused by US air strikes on towns and cities."[36]

As the human costs of the war continued to rise, economic costs rose as well. On a global scale, UN agencies estimated what they could do with something close to the war budget the US Congress had authorized the Pentagon to spend in Iraq. The UN's Food and Agriculture Organization (FAO) estimated it could cut world hunger in half with $24 billion annually. That would translate to 400 million malnourished people finding access to sufficient food, many for the first time in their lives.[37] The director of UNAIDS, Dr. Peter Piot, said he needs only $10 billion annually to launch a truly global, comprehensive program to respond to HIV/AIDS.[38] The UN Children's Organization UNICEF estimates that it would take a mere $2.8 billion annually to provide immunization for every child in the developing world.[39] To provide clean water and functioning sewage systems to the world's population, the World Water Council estimates an annual cost of $37 billion.[40]

Combined, these efforts to provide basic food, HIV/AIDS medicine, childhood immunization, and clean water and sanitation, transforming the lives of impoverished and desperate people around the world, would cost $74 billion dollars a year—about 15 months worth of 2005 levels of US spending on war in Iraq.[41]

So Does the United Nations Defy US Power?

The necessary lesson from the UN's shift away from resisting US power is not that the UN should be attacked or even abandoned by the central and most important sector of that movement—the people in the streets in every country—but rather that the global movement must keep up the pressure on its governments and on the UN itself to keep it accountable to the world's agenda for peace.

Mobilized and empowered internationalism must be the basis of the opposition to empire. And within the multifaceted understanding of internationalism, there is an important role for multilateralism, or the coalescence of governments. That multilateralism is only one part, and not close to being the strongest part, of internationalism, but it is a necessary one. The world is still organized through nation-states, and despite the rise in power of multinational corporations and their international financial institutions, any internationalist movement needs an inter-governmental sector as part of its strategic challenge.

Like all inter-governmental organizations, the UN was created to reflect, not to challenge, the power realities of its founding moment. And certainly the UN bears all of the limitations inherent in an organization crafted to reflect the post-World War II balance of power, and later seized and held hostage by Washington's unchallenged global reach. But imagine how much weaker, how much less able to stand up to US pressure, would be a "United Nations-Lite"—inevitably constructed to reflect the 21st century's reality of vastly expanded, untrammeled US power?

Certainly the United Nations must be defended. But "defending" the UN must itself be broadened and redefined to signify protecting the organization against the domination of its most powerful member, the commanding force within it. Defending the UN has to mean organizing opposition to the role the UN is sometimes forced to play, especially its imposed role as legitimator of the US expansion of empire. It has to mean mobilizing within civil society and finding at least a few member states to rebuild the conditions that made possible the UN's remarkable eight and a half months in 2002 and 2003, of doing what its Charter mandates: standing defiant against the US to "prevent the scourge of war."

And defending the UN also does not mean complacency about the organization's huge weaknesses. Those weaknesses are less problems of "bloated bureaucracy" and "unaccountable staff" that US and other western pundits and officials speak of, than of the power the US holds within the organization. Real reform of the UN does not mean slash-and-burn "downsizing" of UN staff, or imposing corporate-style CEOs to restyle UN management. Real reform means fighting for democratization and transparency at the UN. Defense of UN democracy means defending those voices and agencies within the organization that can speak for the disenfranchised global South, defending the use of UN resources to protect the interests of the weakest of nations and the poorest of peoples. It means fighting to make the dollar-controlled multilateral institutions—the IMF, the World Bank, the WTO—accountable, at last, to the UN's Economic and Social Council as the UN Charter envisioned, rather than to the powerful corporations they now serve.

Security Council reform must be redefined. Adding one or two more wealthy northern countries will not make the Council more representative. Bringing in the largest and most powerful countries of the global South as second-class permanent members while the same five powerful countries maintain the veto will not make the Council more democratic. Real Council reform means working to get crucial issues out of the US-dominated stranglehold of the Council altogether, and into the veto-less General Assembly.

Democratizing the UN also means working to reverse John Bolton's affirmation that

> There is no United Nations. There is an international community that occasionally can be led by the only real power left in the world, and that is the United States, when it suits our interest, and when we can get others to go along... When the United States leads, the United Nations will follow. When it suits our interest to do so, we will do so. When it does not suit our interests we will not.[42]

Democratizing the UN, if serious, must result in overturning that arrogant reality and defending the internationalist integrity of the global organization.

In early 2005 Bush nominated Bolton, who was the former chief of relations with international organizations in the State Department, and under George W. Bush the assistant secretary of state for arms control, to replace Negroponte as US ambassador to the United Nations, despite—or perhaps because of—his hubris, his aggressive style, but especially his passionate and well-documented history of antagonism to the global organization and his disdain for international law. Bolton had argued in the *Wall Street Journal* that even treaties signed and ratified by the US are not legally binding commitments, but rather simply "political obligations."

Bolton's nomination sharply divided US foreign policy elites and the intelligence communities, and for months the Senate refused to confirm him as ambassador, even resorting to the rarely-used filibuster to prevent the appointment from going through. Aside from his overall attack-the-UN orientation (endearing to many conservatives) Bolton had orchestrated the firing of Jose Bustani, chief of the UN's Organization to Prohibit Chemical Weapons, for daring to insist that the US accept the same kind of inspections of chemical plants that Washington demanded for other countries. Elected in 1997 and reelected in 2000, Bustani had achieved enormous success in locating and destroying chemical weapon manufacturers. He reported pressure from the US beginning in mid-2001, in response to efforts to bring the US into compliance with the treaty. In March, the US proposed a no-confidence vote in the OPCW to remove Bustani. Eventually, Bustani reported, "Bolton... told me, 'Washington wants you to leave OPCW tomorrow.' I asked him to be more precise and he responded that he did not need to explain anything."[43]

On one remarkable occasion publicized at the height of the furor over Bolton's nomination, but carefully ignored by even the staunchest anti-Bolton Democrats and the broad activist StopBolton coalition, Bolton actually succeeded at preventing then-Secretary of State Colin Powell from hearing the views of his own State Department analysts regarding a likely breach of US law by Israel. The incident, in July 2002, followed the Israeli military's highly publicized use of a US-provided F-16 jet to bomb a crowded residential quarter of Gaza at 3:00 AM, ostensibly to assassinate a Hamas leader, Salah Shihadeh. Shihadeh was indeed killed; fourteen civilians were also killed in their sleep, thirteen of them young children. Some at the State department worried that the act might violate the US Arms Export Control Act's prohibition on using US-provided arms for anything other than immediate self-defense. They wrote a memo to Powell outlining their concerns, and including opposing views to make it a "split" memo. Bolton got the memo, stripped it of the critical analysis, and sent it on to Powell with only the "don't worry, no problem, no violation" component of the memo.[44] (One might certainly argue that Powell should not have required a memo to realize Israel's violation, but that is a separate matter.)

In other incidents Bolton had attempted to falsify and then claim publicly allegations that Cuba possessed biological weapons, a charge denied by all US intelligence agencies. He consistently attempted to find non-existent evidence of Syrian weapons of mass destruction, and on occasion attempted to fire intelligence analysts who could not produce what he wanted.

Most of the opposition to Bolton focused on his propensity to attack subordinates with whom he disagreed, and his efforts to concoct false intelligence to bolster pre-existing views. Many of the arguments were rooted in the view that Bolton, clearly an extremist, was not a good representative of the US government. The problem, of course, was that while he did represent the most extreme wing of a thoroughly extremist administration, his views—and indeed his tactics—were well within the range of the White House he would serve. Bolton would bring to the UN the same tactics, corroborated in the Downing Street Memo, in which "the intelligence and facts were being fixed around the policy" that the entire Bush administration had relied on to justify war in Iraq.

No one could really claim he did not accurately represent his president. But if indeed the strong anti-Bolton campaign lost, and he was indeed confirmed as US Ambassador to the UN, the consolation prize would be that he would have virtually no capacity to win over diplomatic, let alone public, opinion in the rest of the world. Colin Powell had managed to convince many at the UN that, whatever they thought of George Bush, his, Powell's, was somehow a different, more reliable and honest voice. John Bolton would have no such luck.

The UN in the New Century

When the UN celebrated its 50th year in 1995, it was in the middle of the decade of "humanitarian interventions," in many of which the UN was sent in to clean up the aftermath of disastrous policies and invasions orchestrated by the US and its allies. The anniversary led to a process of public rethinking and reassessment of the organization's goals, functions, successes, and failures in many places across the globe. In the US, much of the public rethinking in the media and the various academic and policy-oriented journals was limited to various levels of criticism and blame for what were called the "UN's failures" around the world. Some focused on financial mismanagement or inefficiency in relief activities, on charges of corruption or the ever-popular "bloated bureaucracy" argument. Other than the last, of course, most of those problems were in fact real, and deserving of serious consideration. The problem was, they were not the fundamental challenges facing the UN, and solving them would not, ultimately, protect the UN's integrity, legitimacy, and influence in the uni-polar post-Cold War world of untrammeled US unilateralism and power.

The key UN problem, so consistently missing from those pages of print and flashes of sound-bite analysis, was the question of power. Virtually no official voices were prepared to state directly that the UN succeeded or failed, that it succeeded in vaccinating children in Bangladesh or failed to bring peace to Somalia, because of what the US and its allies, the wealthy and powerful of the UN, would allow it to do.

A similar kind of analytical attention to the UN emerged in the run-up to the war in Iraq in 2003, as many in the US examined what role the UN should or could play in the post-September 11 world of rising US empire. But this time around the debate was different. Bush himself deemed the UN "irrelevant" for its refusal to endorse his war. US conservatives and others excoriated the UN for its "failure" to back Washington's war in Iraq. Mainstream US critics of the war mostly urged support for continued UN arms inspections but paid little attention to the role of the UN as a whole. It was left to the activist community and the international progressive movement and analysts to examine seriously the new potentials of the global organization, the new relevance made possible by the UN standing alongside governments and a global social movement, defying US demands to go to war.

A contradiction was built into Washington's own goals. To maximize the value of the UN as a legitimating agent for its own unilateral actions, Washington had to maintain at least the appearance of the UN's credibility as a global institution. The US, already the only superpower and unassailably the most powerful member state of the organization, couldn't "use" the UN with open impunity and still expect it to maintain its legitimacy as a multilateral organization, the legitimacy that Washington wanted to derive from the UN to itself.

The power of the US to pick and choose when, how often, and how intensely to manipulate the UN's role in the world does not apply to the rest of the world. For most countries, the UN is the only venue in which they have any chance of joining with others to challenge that unilateral US power. There is little question that the large majority of countries and certainly the majority of the world's people would like the UN—a reconfigured and democratized UN—to play a larger part in the collective global opposition to Washington's drive toward empire. But few diplomats, whether in the UN or in far-flung capitals, will say so out loud.

Bush Empire Strikes Back

Beginning only months after the US invasion of Iraq, the US launched a vicious assault on the legitimacy of the United Nations focused largely on the secretary-general. Six separate congressional investigations were launched, alongside a major independent investigation initiated by the UN itself, examining charges of corruption regarding the "oil-for-food" program that had provided basic humanitarian supplies to the people of Iraq, paid for with Iraqi money, throughout the dozen years of crippling economic sanctions.

While billed as a reform corrective to the oil-for-food "scandal," the escalating attacks, including calls for Annan's resignation, were not responses to any financial misdeeds. Rather, they represented a major coordinated attack on the United Nations as a whole, a punishment for refusing to back the Iraq war. While they were orchestrated first by right-wing elements in Congress and the media, rather than the Bush administration directly, they reflected a growing anger among many in official Washington that the UN had gone too far in challenging US legitimacy and credibility.

The independent UN investigation, led by consummate Washington insider former Federal Reserve Chairman Paul Volcker, largely absolved Annan of any serious wrongdoing. The accusations focused on the claim that the oil-for-food program had allowed Saddam Hussein to skim several billion dollars, over a dozen years, from the oil sales the program oversaw. The *New York Times* actually had it right. Its December 5, 2004, lead editorial acknowledged that

> Iraq accumulated far more illicit money through trade agreements that the United States and other Security Council members knew about for years but chose to accept.... The United Nations bureaucracy had no power to prevent these illicit oil or arms deals outside the oil-for-food program. It was the responsibility of member nations... Thus the primary blame for allowing Iraq to accumulate illicit billions lies with the United States and other Security Council members.

The ideologically driven attacks were led by right-wingers in Congress as well as columnists William Safire in the *New York Times*, Claudia Rosset in the *Wall Street Journal*, Charles Krauthammer in the *Washington Post*, and the pundits of the

American Enterprise Institute. But much of the background came from documents made public by the dubious Ahmad Chalabi, the former CIA asset and Pentagon favorite. When he returned to Iraq shortly after the US invasion under Pentagon protection following decades in CIA-backed exile, the US military had turned over to Chalabi massive quantities of alleged Iraqi government files. Among those documents, Chalabi claims, were lists of people and international corporations who were offered the right to sell Iraqi oil allocations by Saddam Hussein's regime.

The effect of the right-wing campaign was to focus public and media attention on the responsibility of the UN secretariat, especially Kofi Annan personally, for alleged corruption in the oil-for-food contracting arrangements. That kept the spotlight away from the role of the US and other Security Council members, which held the ultimate power to approve or reject all oil-for-food contracts. The US and Britain routinely and publicly used their power to delay or cancel contracts based on their often-cited (though rarely substantiated) claim of "dual use," meaning items that had potential military as well as civilian use. But there were no known reports of the US or any other Council member putting holds on a contract because of the widely known practice (typical of the global oil industry) of kickbacks and surcharges.

In fact, far more billions of dollars went directly into Iraq's treasury outside of the oil-for-food program altogether, from the massive US- and Council-approved Iraqi oil sales to Turkey and Jordan. But the real scandal, even beyond US or Council involvement in enriching Saddam Hussein's treasury, was the US-orchestrated imposition of economic sanctions in the first place, and how, even after the genocidal impact of the sanctions became widely known, Washington manipulated the Security Council to maintain them.

It was certainly not a coincidence that even though they were responding to UN resistance to the Iraq war, the anti-UN attacks escalated particularly after the 2004 US election. During the campaign, some accountability to widespread US support for the UN would have had to be taken into account. The campaign to undermine the UN also escalated following Annan's public recognition that the US war in Iraq was illegal.

The UN's Own Reform Panel

In the face of the relentless attacks from the US, efforts to reform the UN continued. At the official level, proposals for wide-ranging reforms were in preparation ahead of the September 2005 meeting at the UN at which heads of state in the General Assembly would assess progress toward meeting the Millennium Development Goals established in 2000.

Along with drafting his own proposals for reform of the United Nations, the secretary-general had commissioned a "High Level Panel on Threats, Challenges and Change" to develop a reform agenda. The release of the Panel's report in anticipation of the September 2005 Millennium Plus Five meeting of the General Assembly brought to the front of the multilateral agenda a set of interlocking issues involving poverty, disempowerment, environmental degradation, and more. The media attention focused almost exclusively on the report's discussion of Security Council expansion, ignoring much more important analyses. It was significant, for instance, that the report explicitly rejected the idea of "security being best preserved by a balance of power, or by any single—even benignly motivated—superpower."

The panel recognized that

> the refusal of the Security Council to bow to United States pressure to legitimate the [Iraq] war is proof of its relevance and indispensability: although the Security Council did not deter war, it provided a clear and principled standard with which to assess the decision to go to war. The flood of Foreign Ministers into the Security Council chambers during the debates, and widespread public attention, suggest that the United States decision to bring the question of force to the Security Council reaffirmed not just the relevance but the centrality of the Charter of the United Nations.

The panel failed in key areas of improving UN democracy. It called for strengthening the thoroughly undemocratic Security Council, calling on it to be "more proactive" in the future. But instead of encouraging a greater role for the General Assembly, by far the most democratic of UN agencies, it charged that the Assembly has "lost vitality and often fails to focus effectively on the most compelling issues of the day." This despite the crucial role played by the Assembly, even without specific resolutions, in building UN and international rejection of Bush's Iraq war, and despite the potential for greater UN relevance by further empowering the far more democratic Assembly.

An important contribution of the panel's report was its assessment of the breadth of threats facing the UN and the 21st-century world. They recognized that the world's dangers are not limited to terrorism, as the Bush administration continued to claim, but a range of interconnected risks including poverty; infectious disease, especially HIV/AIDS; environmental degradation; inter-state conflict; internal conflicts including civil war and genocide; nuclear, radiological, chemical, and biological weapons; terrorism; and transnational organized crime. By recognizing these broad social crises, and the inter-connected and indivisible nature of them, the report raised an important challenge to Washington's insistence on a myopic focus on international terrorism.

The report was not entirely progressive, however. A crucially significant, and potentially dangerous, development in the report had to do with redefining the legitimacy of the use of preemptive or preventive force. It was important that the panel did not favor abandoning, or even officially reinterpreting, Article 51 of the UN Charter, which outlines the very restrictive conditions in which a nation can legitimately use military force in self-defense. (Article 51 states that self-defense can be used only "if an armed attack occurs," and only "until" the Security Council can meet to determine a collective response.)

The report acknowledged that Article 51 should be understood to include self-defense by a state facing an imminent threat—such as a hostile state loading ballistic missiles onto launch pads. But crucially, the report ultimately failed to answer the fundamental question of what to do when a state claims to face an imminent threat and uses that threat to justify self-defense, but in fact the claim is false. It failed to specify who has the right to determine the legitimacy of such a self-defense claim. The report dangerously implied that any country, asserting the kind of lies that undergirded Washington's and London's claims of Iraq's imminent threat (remember Tony Blair's claim of 45 minutes for Iraq to launch a missile?), might have the right to simply announce to the world that X country represents an imminent danger and therefore claim the right to go to war. The report said nothing about who might hold governments accountable for such false claims.

Another key unanswered question was whether the panel was implicitly recognizing as acceptable the kind of double standard that characterizes so much of UN policy—in which the veto-wielding members of the Security Council are held to a lesser standard of accountability to UN decisions and international law than other countries.

The panel also began to establish criteria for determining the legitimacy of military force. The guidelines were proposed for UN authorization of force, but the panel urged governments to accept them as well. They included the threat being serious enough to justify the use of military force; clarity that the primary purpose of the proposed military action is in fact to halt the threat; ensuring that every non-military alternative has or will fail; that the military force is proportional to the threat; and that there is a "reasonable consequence" that the military action will work against the threat and the consequences will not be worse than the consequences of inaction. But again there was no proposal for holding governments accountable to violations of those guidelines, let alone how to deal with rogue governments taking military action in defiance of any guidelines, such as Washington's war in Iraq.

Even more dangerous, the report seemed to suggest that the UN itself, relying on those criteria, might become a more regular participant in military action. Instead of limiting the deployment of UN peacekeeping or other forces, the new guidelines hinted at a greater willingness to rely on the use of military force.

The report began by appropriately distinguishing "preemptive" military force, used unilaterally by a country claiming to face an imminent threat, from "preventive" force, used in "anticipatory self-defense," meaning a longer-range threat that is not claimed to be imminent. But then it went on to anticipate that even without rewriting Article 51 on self-defense, the Council may authorize the use of preventive force— something never before considered as legitimate in international law. "The short answer," as the panel described it, "is that if there are good arguments for preventive military action... they should be put to the Security Council, which can authorize such action if it chooses to." Such authorization, if the Council granted it, would compromise even further, perhaps irreparably, United Nations credibility.

In the diplomatically difficult area of genocide and ethnic cleansing within an ostensibly sovereign state, the panel broke some new ground in defending the obligation of the international community to protect endangered peoples. It stated that

> there is a growing recognition that the issue is not the "right to intervene" of any State, but the "responsibility to protect" of every State, when it comes to people suffering from avoidable catastrophe—mass murder and rape, ethnic cleansing by forcible expulsion and terror, and deliberate starvation and exposure to disease. And there is a growing acceptance that while sovereign Governments have the primary responsibility to protect their own citizens from such catastrophes, when they are unable or unwilling to do so that responsibility should be taken up by the wider international community—with it spanning a continuum involving prevention, response to violence, if necessary, and rebuilding shattered societies.

It remained unclear whether this language might be used to strengthen calls for the UN to provide international protection to Palestinians living under Israeli occupation.

In other areas there were significant advances in the panel's report, including the recognition that the Non-Proliferation Treaty's Article VI requires the US and other acknowledged nuclear powers to move toward full and complete nuclear disarmament. The report bemoans the weakening of the NPT overall. But by recognizing the obligations of the most powerful nuclear weapons states rather than focusing, as US policy does, only on the possible proliferation of such weapons to other non-nuclear weapons states, the UN panel supported a more equitable global accountability for compliance with the NPT.

The sections that dealt with changing Security Council composition provided two parallel proposals for Council expansion to the existing structure of five permanent, veto-wielding members, and ten non-permanent members elected for two-year terms; both proposals would have added a total of nine new Council seats. One called for adding six new permanent but non-veto seats (two from Africa, two from Asia, one from Latin America, and one from Europe), plus three additional non-permanent seats. The other called for eight new four-year, renewable seats (giving more powerful countries a kind of "illusion of permanence") without veto rights, as well as one new two-year non-permanent seat. The panel did not recommend any expansion of veto power, but they also did not propose methods of ending the anti-democratic veto arrangement altogether.

The panel claimed that any expansion of the Council should "give preference for permanent or longer-term seats to those States that are among the top three financial contributors in their relevant regional area to the regular budget, or the top three voluntary contributors from their regional area, or the top three troop contributors from their regional areas to United Nations peacekeeping missions." These criteria would undermine the long-standing UN principle that financial support for the organization is based on an "equity of pain" principle—that holds that it is equally difficult for the US to pay its several-hundred-million dollar 22 percent of the UN budget as it is for impoverished Chad or Laos to pay the tiny fraction of one percent that constitutes their share. They would privilege the wealthiest states and in a few instances those with a military big enough to send troops for years abroad on UN missions.

Various combinations of countries have teamed up in the campaigning for new permanent Council seats. The most influential, combining Germany, Brazil, India, and Japan, of course favor the plan for four new permanent seats. But by spring of 2004 China had made clear it would not accept Japan as a permanent member, and while the US backed Japan it made clear that Germany was not on Washington's list. Payback for Berlin's anti-war stand regarding Iraq was a clear subtext. The possibility of Brazil and India joining the Council alone remained unlikely. And further, among other governments in the South, opposition to the Big Four was a constant murmur.

By July 2005 the Group of Four, along with France and some additional small nation support, had introduced a resolution in the General Assembly calling for six new permanent seats and four non-permanent seats. The new permanent seats would be assigned to Asia (two—presumably

Japan and India), Africa (two—presumably two out of South Africa, Nigeria, Egypt), Latin America (one—presumably Brazil) and "Western European and Others" (one, presumably Germany). The problem, of course, was that neither Mexico nor Argentina was thrilled about Brazil emerging as the recognized continental leader, just as Pakistan was not prepared to sit quietly while its longtime regional rival rose to international stature. Aside from the US opposition, Italy fumed over Germany's role, and Indonesia was not happy about Japan joining China as permanent Council members. And the Africa Group had deadlocked not only between South Africa, Egypt, and Nigeria, but as well with Senegal and Angola as permanent Council aspirants.

In fact it remained unlikely that either proposal for Council expansion would come to full fruition in the foreseeable future. The panel report did fuel an important global discussion of the undemocratic and illegitimate nature of the current Council composition. But the more realistic possibility of dealing with that imbalance of power lay with a broader campaign—which would require civil society as well as governmental backing—to delegitimize Council power in favor of reimpowering the far more democratic General Assembly.

Real UN Reform

The question for global civil society and international social movements must be how to redirect UN reform away from technical tinkering to fundamental transformations. The goal must be to reclaim the UN as part of the global mobilization against empire, and to return it to the defiant role it played during the 2002–2003 run-up to Washington's war in Iraq. That will strengthen the UN institutionally and democratically, while making the global organization the partner of international civil society, where independent non-governmental organizations and social movements work to transform the world. Joined by a few occasionally supportive states and governments, and united with a reformed and democratized United Nations serving as both venue and player in the search for peace and justice, global civil society anchors the key position in the triad of forces collectively capable of challenging the US.

Support for the UN cannot be reduced either to

cheerleading or dismissing the possibility of any reform because it won't be enough. It is true that none of the reforms that seem conceivable today would, alone, bring about real, fundamental democratization of the UN—the organization remains a reflection of a US-dominated world moving toward consolidation of a mighty US empire. But some changes are possible, and the most significant among them would make a real difference in the UN's capacity to mobilize against wars and to protect the impoverished, occupied, and marginalized countries and peoples of the global South.

Those serious reforms in the organization must aim at creating a level of international democracy rarely seen in multilateral decision-making. UN democracy must in the longer term mean broader representation in the Security Council, less power for its veto-wielding permanent members and eventually less power for the Council itself. That is not likely to happen anytime soon, and in the meantime the UN must create an outside monitoring agency to oversee the Council's conclusions. Such an agency, made up of globally respected international lawyers accountable only to the UN and not to their countries of origin, must be vested with the enforcement power of international law. They must be empowered to prevent Council decisions—such as the imposition of economic sanctions or the decision to authorize war—that might themselves violate the UN Charter, as has happened so many times before. Such power would have prevented, for instance, the US bribing, threatening, and punishing enough governments to pass Security Council Resolution 678 "authorizing" war against Iraq in 1990–1991. It would have stopped the imposition of genocidal economic sanctions against post-war Iraq, sanctions that the US eventually acknowledged were responsible for the deaths of over 500,000 Iraqi children under the age of five.

UN reform must also involve re-empowering the General Assembly, returning the UN's most democratic body to the central position it occupied in the UN's first decades. UN reform means demanding that the UN reclaim its Charter-granted right to oversee—and overturn—the decisions of the Bretton Woods organizations, so that global macro-economic policy is not set by the wealthy countries alone.

The US, as the UN's most powerful member, should be

pressured to increase its financial and diplomatic support for the UN's work in humanitarian and development areas, while abjuring its insistence on control. And UN peacekeeping should be seen in that same context of humanitarian work: as part of a proactive process aimed at identifying potential crises early enough to not only identify but begin to rectify the instabilities so often rooted in inequity, economic dislocation, and political disempowerment, before they explode into violence and require military force.

UN peacekeeping has come under harsh criticism in recent years because of charges of sexual assault, child prostitution, and other horrific behaviors by peacekeepers. The notion of forcing desperate refugees to exchange sex for food or otherwise attacking the most vulnerable populations the UN soldiers are sent to protect is especially reprehensible. Several contingents of the peacekeeping mission in the Democratic Republic of Congo were particularly condemned for exactly that kind of action. Much of the criticism, however, particularly that from the right-wing anti-UN faction in the US Congress in 2004 and 2005, ignored the reality that the United Nations itself is given no authority over the Blue Helmeted peacekeepers it recruits from national armies and sends into far-flung conflict zones. In the case of the Congo, for instance, all the UN commanders could do on the ground or back at the Department of Peacekeeping Operations in New York was ask the relevant governments to send home any soldier accused of even the most heinous crimes. The UN could not bring charges or arrest such peacekeepers or hold them in any way accountable for their violations.

Certainly UN peacekeepers are no more likely to commit such acts than soldiers in any national army—but unfortunately they are no less likely precisely because they are deployed to serve with the UN directly from those national armies. The military culture of every country's army is replete with violence. What is called for is not less of a role for the UN in peacekeeping operations, but a transformed and empowered, greater responsibility for peacekeeping. Certainly the UN should have authority over the military forces operating under its command; but few governments in the world today are prepared to turn their soldiers over to another's command.

For the long term, what is needed is an entirely new way of

fielding peacekeeping missions. UN peacekeeping missions should no longer be carried out by contingents of soldiers trained (often badly), armed (usually inadequately), and conditioned (always violently) by ordinary national armies. Instead, peacekeeping should be done by a new UN military and police peace force, to which young people from all over the world would be recruited to join on their own, not deployed by an existing army. They would attend school in a UN-run university that would include training in police and military skills, but would also be educated in internationalism and the understanding that military force is always a last resort. They would graduate accountable to, and loyal to, the United Nations as an institution before any national army.

Creation of a UN military peace force should not be translated, however, to mean increasing UN endorsement of unilateral military interventions by its major powers as a replacement for direct UN involvement. If, in violation of international law and the UN Charter, the US storms across the Iraqi desert, or France re-occupies part of Rwanda, or the US invades Haiti—whether or not the actions are carried out in the name of "restoring democracy" or "providing hope"—it should be made clear to the world that they did so without UN approval and authority. And if the US deliberately chooses to go to war without UN approval in search of non-existent weapons of mass destruction or to "liberate" the Iraqi people through military occupation, the UN should not serve as an enabler of countries wishing to collaborate in occupation. The UN should refuse to serve as a blue-helmeted clean-up squad sent in to mop up Washington's messy aftermath. Illegal wars should remain illegal and be opposed as such—and the UN should maintain its Charter obligations to prevent the scourge of war and should hold the perpetrators of wars accountable for their violations of the international crime of aggression.

Sometimes, just sometimes, such a role for the UN might be possible. There are no magic solutions. But the result of these changes would mean at least the beginning of UN democratization. We need the UN to at least try to provide some level of that international collaboration, some level of protection for impoverished countries and peoples of the South, some level of what the founders claimed they were interested in:

to end the scourge of war—not to increase the might of the world's sole hyper-power.

There is no question that the UN should have claimed, and the US should have accepted, the centrality of UN decision-making years ago, in Iraq, in Palestine, in Haiti, and elsewhere. There is no question that despite its flaws the UN represents a far more democratic expression of the "international community" than does Washington alone, or NATO's North Atlantic Council or George W. Bush's "coalition of the willing." The US and the other powerful nations should have supported UN-controlled efforts (along with those of the OSCE, the African Union, the Arab League, and other regional organizations) to respond proactively and collaboratively to emerging humanitarian crises. The US and its allies should have supported the creation of a UN Department of Preventive Diplomacy and a standing, independent UN-controlled rapid-response military/police peace force. There is no question that the United Nations, not the US alone or a US–UK partnership or even a so-called quartet created under Washington's control, should be orchestrating international protection and the enforcement of international law to end Israel's occupation of Palestine. There is no question that the UN should be helping the Iraqi population rebuild its destroyed state structures and reclaim its sovereignty on Iraqi terms, rather than the Pentagon continuing its illegal occupation. There is no question that the General Assembly should claim the right to address a far greater share of UN decision-making too often left to the veto-distorted, undemocratic Security Council.

There is no question that those things would make the UN—a stronger, more democratic, and more empowered UN bolstered by international social movements and far-flung citizens' organizations throughout the world—a vital component of a new inter-nationalism that together would stand in strategic challenge to Washington's empire. And there is no question that strengthening the United Nations is definitely not on the agenda of Washington's rising empire. Precisely for that reason, defense of the UN must remain a priority for internationalists across the globe.

The bottom line, once again, is that of power. The US has a virtually unlimited arsenal of weapons to enforce its will on other countries outside the UN framework—no other country's reach comes even close. The UN exists squarely within, not outside, of that power disparity, but the ability for collective resistance action among its member states makes it a potential, if not always reliable, venue of challenge to US power. So strengthening the United Nations must be a priority precisely to reinforce some level of international balance in our extraordinarily unbalanced and asymmetrical world.

The call from civil society to the global organization should challenge the UN to heed the voices of its partners in the "second superpower" above that of the first. Civil society must take that stand, for the stark reason that there is nothing else to provide a multilateral voice for the majority of the world's countries—and sometimes, albeit rarely, of the world's peoples. For progressives and democrats and civil society—most especially those in US civil society whose government remains the imperial world power—the commitment must be to a new kind of internationalism, linking the UN with willing governments and an empowered global civil society. However flawed the UN of the 21st century may still be, it remains a crucial part of any potentially successful effort to mount a serious challenge to US empire.

5
INTERSECTIONS

In January 2005, Arundhati Roy spoke to tens of thousands of people at the opening of the World Social Forum in Mumbai. Celebrating the success of social movements in preventing expansion of the World Trade Organization's power at the ministerial meeting of the WTO in Mexico sixteen months earlier, she said "what Cancún taught us is that in order to inflict real damage and force radical change, it is vital for local resistance movements to make international alliances. From Cancún we learned the importance of globalizing resistance."[1]

The powerful Indian novelist and peace campaigner's words frame a wide understanding of how global resistance, operating in a globalized world, can challenge the US hyper-power's drive toward war and empire. And although, as she noted, "governments try to take the credit" for such change, the centerpiece of resistance remains what Roy called "the years of struggle by many millions of people in many, many countries."

Ultimately changes in social policy mean governments changing their ways, even if for opportunistic or politically motivated reasons—something that requires relentless pressure to be brought to bear on those governments. To change people's lives demands changes at the governmental level. It is therefore not enough for people to mobilize in the street: the mobilization must demonstrate enough strength to force those in power to change. And when the government's power affects people across the globe, as is the case with the United States and its willingness to wage war for the expansion of power, other governments must be pushed to join with people's movements to say no to US wars. Then those governments can unite to challenge the US collectively. And that coming together of governments can only take place in the multilateral context of the United Nations, which similarly can change only when enough governments force it to become a venue in that global resistance.

The question for the global movements, then, is how to pressure governments successfully enough that they are forced to stand up to US unilateralism and militarism, and then how to push enough governments into that position that they take over the initiative and seize the United Nations out from under US domination. The role of the social movements remains central—any alliance with governments or the UN will always be short-term and tactical. But the intersection of activist movements—national, regional, and international—with those national and multilateral power centers remains a key weapon for global resistance.

People and Governments

The history of social movements almost always begins with campaigns to pressure governments—to make good on too-often false promises of reform or democracy or economic justice, or to stop trajectories of war, oppression, human rights violations, or denials of basic rights. Less frequently have popular movements found themselves in alliance with governments, but in the context of a global campaign against a world-wide power, such alliances become important.

In the run-up to the Iraq war, local and national pressure in countries around the world combined with governments recognizing the dangers posed by the looming US–British war to create the basis for many governments opposing the war. That put them, tactically, on the side of the social movements that provided the strategic center to the expanding international mobilization against war in Iraq, and required new ways of social movements interacting with governments.

In many instances it meant that "alliance-based" relationships with those governments were forged outside their own countries, while at home anti-war campaigners kept up the pressure to make sure the government didn't falter. One example was visible during the focus on the "Uncommitted Six" members of the Council who were facing enormous US pressure to endorse the war. In Mexico, in Chile in particular, as well as in the three African countries and Pakistan, local protests continued, opposing Bush's war and demanding that the governments maintain their defiance. In Washington at the same time, the women's peace organization Code Pink was organizing a roving parade of supportive demonstrations at the embassies of the key countries. They brought croissants to the staff of the French embassy and flew French flags when the House of Representatives cafeteria began serving "freedom fries," they brought flowers to the embassies of Mexico, Chile, and Angola. The flowers and treats certainly didn't determine those governments' willingness to resist US pressure, but it was a public reminder—not least from the resulting press coverage—that many Americans viewed those anti-war governments as friends and partners, not as adversaries or even enemies.

During the same period Cities for Peace organizers in 165 US cities succeeded at winning city council resolutions against war in Iraq. The campaigns created new alliances between local activists and municipal government officials, many of whom became key participants in national and international peace mobilizations. In New York, City Council members hosted activists from United for Peace and Justice for a reception the night before the February 15 events, and a Chicago city council member traveled to Italy for a speaking tour coordinated by the Italian Peace Roundtable (Tavola della Pace) and its 400-plus constituent municipalities committed to peace education. In the US, the Cites for Peace council members played an active role in challenging the Bush administration. Just weeks before the US invasion of Iraq in the winter of 2003, dozens of mayors and city council members from across the country converged on Washington to march on the White House and present their official resolutions. White House guards refused to allow the officials to enter, and even refused to accept the documents—and the wide-ranging national press coverage of the local officials being denied access to the federal government showed an important and credible component of the peace movement as well as demonstrating new schisms within official governmental circles.

Elsewhere in the world, national governments emerged as serious partners with civil society and social movements on specific issues. One of the clearest examples was Malaysia, whose government emerged as a strong supporter of Palestinian rights in the UN years ago, and in the period since the second intifada began in 2000 became involved as well in supporting Malaysian and international civil society campaigns for Palestine. A major conference in Kuala Lumpur in 2004 brought together hundreds of activists from dozens of Asian countries, especially from within Malaysia itself, as well as from Palestine and Israel and a few from other parts of the world. The conference was initiated by the Kuala Lumpur-based International Movement for a Just World in collaboration with Peace Malaysia (both NGOs active in the peace movement), but the conference was supported by the Malaysian government and featured major presentations by the prime minister and other government officials. Given the government's history of domestic repression, it would have been hard to imagine even a tactical alliance on any other issue. But in this case the collaboration worked, and the conference resulted in the launching of a plan for a new resource center on Palestine to be created in Malaysia, aimed at providing material, information, and campaign support for Palestine support movements in the global South.

Other examples were more complex. In the context of both opposing the war in Iraq and supporting Palestine, the ANC-led South African government has played a vital role in the United Nations, leading the Non-Aligned Movement and helping to shore up weaker governments wavering under US pressure. South African diplomats developed strong working relationships with civil society organizations and activists operating within or even outside the UN framework, collaborating on education and mobilization campaigns. Within South Africa, however, things were more complicated. The governmental involvement, especially on the Palestine issue, remained strong, but the powerful South African civil society organizations supporting Palestine worked on parallel rather than intersecting tracks. Many of the activists working on the Palestine issue were simultaneously involved in challenging the government's sometimes neo-liberal economic programs responsible for keeping so many South Africans impoverished even after the end of apartheid. That meant that their work challenging official policies resulting in corporate domination and economic inequality targeted the same government that took a principled and internationalist stand in support of Palestinian rights. It was not an easy basis for even a tactical partnership. But within the global movements, a sophisticated understanding emerged based on recognizing the need for a nuanced "inside-outside" strategy. People in the streets empowered others in the suites. In the South African model, for example, that meant that the consistent pressure of social movements supporting Palestine inside South Africa kept the government willing to play a role outside South Africa as partners of international or UN-based movements fighting for the same issue. International activists working in New York or Geneva had to understand that their South African counterparts maintained a very different relationship to their government than those external players, and were what made possible South Africa's consistent stance. At the same time the South African activists recognized that the United Nations represented a very different political arena than Pretoria, and that cooperating with the government in that context did not equal betrayal of internationalism.

Building the collaboration between the three components of the second superpower was never going to be easy.

People and Multilateral/Regional Organizations

At the regional level things are often more confusing. In Europe, the 2005 referendums defeated the proposed constitution of the European Union in France and the Netherlands. In both cases, progressive social movements had mobilized widely on a national basis, but working in close coordination between European countries, to defeat the constitution. The notion of strengthening EU unity as a means of increasing Europe's ability to challenge the US was and remains an appealing one. But the constitution was widely understood to be aimed far less at strengthening Europe's capacity to provide a political and social challenge to the US, than at consolidating neo-liberal economic policies and expanding Europe's military capacities and arms industries. In this case the governments of every European country—from socialists and social democrats in Spain and Germany to Gaullists in France and conservatives in Italy—supported the constitution, so alliances with governments were not on the agenda. What was required, instead, was a European-wide mobilization of progressive forces (right-wing anti-immigrant, anti-Muslim, and other racist elements also opposed the constitution as a statement against Turkey's admission to the EU) cooperating on the basis of building a "social Europe" as an alternative.

Earlier, in Cancún in the fall of 2003, when the World Trade Organization's trade ministers met to try to expand the power of the WTO, the regional alignments were different. During that meeting, Europe and the US returned to the strategic unity that had been shaken but not splintered despite the seriousness of the divisions over Iraq. The two major economic powers joined to ratchet up the pressure on countries of the global South—but, bolstered by the collective opposition to war earlier that year and the fact that the US had not implemented the various threats Washington had made, the South banded together and said no. It came to be known as the Group of Twenty, or G-20, in which Brazil, India, China, Argentina and others led the strongest of the South in opposition to the US–European northern bloc. The G-20 gained much of its strength and backbone from its alliance with the scores of thousands of protesters who filled the streets of Cancún. Those opponents of corporate-driven globalization, themselves from northern as well as southern countries, shared the goals of the southern governments: to prevent the expansion of WTO regulations to even more sectors of global trade. And the informal coalition that provided the backbone of opposition thus led to the collapse of the Cancún summit. It was a major victory for at least two-thirds of the second superpower.

The People and the UN

The Cancún victory did not involve the UN. But the emergence of the new internationalism, whose birth was heralded by the *New York Times* after the global mobilization of February 15, 2003, was shaped very much by the involvement of people in, and the success of people's influence on, the United Nations.

By the time the anti-war movements of the early 21st century were underway, there was a longstanding relationship between individual people and groups of people around the world and the United Nations. Some of the connection was immediate and direct, some based on long unfulfilled dreams. In refugee camps people understood the role of the UN in providing for immediate needs of vaccinating children, providing fresh water and emergency food aid. In impoverished countries people looked for development assistance to rebuild after wars or to help build schools and clinics, sometimes for the first time.

In wealthy northern countries with little need for direct help from the global organization, the UN was long seen as the repository of international law. A few years after the 1991 Gulf War, the US public television network rebroadcast an extraordinary series, *Eyes on the Prize*, about the history of the US civil rights movement. It opened with an old black-and-white film clip, apparently from the early 1950s, showing a small group of black sharecroppers marching, somewhere in the deep American South. They could have been almost anywhere in the world: their clothes were ragged, they were badly educated, they were desperately poor. They carried with them a few crudely-drawn signs, asking for simple justice, for the right to vote. And they carried a single tattered flag, the blue and white banner of the United Nations. It represented their hopes, at a time when their government offered no hope at all for a better life.

The UN wasn't able to provide more than an occasional forum for voting rights advocates and their counterparts around the world, although there were times when an international forum proved crucial. In 1951 the great African-American leaders Paul Robeson and William L. Patterson decided to bring to the United Nations their petition entitled "We Charge Genocide: The Crime of Government Against the Negro People." Drafted by the Civil Rights Congress, which Patterson directed, they presented the signed petition simultaneously to UN officials in New York and to the General Assembly in Paris.

Only three years earlier, responding to the carnage of World War II and the Holocaust, the UN had passed the Convention Against Genocide, codifying such acts for the first time as international crimes. Robeson and Patterson realized they could claim this new UN commitment as their own, on behalf of an impoverished and dispossessed population still only a couple of generations removed from chattel slavery. "Out of the inhuman Black ghettos of American cities," the introduction began, "out of the cotton plantations of the South, comes this record of mass slayings on the basis of race, of lives deliberately warped and distorted by the willful creation of conditions making for premature death, poverty and disease..."[2]

Bringing the petition to the United Nations certainly did

not end racism in the United States. But it did put the issue of racism, racist violence, and racial oppression squarely at the forefront of the world's human rights agenda. It was because of the "We Charge Genocide" petition, as much as anything else, that exposure of US institutional racism became a key weapon of Washington's opponents in the Cold War. US charges, sometimes true but as often false or exaggerated, of social ills in the Soviet Union were answered by accounts of how the self-described greatest democracy in the world treated people of color. The petition, and the attention it garnered in UN circles, helped strip away the carefully constructed US mythologies of equality and fairness.

Demands for greater involvement of civil society in the work of the United Nations increased during the 1990s, partly in response to the higher profile of the UN in the post-Cold War era and partly as the "humanitarian interventions" of that decade raised more questions about the role of the UN in the world, and especially in the context of the sequence of global conferences that took place at that time. The demands were for access to meetings, then for a voice, and ultimately for some role in decision-making processes. They didn't all succeed. The call for access was answered only partly throughout the UN conferences, where NGO and civil society representation was limited to separate parallel conferences, usually far from the official conference sites. The conference process began in 1990 with the Summit for Children (which was quickly derailed to become a venue for the US to bribe governments for support of their planned war against Iraq.) In 1992 came the Earth Summit in Rio, followed in quick succession by the 1993 Human Rights Summit in Vienna, the 1994 Population Summit in Cairo, and in 1995 Social Development Summit in Copenhagen and the Fourth International Women's Conference in Beijing.

None of the conferences, which all faced serious undermining by US efforts to avoid any binding commitments to international law or justice, succeeded in transforming the social and political crises they were designed to address. But they did provide some new international attention to those often hidden issues, and provided a venue for world-wide networking among civil society organizations. Those contacts, strengthened in the years that followed by the creation and expansion of the internet, set the stage for the emergence of the World Social Forum movement, which also began as a civil society response to the exclusivity of those in power—meeting in the glittering chateaux of Davos at the annual World Economic Forum.

Other collaborations between the UN and civil society have been more successful, both in joint work and in preventing UN disasters. The longstanding relationship between the General Assembly's Committee on the Exercise of the Inalienable Rights of the Palestinian People (one of the worst examples of bureaucratic UN-speak around) and its secretariat staff in the Division for Palestinian Rights have for years maintained close working relations with scores of organizations all over the world working on the UN- and international law-related aspects of the Palestinian issue. The committee hosts an annual conference of global NGO activists, and however limited the official agenda may be because of diplomatic cautiousness, the opportunity to meet, talk strategy, and craft unified programs is unmatched. Taking its lead from recent developments on the ground, the work of the NGO network focuses on such issues as demanding Israeli compliance with the advisory opinion of the International Court of Justice, which held that Israel's separation wall built to snake through the occupied West Bank in a major land grab, was illegal.

The committee also ensures civil society representation within the annual official General Assembly commemoration of the International Day of Solidarity with the Palestinian People. That participation provides a rare opportunity for representatives of the Palestinian rights movements to address the Assembly delegates directly, in many cases identifying and challenging the Assembly's failures to act more assertively to defend Palestinian rights.

Stopping UN Corporatization

Success of a different kind could be seen in the work of a civil society advisory committee convened by the leadership of the UN Development Program. In the 1990s' drive toward privatizing and corporatizing UN activities, few UN agencies had gone farther in recreating their identity as corporate partner than the UNDP. In early 1999, UNDP created blueprints for a "Global Sustainable Development Facility," designed officially to show corporations that "helping the poor in developing countries can also be profitable."[3] In fact, the corporations who would join the effort, for an insignificant $50,000 contribution, would gain access to UNDP's network of high-level contacts and, even more valuable, a chance to "bluewash" their often appalling environmental, labor, and human rights records with the UN flag. The increasingly visible global networks of northern and southern economic justice advocates launched a highly public and very embarrassing attack on the project. The UNDP leadership began to backtrack, and only days before his resignation, in a meeting with a group of civil society representatives, the program's administrator, James Speth, went to great pains to describe the project (to which he had already assigned three full-time staff people) as still in the preliminary stages.

But however defensive the UNDP leadership became, the planning and development of the GSDF project did not stop. Speth's successor, Mark Malloch Brown, came to the agency in July 1999 directly from a career as a high-ranking public relations official for the World Bank. He was even more interested than Speth had been in building corporate partnerships for the UNDP. A favorite in Washington, Malloch Brown brought even the language of corporate culture directly to the development agency. In his inaugural speech on the day he took up his position as UNDP Administrator, he told the assembled UNDP headquarters staff and those in far-flung field postings brought in through video-conferencing, "We must work to develop a universal corporate focus and a corporate standard for country offices... Re-building UNDP's franchise and reputation for excellence starts with field entrepreneurship." But the anti-globalization movements that came to such unified fruition in Seattle later that year turned their focus on the United Nations as well as individual governments, and Malloch Brown's PR background helped him realize his agency's vulnerability in public perception. He convened his own group of civil society advisers, made up of strong critics of corporate domination but supporters of the UN, who were able to convince him to cancel the UNDP's plan for corporatization.

Article 14

Of course not all of the efforts of civil society to pressure the United Nations end so well. The UNDP's cancellation of its

GSDF was an important victory, but it did not herald the end of other UN efforts toward corporate partnerships. One of the most ambitious campaigns was launched by the secretary-general himself, with the announcement of the Global Compact to link the UN with corporations that would then have the right to use their UN endorsement for advertising. The theory was that mere involvement with the UN, statements of intention to abide by a set of goals involving labor and environmental rights, and posting good ideas on a website would somehow turn ruthless corporations into warm and fuzzy global neighbors. But there was no enforcement of the rules, no accountability to the goals of the UN. Civil society wasn't buying it. And, as it turned out, neither were most corporations. By July 2005 just over 2,000 businesses were listed, the vast majority of them without posting any of the "best practices" the compact supposedly encouraged. The lack of significant corporate interest (particularly from US-based corporations who saw little advertising advantage to be gained from UN connections) reduced the grand scheme to an organizational shell limping along with little influence or credibility, but the project was not yet disbanded.

An earlier effort at civil society enforcement of UN decisions also didn't accomplish quite what it set out to do. During the inter-war years of economic sanctions in Iraq, a global movement to stop the sanctions grew around the world. One of the key actors in that movement was Denis Halliday, the former UN assistant secretary-general who had been in charge of the oil-for-food program in Iraq during 1997 and 1998. After 13 months on the job he resigned in protest of the genocidal impact of the sanctions on the people of Iraq, particularly the most vulnerable, children and old people, and the inability of the program to alleviate the suffering. Within weeks of his return to New York, Denis and I started a six-week, 22-city speaking tour across the US to mobilize the anti-sanctions movement. One of our key arguments was based on Article 14 of the famous UN Security Council Resolution 687, which US President George H. W. Bush had imposed on the Council in April 1991 calling for Iraq's disarmament and for UN authorization to continue post-war sanctions against Iraq.

A largely unnoticed section of the resolution, Article 14, put the entire Iraq crisis in a new light. It said that the disarmament actions to be taken by Iraq should lead "toward the goal of establishing in the Middle East a zone free from weapons of mass destruction and all missiles for their delivery and the objective of a global ban on chemical weapons." The establishment of such a zone would certainly include the abolition of Israel's huge but unacknowledged nuclear arsenal of between 200 and 400 high-density nuclear warheads. Yet despite all the US bluster regarding the consequences of Iraq's non-compliance with Resolution 687 (it was eventually one of the myriad rationales for the 2003 invasion), despite the fact that the US had drafted the text of the resolution, no UN campaign even to force Israel to officially acknowledge the nukes was ever taken up. Denis and I raised the issue repeatedly, and it picked up some currency within the broad, largely faith-based movement.

Eventually the question came up following a presentation sponsored by the Council on Foreign Relations. A member of the audience identified himself as a State Department official who had helped to draft 687. After the official talk, we asked him, "What were you thinking? Why would you include language like Article 14?" It was no problem, he said: "We knew no one would take it seriously." On one level he was right; the fact that the activist movement took the issue seriously was not a problem for the State Department. On the other hand, when hypocrisy and double standards in enforcement of UN resolutions emerged as part of the challenge to the second Bush's war in Iraq, at least a few people remembered the history of Article 14. For broadening public awareness of Israel's dangerous nuclear arsenal, the US-drafted United Nations resolution turned out to be a useful tool.

War in Iraq

During the run-up to the 2003 invasion of Iraq, the global peace movement interacted in myriad ways with the United Nations. One of the most consistent in the United States was in the widespread public understanding that the looming US war was being waged without UN authority and thus in violation of the UN Charter and international law. The Cities for Peace campaign, which orchestrated city council resolutions in huge industrial cities and tiny rural towns and everything in between, recognized the importance of each city's campaign being built around its own articulation of resistance to war. As a result, the language differed in each city, but what linked all of the resolutions was an explicitly stated rejection of an illegal unilateral war launched without United Nations authority. It was clear that if the US had succeeded in forcing a Security Council imprimatur to the war, far fewer municipal officials, mayors, and city council members would have been prepared to challenge the war as directly. Cities for Peace might still have managed to pass resolutions against the war on the basis of morality, governmental lies, and overt opposition to US empire, in Berkeley, in Boulder, Colorado, in Madison, Wisconsin, and perhaps a dozen other small, progressive, often college-based towns. But the power of recruiting a range of cities from New York to Chicago to Baltimore to Atlanta to Los Angeles to Detroit to Seattle to Cleveland—huge diverse industrial and financial centers that collectively are home to 40 percent of Americans—would have likely remained out of reach.

Not Quite Uniting for Peace

Even in the extraordinary context of the run-up to the war and the period around February 15, of course not all the campaigns were successful. One such educational but ultimately insufficient effort was the attempt to mobilize support for a move in the General Assembly to use an old UN precedent, known as the Uniting for Peace resolution, to get the issue of war in Iraq out from under the control of the veto-deadlocked Security Council and into the General Assembly.

Given the origins of the Uniting for Peace precedent, it was particularly ironic to imagine it being used successfully to prevent a threatened US war. The Uniting for Peace resolution 377 was originally a US weapon for the Cold War. With the Security Council largely paralyzed, the Assembly was Washington's agency of choice in 1950 in obtaining the UN's multilateral credential to go to war in Korea. Under the terms of Chapter VII of the Charter, the Security Council alone holds the ultimate power of deploying UN military force. But the Council was already locked in a paralysis born of Cold War and colonial interests' conflicts, so it was deemed an unlikely agency to provide Washington with the desperately sought international endorsement. Instead luck, in the form of fortuitous timing, was on the Americans' side. At the moment the US tabled a resolution in front of the Council, its Soviet nemesis was temporarily boycotting Council meetings, in protest over Washington's refusal to accept the People's Republic of China as the legitimate representative of China, rather than the Nationalist government now located in Taiwan.

US diplomats grabbed the opportunity of the Soviets' absence to gain the Council's imprimatur. When the Soviets returned to the Council a few weeks later and not unexpectedly rejected the US-imposed decision, Washington turned to the Assembly. The US introduced the Uniting for Peace resolution authorizing the General Assembly to meet on short notice in an emergency in which the Security Council could not act and to recommend collective measures, including the use of armed force. Inevitably, the pliant, pre-decolonization Assembly passed the US-sponsored resolution. The result was that, despite the Soviet position that the Council's action was illegal and the active Soviet opposition that followed in the Council, the US relied on the Assembly resolution to legitimate its claim that its own involvement in the Korean War was somehow mandated by the international community.

The language of Resolution 377 states that, if there is a "threat to peace, breach of the peace, or act of aggression" and the permanent members of the Security Council do not agree on action, the General Assembly can meet immediately and recommend collective measures to "maintain or restore international peace and security."[4]

The next time the 377 precedent was used was also a US initiative. But this time, in 1956, it reflected a Cold War-era, shaken-up set of relations in the Middle East, in which the US found itself opposing its Israeli and European allies and opposing war. When Egypt nationalized the Suez Canal in 1956, Britain and France, backed by Israel, invaded Egypt and began advancing on the canal. US President Eisenhower demanded an end to the invasion. Ceasefire resolutions in the Security Council were vetoed by France and Britain. Then the US proposed a ceasefire resolution in the General Assembly, which met in emergency session and passed Washington's resolution, including a call for the invading troops to withdraw. Within a week the foreign troops were out of Egyptian territory.

The run-up to war in Iraq in 2003 seemed a perfect opportunity to use the precedent once again to avert, or later stop, a war. Civil society organizations, primarily those focused on issues of UN reform and global governance, began mobilizing public support for a Uniting for Peace move into the General Assembly.[5] But implementing 337 takes political will, and political courage, two items in increasingly short supply in UN diplomatic circles as the war grew closer, as the toll of months of opposition continued to rise. The Non-Aligned Movement's summit on February 25 "emphasized the urgent need for a peaceful solution of the issue of Iraq in a way that preserves the authority and credibility of the Charter of the United Nations and international law as well as peace and stability in the region" and "affirmed their categorical rejection of assaulting Iraq."[6] But they did not move the issue into the General Assembly.

By the time the war began in mid-March, no action had been taken at the UN. Discussions continued after the US invaded Iraq, and a week later the Arab League foreign ministers condemned the invasion and called for an immediate and unconditional withdrawal. Eventually discussions were held on the margins of the Council and of the Assembly, but no resolutions condemning the war or calling for withdrawal of the invading troops were put on the table. There was fear by the war's opponents—including at various points the Arab League, the Non-Aligned Movement, and the Organization of the Islamic Conference—that the inevitable defeat of such a resolution in the Council by US and UK vetoes could lead to the appearance of a UN endorsement of the war. There was no such problem in the General Assembly, however, where there are no vetoes; there, it was a matter of the failure of political will and the success of US threats to any country that might even consider bringing the issue to the Assembly. The US spent enormous diplomatic energy both before and immediately after the war began aggressively pressuring governments to prevent an Assembly initiative. It was in this period that the letters were sent to governments threatening that "the United States would regard a General Assembly session on Iraq as unhelpful and as directed against the United States."

For Iraq, the UN's strategic collapse in May 2003 with the

passing of Resolution 1483 "recognizing" the US–British occupation, remained unchanged. The Uniting for Peace precedent was never introduced at all. The civil society campaign did help to popularize understanding of how it could be used, and overall helped to build support for claiming United Nations authority on behalf of the anti-war mobilization rather than to legitimize war. So it set some potential for future collaboration.

New Collaborations

In the years following the US invasion, while the US–British occupation of Iraq continued, other forms of collaboration between people's movements, governments, and the UN continued. In February 2005 the Framework Convention on Tobacco Control (FCTC) came into force after a three-year process involving hundreds of NGOs as well as governments from Asia and the Pacific, the Caribbean, and the Middle East. According to Kathryn Mulvey, executive director of the US-based Corporate Accountability International, "The FCTC is the first global health and corporate accountability treaty that challenged the abusive practices by transnational corporations." It was made possible by collaboration between governments and global social movements, targeting internationally powerful tobacco corporations.[7]

And civil society and social movements also continued to build cooperation—critical cooperation—with the United Nations. In preparation for the September 2005 "Millennium Plus Five" summit meeting at the UN, devoted to assessing progress toward meeting the eight Millennium Development Goals from 2000, social movements of anti-poverty activists, indigenous peoples, women's organizations, trade unions, peace mobilizations, anti-corporate campaigners, and many more from across the globe came together to forge a parallel effort to "make poverty history." Building a people's infrastructure of national, regional, and international collaboration, coalitions such as the Global Call Against Poverty (G-CAP) emerged to simultaneously use the moment of the UN summit to shape new mobilizations against poverty, to demand full implementation of the Millennium Goals, and to critique seriously the insufficiencies inherent in the goals themselves. It was a daunting challenge.

Part of the work involved fighting for a direct civil society voice within the UN negotiations; two days of hearings sponsored by the president of the General Assembly in June 2005 represented a small step in the long process of making that goal a reality. But understanding was clearly growing in the UN about the necessity of taking seriously the role of civil society actors and social movements on the global stage. Secretary-General Kofi Annan's description of civil society as "the world's new superpower" in a speech at a McGill University conference of international NGOs reverberated through the corridors. "After decades of undemocratic and ineffective global governance on key global issues—ranging from development and environment to human rights, trade, and security—now is the time to privilege and highlight the visions and views of civil society leaders around the world," one participant told the conference.[8]

There remains a huge challenge within the global justice and peace movements around the world: to educate people about why the United Nations does not have to remain the "tool of US foreign policy" that Madeleine Albright once described. It will often be used that way. But sophisticated, committed global people's movements, sometimes with a few governments beside them, have the capacity to defend the UN from US domination, not collaborate in its destruction. In building internationalism, people's movements, defiant governments, and the UN all have a role to play. The people's movements, of course, stand at the center. But our movements' fight against the US drive toward war and empire must include providing backbone to those rare resisting governments, and reclaiming the United Nations, as Bishop Tutu urged us, as our own. Together, that will create the three-part internationalist superpower capable of defying war and empire.

NOTES

1. INTRODUCTION

1 "Largest Coordinated Worldwide Anti-War Protest in History," Norm Dixon, *North Bay Progressive*, 25 February–25 March 2003, available at www.thirdworldtraveler.com/Dissent/Largest_Antiwar_Protest.html.

2 *Green Left Weekly*, 26 February 2003, available at www.greenleft.org.au/back/2003/527/527p21c.htm.

3 "Global Protests Against War in Iraq," Factbites, available at www.factbites.com/topics/Global-protests-against-war-on-Iraq.

4 The following cities participated in the February 15, 2003, protests:

Africa: Bloemfontein, Bulawayo, Cairo, Cape Town, Durban, Harare, Johannesburg, Kigali, Lagos, Lusaka, Nairobi, Niamey, Rabat, Reunion Island

Asia/Middle East: Amman, Aligarh, Baghdad, Bahawalpur, Bangalore, Bangkok, Beirut, Bombay, Busan, Daegu, Daejeon, Damascus, Dili, Faisalabad, Gaza, Gojranwala, Gwangju, Hong Kong, Hyderabad, Islamabad, Istanbul, Jakarta, Karachi, Kharian, Kuala Lumpur, Kumamoto, Lahore, Larkana, Layya, Muharraq, Manama, Mandi Bahaudin, Manila, Matsumoto, Multan, Naha, Okara, Osaka, Otsu, Penang, Peshawar, Pune, Qasur, Rafah, Ramallah, Sahiwal, Sargodha, Seoul, Sheikhupura, Taipei, Tel Aviv, Tokyo, Wonju

Europe: Aalborg, Aarhus, A Coruña, Aix-en-Provence, Agen, Akureyri, Albacete, Alcalá, Alfta, Algeciras, Alicante, Almería, Alta, Amsterdam, Andorra, Angouleme, Antwerp, Arendal, Arjeplog, Arosa, Arrecife, Athens, Ávila, Azuqueca de Henares, Bad Kreuznach, Baiona, Bagnols-Sur-Ceze, Bangor, Barcelona, Belfast, Beoria, Bergen, Berlin, Berne, Bilbao, Bochum, Boden, Bodoe, Bodx, Bonn, Bordeaux, Bores, Borldnge, Bratislava, Briviesca, Brussels, Brxnnxysund, Brxnshxj, Bucharest, Budapest, Burgos, Cádiz, Castellón, Ciudad Real, Ciutadella, Clermont Ferrand, Cluj-Napoca, Coimbra, Copenhagen, Cordoba, Corinth, Cuenca, Darmstadt, Donosti, Dublin, Dülmen, Düsseldorf, Elche, Elesund, El Hierro, El Rosario, Elverum, Erftstadt-Lechenich, Erfurt, Erlangen, Es, Esbjerg, Eskilstuna, Euskal Herria, Évora, Falun, Faro, Ferrol, Florx, Fraga, Fredericia, Fredrikstad, Gagnef, Galicia, Gazteiz-Vitoria, Gällivare, Gdvle, Gelsenkirchen, Girona, Gislaved, Gjxvik, Glasgow, Gothenburg, Granada, Guadalajara, Halmstad, Hamar, Hammerfest, Hania, Harstad, Haugesund, Hdrnvsand, Hedemora, Heide, Heilbronn, Helsingborg, Helsinki, Hereford, Hückelhoven, Huelva, Huesca, Hjxrring,

Honningsveg, Hudiksvall, Ibiza, Idar-Oberstein, Igualada, Ioannina, Irakleio, Iruña-Pamplona, Isafjordur, Iserlohn, Jaén, Joensuu, Jvnkvping, Jyväskylä, Kaiserslautern, Kalamata, Kalmar, Karlshamn, Karlskrona, Kavala, Kemi, Kerkyra, Kiev, Kirkenes, Kiruna, Kolding, Konstanz, Kragerx, Kristiansand, Kristiansta, Kundgebung, Kuopio, Lancaster, Landau, Landshut, La Rochelle, Las Palmas, Leer, Le Mans, Levanger, Lillehammer, Limoges, Lingen, Lisbon, Ljubljana, Lleida, Lloret de Mar, Logroño, London, Longyearbyen, Ludvika, Lugo, Lulee, Lund, Luxembourg, Lyon, Macapá, Madrid, Mahón, Mainz, Málaga, Malmö, Malmv, Mandal, Mariehamn, Marl, Marseille, Mataró, Melilla, Menden, Meppen, Moers, Mo i Rana, Molde, Monforte de Lemos, Montluconm, Moscow, Motala, Moulin, Mundaka, Murcia, Mytilini, Nantes, Narbonne, Narvik, Navplio, Ndssjv, Neuwied, Nice, Nimes, Nokia, Nordhorn, Norrkvping, Nxrrebro, Ockelbo, Oslo, Ostrava, Otta, Oulu, Ourense, Oviedo, Paderborn, Palencia, Palma de Mallorca, Pamplona, Paris, Patras, Pecs, Peiraias, Perpignan, Piedralaves, Pitee, Ponta Delgada, Pontevedra, Porsgrunn, Porto, Poznan, Prague, Puertollano, Randers, Ratingen, Ravensburg, Rethymno, Reykjavik, Risør, Rissa, Risxr, Rodos, Rognan, Rome, Roros, Roskilde, Rovaniemi, Rxrvik, Saint-Gaudens, Salamanca, Sandnessjxe, Sandviken, San Sebastian, San Sbtián. de Gomera, Santa Coloma, Sta. Cruz de la Palma, Sta. Cruz de Tenerife, Santander, Stgo. de Compostela, Saone et Loire, Sarpsborg, Savolinna, Schwäbisch Hall, Segovia, Seinäjoki, Sevilla, Shetland, Siegen, Siero, Silkeborg, Simrishamn, Skelleftee, Skien, Skopje, Sofia, Soria, Sortland, Sparti, Stavanger, Steinkjer, Stockholm, Stokmarknes, Strasbourg, Struer, Stuttgart, Sundsvall, Svderhamn, Svolvfr, Sykkylven, Tampere, Talavera de la Reina, Tallinn, Tarragona, Tavagnacco, Teruel, Thessaloniki, Toensberg, Tomelilla, Toledo, Tornee, Tortosa, Toulon, Toulouse, Tours, Tripoli, Tromsoe, Tromsx, Trondheim, Turku, Txnsberg, Uddevalla, Ulvik, Umee, Valby, Valence, Valencia, Valetta, Vdsteres, Vdxjv, Vegan, Vege, Viborg, Vichy, Vienna, Vienne, Vigo, Villingen, Vilnius, Visby, Vitoria, Volos, Voronezh, Voss, Vstersund, Warsaw, Wetzlar, Wroclaw, Wuppertal, Xrsta, Zagreb, Zamora, Zaragoza

Latin America & the Caribbean: Aguascalientes, Bahia, Bariloche, Bauru, Bermuda, Bogotá, Buenos Aires, Caracas, Caxias do Sul, Chihuahua, Ciudad Juárez, Cuernavaca, Goiania, Guadalajara, Havana, Kingston, Lima, Martinique, Mexicali, Mexico City, Monterrey, Montevideo, Outre-Mer Guadeloup, Quito, Rio de Janiero, Rio Grande do Sul, San Cristóbal, San Jose - CR, San Juan - PR, San Luis Potosí, San Miguel, San Salvador, Santa Cruz - Bol., Santiago, Santo Domingo, Sao Paulo, Tijuana, Veracruz, Xalapa

USA and Canada: Akron, Amarillo, Anapolis Royal, Antigonish, Arcata (CA), Armidale, Asheville, Ashland, Athens, Atlanta, Austin,

Baltimore, Barrie, Beavercreek, Bellingham, Billings, Biloxi, Binghamton (NY), Birmingham, Bisbee, Blacksburg, Bloomington, Boise, Boulder, Brampton, Brandon, Burlington, Butler, Calexico, Calgary, Canmore, Canton, Canton (NY), Cape Cod, Cape Girardeau, Capt. Cook, Carbondale, Castlegar, Cedar Rapids, Charleston, Charlotte, Charlottetown, Charlottesville, Chatanooga, Chicago, Chico, Cincinnati, Cleveland, Coburg, Colorado Springs, Columbia (MO), Columbia (SC), Columbus, Comox Valley, Concord, Cornwall, Corpus Christi, Cortez, Corvallis, Cranbrook (BC), Croton-on-Hudson, Cowichan, Cumberland (MD), Dallas, Dayton, Daytona Beach, Deland, Denton, Detroit, Dubuque, Durango, Edmonton, Ellensburg (WA), Elkins (WV), Encino, Erie (PA), Eugene, Fairbanks, Farmington, Fayetteville, Fillmore, Findlay (OH), Flagstaff, Fort Lauderdale, Fort Smith, Fort Wayne, Fredricton, Fresno, Gainesville, Galesburg, Galveston, Geneva (NY), Grand Forks (BC), Grand Junction, Grand Prairie, Grand Rapids, Guelph, Hadely, Halifax, Hamilton, Hilo, Holland, Honolulu, Houston, Hull, Huntington, Huntsville, Indianapolis, Ithaca (NY), Jasper, Jefferson City, Jersey City, Johnston (NY), Juneau, Kamloops, Kansas City, Kelowna, Kezar Falls, Kingston, Kitchener, Knoxville, Lafeyette, Lancaster, Lansing, Las Cruces, Las Vegas, Lawrence (KS), Leavinsworth, Lethbridge, Lexington, Lilloet, Lincoln, Little Rock, London, Long Beach, Los Angeles, Louisville, Macomb, Madison, McAllen, Meadville (PA), Medicine Hat, Medford (OR), Melbourne, Memphis, Minneapolis, Miami, Midland, Milwaukee, Minden (NV), Mobile (AL), Moncton, Montague Center, Montpelier, Montreal, Mount Vernon (OH), Nanaimo, Naples, Nashville, Nelson, New Britain, New Carlisle, New Orleans, New York City, Newark (DE), Niagra, Norfolk (VA), North Bay, North Newton, Olympia, Orange, Orangeville, Orillia, Orlando, Ottawa, Palm Desert, Parker Ford (PA), Parry Sound, Pensacola, Penticton, Peoria, Peterborough, Philadelphia, Phoenix, Pittsboro, Plattsburg, Portland (ME), Portland (OR), Port Perry, Portsmouth, Powell River (BC), Prince Albert, Prince George, Qualicum Beach, Quebec City, Racine (WI), Raleigh, Red Deer, Regina, Richland Center, Riverview, Rockford, Rolla, Sackville, St. Augustine, St. Catherines, St. Charles, St. Joseph, St. Louis, St. Paul, St. Petersburg, Saguenay, Salem, Salmon Arm, Salt Lake City, Saltspring Island, Sacramento, San Antonio, San Diego, Sandpoint (ID), San Francisco, San Jose, San Luis Obispo, Santa Barbara, Santa Cruz, Santa Fe, Santa Monica, Sarasota, Saskatoon, Sault Ste. Marie, Savannah, Seattle, Sherbrooke, Silver City, Sioux Falls, Sitka, Sonora, South Bend, South Haven, Spokane, Springfield, Starkville, St. John's, Sudbury, Summertown (TN), Sydney (NS), Tacoma, Tallahassee, Taos, Tehachapi, Temple, Thornbury, Thunder Bay, Tofino, Toronto, Trois-

Rivières, Truro, Tulsa, Tucson, Uxbridge, Valdosta (GA), Vallejo, Vancouver (BC), Vancouver (WA), Victoria, Vineyard Haven, Watertown, Wausau, Waterloo, West Palm Beach, Westbank (BC), Whitehall, Whitehorse, Wilkes-Barre, Williamsburg, Williamsport, Williamstown, Wilmington, Windsor, Winnipeg, Wolfville, Yakima, Yarmouth, Yellowknife, York (PA), Youngstown

Oceania: Adelaide, Alice Springs, Armidale, Auckland, Bellingen, Brisbane, Bundaberg, Byron Bay, Cairns, Canberra, Central Coast, Christchurch, Dannevirke, Darwin, Dunedin, Forster-Tuncurry, Geelong, Gisborne, Greymouth, Hamilton (NZ), Hastings, Hobart, Kelowna, Kempsey, Launceton, Lismore, Maroochydore, Melbourne, Motueka, Nambucca Heads, Nelson, Newcastle, Noosa, Opotiki, Palmerston North, Perth, Rockhampton, Rotorua, Saint Helens, Strahan, Tasmania, Sydney, Takaka, Tamworth, Taree, Tauranga, Thames, Timaru, Ulladulla, Wagga Wagga, Wanganui, Wellington, Westport, Whakatane, Whangarei, Wollongong

Antarctica: McMurdo Station

TOTAL: 794 locales [4] Source: Wikipedia

5 Patrick E. Tyler, "A New Power in the Streets," *New York Times*, 17 February 2003.

6 Some of these concepts regarding the role of US citizens rely on ideas developed in Robert Jensen's *Citizens of the Empire: The Struggle to Claim Our Humanity*, (San Francisco: City Lights Books, 2004).

7 Eqbal Ahmad, "Portent of a New Century," Introduction from Phyllis Bennis and Michel Moushabeck, eds., *Beyond the Storm: A Gulf Crisis Reader* (Northampton, MA: Olive Branch Press, 1991).

8 Bob Woodward and Dan Balz, "'We Will Rally the World'," *Washington Post*, 28 January 2002.

9 Many reports, aimed at discrediting the UN Human Rights Commission, falsely claimed that the US "was replaced by Sudan" on the Commission. In fact, membership in the Commission is determined by election within regional groups. Sudan was elected by the African group, which uses a rotation system including all its members. Washington lost its seat in a completely separate process, when members of the Cold War-era "Western Europe and Others Group" voted for Sweden rather than the US.

10 David E. Sanger, "House Threatens to Hold Back UN Dues for Loss of Seat," *New York Times*, 9 May 2001.

11 Tom Friedman, "Noblesse Oblige," *New York Times*, 31 July 2001.

12 Jeffrey Gedmin and Gary Schmitt, "Allies in America's National Interest," *New York Times*, 5 August 2001.

13 "Rebuilding America's Defenses: Strategy, Forces, and Resources for a New Century," Project for the New American Century, September 2000.

14 Martti Ahtisaari, Report of the United Nations Mission to Assess Humanitarian Needs in Iraq, 20 March 1991.

15 Dana Priest, "US Talks With Iraqi Insurgents Confirmed," *Washington Post*, 27 June 2005.

16 April 11, 2003, CNN. Available at www.cnn.com/2003/US/04/11/sprj.irq.pentagon

17 Paul Schroeder, The History News Network, Center for History and the New Media, George Mason University, 3 February 2003

18 Jimmy Carter, "Saving Nonproliferation," *Washington Post*, 28 March 2005.

19 Catherine Toups, *Washington Times*, 13 December 1995.

20 Julian Borger, "March of Triumph Hits Skiddy Patch," *Guardian Weekly*, 29 April–5 May 2005.

21 George Monbiot, *Guardian*, 25 February 2003.

22 James Traub, "The Next Resolution," *New York Times* magazine, 13 April 2003.

2. THE MOVEMENT

1 Joseph Lelyveld, "Interrogating Ourselves," *New York Times Magazine*, 12 June 2005.

2 Excerpted from "first writing since," by Suheir Hammad. Available at www.montrealserai.com/2002_Volume_15/15_2/Article_8.htm.

3 Vanaik interview with Aleksej Scira, Transnational Institute, 21 May 2005. Available at www.tni.org.

4 "Rebuilding America's Defenses: Strategy, Forces, and Resources for a New Century," Project for the New American Century, September 2000.

5 Chalmers Johnson, *The Sorrows of Empire: How the Americans Lost Their Country* (New York: Metropolitan Books, 2003).

6 Nicholas Lehman, "The Next World Order," *New Yorker*, 2 April 2002.

7 Bob Woodward, *Bush at War* (New York: Simon and Schuster, 2002).

8 Johnson.

9 Clyde Haberman, "When the Unimaginable Happens, and It's Right Outside Your Window," *New York Times*, 12 September 2001.

10 James Bennet, "Spilled Blood Is Seen as Bond That Draws 2 Nations Closer," *CounterPunch*, 13 September 2001.

11 Alan Sipress, "Cheney Plays Down Arab Criticism Over Iraq," *Washington Post*, 18 March 2002.

12 Sipress.

13 White House press release, "President to Send Secretary Powell to Middle East," 4 April 2002, www.whitehouse.gov/news/releases/2002/04/20020404-1.html.

14 "President to Send Secretary Powell."

15 Three years later, during his confirmation hearings to become US ambassador to the United Nations, it would emerge that arch-conservative John Bolton, while undersecretary of state for disarmament affairs, had prevented Secretary of State Powell from learning of the potential violations of US law in Israel's use of US-supplied F-16 jets to attack Gaza City in a "targeted assassination" in July 2002. According to *US News and World Report* (9 May 2005), "Senate staffers are now said to be looking into how Bolton, as under secretary of state for arms control, handled a State Department review of a July 2002 missile strike on a Gaza City building that killed the military leader of the Palestinian extremist group Hamas and 14 others." (See Chapter 4).

16 Mary McGrory, "Speaking From the Sidelines," *Washington Post*, 4 April 2002.

17 Alan Sipress and Howard Schneider, "Powell Meets Criticism on His First Stop: Delay in Going to Jerusalem Questioned by Moroccan King," *Washington Post*, 9 April 2002.

18 Sipress and Schneider.

19 "Bush Throws US Support Behind Israel," Agence France Presse, 18 April 2002.

20 Peter Slevin and Mike Allen, "Bush: Sharon A 'Man Of Peace'—Israel 'Responded' To Call for Pullout," *Washington Post*, 19 April 2002.

21 Human Rights Watch, "Jenin War Crimes Investigation Needed: Human Rights Watch Report Finds Laws of War Violations," 3 May 2002.

22 "UN Envoy Says Jenin Camp 'Shocking and Horrifying'," CNN online, 18 April 2002.

23 Physicians for Human Rights Forensic Team, "Preliminary Assessment: Jenin," 21–23 April 2002.

24 Human Rights Watch, "Jenin War Crimes."

25 Physicians for Human Rights, "Preliminary Assessment."

26 "UNSC Avoids Immediate Clash Over Arab Call for Jenin Inquiry," Agence France Presse, 19 April 2002.

27 Human Rights Watch, "Israel: Allow Access to Jenin Camp," press release, 15 April 2002.

28 "Proposed Pentagon Budget Hike More Than Other Countries' Military Spending," Associated Press, 26 January 2002.

29 "Terror Prompts Huge US Military Revamp," BBC, 1 February 2002.

30 Ghada Elnajjar, "Senate Holds Hearings on Reconstruction of Post-Saddam Iraq 31 July 2002," State Department's *Washington File*, 2 August 2002.

31 2002 Actions, National Network to End the War Against Iraq: *March to April 2002, Campaign to Stop the War on Iraq*: The National Network's Coordinating Committee endorsed a campaign initiated by the Rocky Mountain Peace and Justice Center. Phase One (11–31 March) speak up to Congress; general outreach and media work; Phase Two (1–19 April) weekly events at Congressional offices; Phase Three (20 April), join the demonstration in DC; continue visiting Congressional offices.

20 April 2002, Stop the War at Home and Abroad: Estimates of those who marched down Pennsylvania Avenue in Washington, DC, for this event range from 75,000 to 120,000. This event drew together peace activists working to stop various US-funded wars from Colombia to Iraq to Palestine with social justice activists opposing new 'Homeland Security' legislation that weakens our civil liberties and targets racial minorities. Separate events were organized in the early part of the day by the student-led April 20 Mobilization, the International A.N.S.W.E.R. Coalition, and Plan Colombia Mobilization. The A.N.S.W.E.R. contingent included a large Muslim delegation, many waving Palestinian flags and holding signs supporting independence and liberation for Palestine, making this by far the largest pro-Palestinian independence march in the US to date.

25–26 May 2002, Third National Organizing Conference on Iraq: At Stanford University, Palo Alto, CA. Hosted by the Peninsula Peace and Justice Center, Network members met for two days of discussion and planning to lay out an agenda for the coming year. Events planned include decentralized local actions, national actions, a speaking tour, promotion of the Iraq Peace Pledge/Iraq Pledge of Resistance, and a campaign to make Iraq an issue in the fall campaign. The Network undertook a new outreach program in the wake of the conference to build support by drawing in new members.

15–18 June 2002, Iraq Forum: Organized by the Education for Peace in Iraq Center (EPIC), based in Washington, DC. A panel of experts, including former weapons inspector Scott Ritter, spoke during two days of advocacy training. Activists visited over 150 congressional offices, promoting peace with Iraq, an end to sanctions, and a halt to plans for a US invasion of Iraq.

29 July 2002, National Call-In Day for the People of Iraq: The US Senate held hearings on Iraq on 31 July and 1 August 2002. Thousands of Network members called in to Congress to insist that these hearings include experts like Denis Halliday. The Senate Foreign Relations Committee agreed to include written statements from some of the experts we were asking to have present to the hearings.

2–11 August 2002, National Days of Action: Act Against Nukes! No War Against Iraq!: Over 35 events in over 31 cities in 21 states or district(s).

3 September–5 November 2002, Congressional Campaign: Leading up to election day in November, the National Network to End the War Against Iraq encouraged its members and all citizens of conscience to meet with their local new and incumbent candidates for Congress, to be present and vocal at public meetings, and to call in to their senators and representatives in Congress as well as the White House and the State Department, to call for an end to the war and the sanctions against Iraq, and a halt to all planning for another major attack on Iraq. Weekly alerts were put out by the Network, with talking points.

29 September 2002, Don't Bomb Iraq! Rally and March in Washington, DC: Between 5,000 and 10,000 people gathered in Dupont Circle for music and speakers, followed by a march up Massachusetts Avenue to the Naval Observatory, DC home for Vice President Dick Cheney. There a brief concluding rally was held across from the gates of the Observatory and the British Embassy. Along the march, the protest stopped at the embassies of Turkey, Japan, Egypt, and South Africa to show support for recent statements made by heads of states of these countries opposing a US invasion of Iraq. Ryan Amundson of Families for Peaceful Tomorrows, along with Mike Zmolek, Outreach Coordinator for the National Network to End the War Against Iraq, met briefly with an official of the British Embassy to deliver a written statement calling upon Tony Blair and the people of Great Britain to oppose a US invasion of Iraq. The Network's website, endthewar.org, hosted the dedicated page for this event.

7–11 October, National De-Centralized Days of Action: Anticipating the October 10–11 vote in Congress to grant President Bush authority to take the US to war against Iraq, the Network put out an emergency call for local protest actions across the US, combined with calls for continued messages to Congress. Major rallies took place in San Francisco, Portland, and many smaller towns like Bloomington, Indiana. A campaign of sit-ins at Congressional offices put pressure on Congressional representatlves and senators to vote against the war resolution, as most House Democrats did.

26 October 2002, International Day of Action to Stop the War Against Iraq: Network members came to Washington, DC, San Francisco, Denver, and held local rallies across the US on this day of protest around the globe. Events in the US were organized primarily by the International A.N.S.W.E.R. Coalition. Estimates of the Washington, DC crowd ranged between 100,000 and 200,000. The day before the rally, at a meeting in Washington, DC, the United for Peace and Justice Campaign was initiated.

14 November 2002, No Invasion of Iraq! An Urgent Call to Action: In response to the beginnings of a serious build-up of US forces in the Gulf, the Coordinating Committee of the National Network issued a call to action, urging Network members and non-members alike "to organize protests and/or nonviolent civil disobedience actions to prevent US aggression against Iraq."

10 December 2002, International Human Rights Day Actions: Network member groups staged local demonstrations as part of a national call to action from many organizations. All in all, over 150 cities across the US commemorated International Human Rights Day. UFPJ coordinated most of the 150 actions and tracked them on their new website. The protests took place only two days after the UN adopted Resolution 1441, giving Iraq a "final opportunity" to comply with previous resolutions, but not specifying precisely what actions would be taken to force compliance.

This summary from www.endthewar.org/wgs/action_wg/past2002.htm Copyright © 2002 National Network to End the War Against Iraq.

32 Steve Schifferes, "World Inequality Rises," BBC online, 17 January 2002.

33 Monte Reel and Manny Fernandez, "More Than 100,000 March in Washington, DC: Antiwar Protest Largest Since '60s," *Washington Post*, 27 October 2002.

34 Chris Toensing and Bilal el-Amine, "Groundswell," *Middle East Report*, Spring 2003.

35 Toensing and el-Amine.

36 Toensing and el-Amine.

37 Tom Bowman, "Unceremonious End to Army Career," *Baltimore Sun*, 29 May 2005. It was of course particularly ironic that the retired general critiquing the "politicization" of the Pentagon chief's office was Rumsfeld's old friend, Jay Garner. Aside from being a "one-time Pentagon adviser," his appointment as the first US pro-consul, officially in charge of reconstruction in Iraq from the beginning of the 2003 invasion, reflected his post-military life as a weapons manufacturer, corporate friend of the Bush administration, personal friend of Secretary of Defense Rumsfeld, and potential large-scale profiteer from the Iraq war. Ten days after the US invasion, the *San Francisco Chronicle* noted that

> The retired general tapped by the Bush administration to oversee rebuilding of post-war Iraq was, until just a few weeks ago, an executive at a leading defense contractor working on missile systems that would be used to bomb Baghdad. Although a Pentagon official said Jay Garner's new role as head of the Office of Reconstruction and Humanitarian Assistance does not constitute a conflict of interest, ethics experts say the appointment raises troubling questions. Garner, 64, a former three-star Army general and friend of Defense Secretary Donald Rumsfeld, served until last month as

president of SY Coleman, a division of defense contractor L-3 Communications specializing in missile-defense systems."

"General reverses his role," David Lazarus, *San Francisco Chronicle*, 26 February 2003.

38 "Troops Put Thorny Questions to Rumsfeld: Troops Grill Defense Secretary Donald Rumsfeld on Armor and Tour Lengths," CNN, 9 December 2004

39 "Amnesty Defends 'Gulag,' Urges Guantánamo Access," Reuters, 2 June 2005. Available at www.truthout.org/docs_2005/060205X.shtml.

40 Scott Shane, "The Costs of Outsourcing Interrogation: A Canadian Muslim's Long Ordeal in Syria," *New York Times*, 29 May 2005.

41 Shane, "The Costs of Outsourcing..."

42 Transcript: President's Weekly Radio Address, 1 May 2004, AP.

43 Burton J. Lee III, "The Stain of Torture," *Washington Post*, 1 July 2005.

44 The torture scandal also provided further evidence of the corruption inherent in the expanding role of the 20,000 or so mercenaries, euphemistically known as private military contractors, in Iraq. Army reports on the interrogators employed by CACI International, one of the largest contingents in Iraq and whose employees were implicated in the Abu Ghraib scandal, only recommend that one of those responsible for abusing prisoners be fired and the other merely disciplined. The military did not recommend criminal action against them, and the Pentagon itself has no actual authority over these intelligence mercenaries. Even the US government's General Accounting Office admits that Pentagon oversight of private contractors is "inconsistent and sometimes incomplete." ("Contractors Provide Vital Services to Deployed Forces but Are Not Adequately Addressed in DOD Plans," United State General Accounting Office, June 2003. www.gao.gov/highlights/d03695high.pdf). The scandal reminded the world that the US remained resolutely outside of, and in fact implacably hostile to, the International Criminal Court. If the US had joined its allies in the ICC and thus was within its jurisdiction, the Court might have been able to hold these corporate-sponsored mercenaries accountable if the US government refused.

45 Timothy Appleby, "Canadian Refugee Board Refuses US Military War Resister Jeremy Hinzman Asylum," *The Globe and Mail* (Canada), 25 March 2005.

46 Amy Goodman, "US Army War Resister Jeremy Hinzman: 'I Have a Duty to Disobey'," *Democracy Now!*, 13 December, 2004.

47 Mission statement, Iraq Veterans Against the War. Available at www.ivaw.net.

48 GSFP website, www.gsfp.org.

49 The germs were sold by the American Type Culture Collection agency in Rockville, MD. Documented in the Senate Banking Sub-Committee hearings of 1994.

50 Evan Thomas and Roy Gutman, "Iraq in the Balance," Evan Thomas and Roy Gutman, *Newsweek*, 22 March 2002.

51 Col. Patrick Lang, speaking at convention of the American-Arab Anti-Discrimination Committee, 28 May 2005.

52 Rory Carroll, "US in Talks with Iraqi Insurgents," *Guardian*, 10 June 2005.

53 Arundhati Roy, "The Most Cowardly War in History," Opening Statement on behalf of the jury of conscience of the World Tribunal for Iraq, 24 June 2005.

54 *Democracy Now!*, 27 June 2005.

55 I first heard this term from Antonia Juhazs, author of the forthcoming *The Bush Agenda: Invading the World, One Economy at a Time.*

56 Neil Mackay, "Firms that Gave to Bush Get Contracts," *Neil Mackay, Sunday Herald*, 13 April 2003.

57 www.iraqbodycount.net

58 Elisabeth Rosenthal, "Study Puts Civilian Toll in Iraq at Over 100,000," *International Herald Tribune*, 30 October 2004.

3. GOVERNMENTS

1 Robert W. Tucker and David C. Hendrickson, "The Sources of American Legitimacy," *Foreign Affairs*, November/December 2004.

2 Dana Priest, "Help From France Key in Covert Operations," *Washington Post*, 3 July 2005.

3 David Gergen, "Bring Back the Junkets!" *US News & World Report*, 27 October 1997.

4 In its effort to ennoble the US troops at the heart of the story, the movie ignored the political roots of the 1992–93 US intervention in Somalia, in particular the US refusal to participate in the original United Nations aid protection effort. It was US troops sent into Somalia under a separate Pentagon command, not sanctioned by the Security Council, whose mission in Mogadishu led to the deaths of close to 1,000 Somalis as well as the 18 US Army Rangers. The movie also ignored the longer history of US involvement in the country, particularly Somalia's role as a Cold War battlefield in which both US and Soviet sponsorship left behind a country awash in poverty and want, with a surplus only of guns, mortars, and landmines.

5 John Vinocur, "Going It Alone: US Upsets France So Paris Begins a Campaign to Strengthen Multilateral Institutions," *International Herald Tribune*, 3 February 1999.

6 Vinocur.

7 Derek Brown, "The US-China Spy Plane Row," *Guardian*, 4 April 2001.

8 "Spy Plane Breakthrough," BBC, 11 April 2001.

9 Powell testimony on US policy toward Iraq, International Relations Committee, House of Representatives, 7 March 2001. Available at www.usembassy.it/file2001_03/alia/a1030817.htm

10 Actually, Cheney's oil-driven loyalties had been clear for years: as a member of the House of Representatives, he supported the 1981 sale of AWACS planes to Saudi Arabia, despite Israeli opposition; in 1979 he voted against the windfall profits tax on oil revenues. And just to fill out the record, Cheney also voted against the Panama Canal Treaty (1979), the Department of Education (1979), South African sanctions (1985) and safe drinking water (1986).

11 Tom Friedman, "Noblesse Oblige," *New York Times*, 31 July 2001.

12 Walter C. Clemens Jr., "How to Lose Friends and Inspire Enemies," *Washington Post*, 20 May 2001.

13 *Washington Post*, 8 June 2001.

14 "A More Assertive Europe," *New York Times* editorial, 30 March 2001.

15 John Hughes, "Cheer Up, Ugly Americans," *Christian Science Monitor*, 20 June 2001.

16 "Containing America," *Christian Science Monitor* editorial, 15 June 2001.

17 "Powell Fails to Persuade NATO on Antimissile Plan," AP, 30 May 2001.

18 "A Wary Atlantic Alliance," *New York Times* editorial, 31 May 2001.

19 Marie Isabelle Chevrier, quoted in Vernon Loeb, "Bush Panel Faults Germ Warfare Protocol," *Washington Post*, 27 May 2001.

20 "President Bush's Arrogant Negotiating Style Is All Take and No Give," *Independent* (London), 26 July 2001.

21 Mike Allen & Steven Mufson, "US Scuttles Germ War Conference," *Washington Post*, 8 December 2001.

22 Keith B. Richburg, "Europeans Object to Bush Approach on Foreign Policy," *Washington Post*, 16 August 2001.

23 Michael J. Glennon, *Washington Post*, 12 August 2001.

24 Thomas E. Ricks, *Washington Post*, 21 August 2001.

25 "With regard to the historical aspects, the European Union profoundly deplores the human suffering, both individual and collective, caused by slavery and the slave trade. They are amongst the most dishonourable and abhorrent chapters in the history of humanity. The European Union condemns these practices, in the past and present, and regrets the suffering they have caused.

"Some effects of colonialism have caused immense suffering which still persist today. Any act causing such suffering must be condemned, wherever and whenever it occurred.

"Through these acts of acknowledgement, regret and condemnation, the European Union, aware of the moral obligation incumbent on the entire international community vis-à-vis the victims of these tragedies, shows its firm determination to honour this obligation and to accept its responsibility. It considers that it is the obligation of each individual to remember the suffering caused by events occurring at different points in history, so that they will never be forgotten. The obligation to remember will make it possible to build the future on solid foundations and to prevent the recurrence of the grave errors of the past."

From the European Commission, General Affairs Council, "Council Conclusions: On the World Conference against Racism, Racial Discrimination, Xenophobia and Related Intolerance," 16 July 2001.

26 Hugh Nevill, "US, Israel, Pull Out of Acrimonious Racism Conference," AFP, Durban, 3 September 2001.

27 Mahmoud Mamdani, "Good Muslim, Bad Muslim—An African Perspective," Insitute of African Studies, Columbia University, October 2001. Available at www.ssrc.org/sept11/ essays/mamdani.entry.

28 Nevill, "US, Israel, Pull Out."

29 Nevill, "US, Israel, Pull Out."

30 BBC World, 4 August 2001.

31 Ofeibea Quist-Arcton, "Delegates Confused by US Stance on Conference," allAfrica.com, 4 September 2001.

32 Bob Woodward and Dan Balz, "'We Will Rally the World'," Washington Post, 28 January 2002.

33 President George Bush, CNN, 23 January 2002.

34 "Proposed Pentagon Budget Hike More Than Other Countries' Military Spending," AP, 26 January 2002.

35 Stockholm International Peace Research Institute, SIPRI Yearbook 2004, 22 September 2004. Available at: http://web.sipri.org/ contents/milap/milex/mex_ trends.html.

36 Elizabeth Skoens, "World Military Spending: Where are We Heading?", World Policy Institute, 11 May 2004.

37 News Hour with Jim Lehrer, 11 March 2002.

38 National Public Radio, 1 March 2002.

39 William Safire, "That Dog Won't Bark," New York Times, 24 February 2002.

40 Address to a Joint Session of Congress, September 20, 2001. Available at www.whitehouse.gov/news/releases/2001/09/20010920-8.html.

41 Human Rights Watch, "Middle East and North Africa Overview—Human Rights Developments," World Report 1999,

Human Rights Watch.

42 Eqbal Ahmad, "Portent of a New Century," in Bennis and Moushabeck, eds., *Beyond the Storm: A Gulf Crisis Reader*, Northampton, MA: Olive Branch Press, 1991).

43 Phyllis Bennis, "Understanding the US–Iraq Crisis: The World's Response, the UN & International Law," a pamphlet of the Institute for Policy Studies, January 2003.

44 Associated Press, 6 November 2002.

45 Figures from the five paragraphs preceding this note all come from Thalif Deen, "US Dollars Yielded Unanimous UN Vote Against Iraq," Thalif Deen, InterPress Service, 9 November 2002.

46 All statements from Council ambassadors come from "Foreign Country Statements from UN Security Council," United Nations Press Release, 8 November 2002.

47 Powell interviewed on CNN's *Late Edition with Wolf Blitzer*, 11 November 2002. State Department transcript available at www.usembassy.it/file2002_11/alia/a2110803.htm.

48 Andreas Zumach, *Die Tageszeitung*, 16 December 2002.

49 David Manning, "The Secret Downing Street Memo," David Manning, *Sunday Times* (London), 1 May 2005.

50 Secretary of Defense Donald H. Rumsfeld, Foreign Press Center briefing, 22 January 2003. Available at, www.defenselink.mil/transcripts/2003/t01232003_t0122sdfpc.html.

51 Martin Aguera, "Collateral Damage?," *Defense News*, 17 February 2003.

52 *New York Daily News*, 17 February 2003.

53 Glenn Kessler, "Rice Apparently Rejects German Bid," *Washington Post*, 17 May 2005.

54 William Matthews, "US Eyes Cutbacks in Europe," *Defense News*, 24 February 2003.

55 US Census Bureau, Foreign Trade Statistics.

56 Glenn Frankel, "Chirac Fortifies Antiwar Caucus," *Washington Post*, 22 February 2003.

57 US Trade Representative, "2002 Comprehensive Report on US Trade and Investment Policy Toward Sub-Saharan Africa and Implementation of the African Growth and Opportunity Act," May 2002.

58 Website of the Sustainable Energy and Economy Network, www.seen.org.

59 Colum Lynch, "Costa Rica Reprimands U.N. Envoy Over Iraq," *Washington Post*, 21 February 2003.

60 Press release, Office of the US Trade Representative, 11 December 2002.

61 EFE News Services, 14 February 2003.

62 *El Mercurio*, 25 February 2003.

63 Dafna Linzer, "US Officials in Security Council Capitals in Diplomatic Drive for Iraq Support," AP, 23 February 2003.

64 K. Alan Kronstadt, "Pakistan–US Relations," Congressional Research Service, 23 January 2003.

65 Note: Congress has not yet brought this bill up for a vote, most likely due to resistance from textile state lawmakers.

66 K. Alan Kronstadt, "Pakistan–US Anti-Terrorism Cooperation," Congressional Research Service, 31 December 2002.

67 Letter obtained from UN-based diplomats in March 2003. Full text available at: http://nowararchive.greenpeace.org/images/scan1_lg.gif.

68 Much of the information in this section was first published in "Coalition of the Willing or Coalition of the Coerced? How the Bush Administration Influences Allies in its War on Iraq," by Sarah Anderson, Phyllis Bennis, and John Cavanagh, Institute for Policy Studies, 26 February 2003. Available at http://ips-dc.org/iraq/coerced.htm.

69 "Non-US Forces in Iraq," GlobalSecurity.org, 15 March 2005.

70 Robin Wright and Bradley Graham, "US Works to Sustain Iraq Coalition," *Washington Post*, 15 July 2004.

71 "Non-US Forces in Iraq," GlobalSecurity.org, 15 March 2005.

72 Testimony before the Senate Foreign Relations Committee, 11 February 2003.

73 US Embassy in Bulgaria web site, "Statement of the Vilnius Group Countries in Response to the Presentation by the United States Secretary of State to State to the United Nations Security Council," 5 February 2003.

74 Marian Chiriac, "Bulgaria and Romania Set to Support Iraq War," InterPress Service, 29 January 2003.

75 Snjezana Vukic, "US Seeks Use of European Air Space," AP, 21 February 2003.

76 Alan Perrott, "Coalition of the Willing? Not Us, Say Solomon Islanders," *New Zealand Herald*, 27 March 2003.

77 William D. Hartung and Michelle Ciarrocca, "Buying a Coalition," *The Nation*, 17 March 2003.

78 Keith Richburg, "Turks Remember Losses from Last War on Iraq: Opposition Rooted in Economic Devastation," *Washington Post*, 23 February, 2003.

79 22nd Africa–France summit—The Heads of State and Government of Africa and France Reassert their Position on Iraq. Paris, 20 February 2003. Text available from Embassy of France in the US at: www.info-france-usa.org/news/statmnts/2003/22som_frafr.asp

80 Reuters, 18 February 2003.

81 Crispian Balmer, "Italy Honours Shot Agent," Reuters, 8 March 2005.

82 "Italy Bids Farewell to Iraq 'Hero'," Agence France Presse, 8

March 2005.

83 Aidan Lewis, "Italy Judge Orders Arrest of 13 CIA Agents," AP, 24 June 2005.

84 www.globalsolutions.org/programs/law_justice/icc/bias/ bias_home.html

85 "35 Nations Losing Military Aid Over World Tribunal Stance," *Los Angeles Times*, 2 July 2003.

86 Heather Hamilton, "Punishing America's Allies," World Federalist Organization, 16 July 2003. Available at www.veterans forpeace.org/ICC_Community_071603.htm.

87 "Non-US Forces in Iraq," GlobalSecurity.org, 15 March 2005.

88 Bloomberg News, 3 June 2004.

89 "Non-US Forces in Iraq," GlobalSecurity.org, 15 March 2005.

90 Walter Pincus, "British Intelligence Warned of Iraq War," *Washington Post*, 13 May 2005.

91 Pincus.

92 Pincus.

93 Steven R. Weissman, "US Is Working to Isolate France in UN Council on Iraq Approach," *New York Times*, 19 September 2003.

94 Weissman.

95 Weissman.

96 Elaine Sciolino, "US and France Set Aside Differences in Effort to Resolve Haiti Conflict," *New York Times*, 2 March 2004.

97 Sciolino, "US and France Set Aside."

98 Resolution 1326 (2003)1, "Europe and the War in Iraq," Parliamentary Assembly/Assemblée parlementaire. Available at http://assembly.coe.int/Documents/Logo130X120.jpg.

99 Sciolino, "United States and Europe Differ."

100 Sciolino, "United States and Europe Differ."

101 "Bush Extends National Emergency with Respect to Iran," US State Department website, 10 March 2005. Available at http://usinfo.state.gov/is/Archive/2005/Mar/14-537635.html.

102 Al Kamen, "What Defeat? Rice Finesses Win-Win at OAS," *Washington Post* 16 May 2005. Available at: www.washingtonpost.com/wp-dyn/content/photo/2005/03/26/ PH2005032604415.jpg.

4. THE UNITED NATIONS

1 Catherine Toups, *Washington Times*, 13 May 1999.

2 Columbia University biography of Virginia Crocheron Gildersleeve. Available at www.columbia.edu/percent7Err91/3567/sample_biographies/virginia_gildersleeve percent20-percent20bio.htm.

3 Gareth Evans, *Cooperating for Peace: The Global Agenda for the 1990s and Beyond* (St Leonards, Australia: Allen & Unwin, 1993) 20.

4 Evans 224.

5 Erskine Childers, "Introduction," in Childers (ed.), *Challenges to the United Nations* (New York: St. Martin's Press, 1995) 3.

6 Harold Hongju Koh, "A Wake-Up Call on Human Rights," Harold Hongju Koh, *Washington Post*, 8 May 2001.

7 David E. Sanger, "House Threatens to Hold Back UN Dues for Loss of Seat," *New York Times*, 9 May 2001.

8 Dennis Jett, "The World's Only Super Pouter," *Christian Science Monitor*, 14 May 2001.

9 Bill Sammon, "Bush Hits UN Corruption," *Washington Times*, 15 September 2005.

10 UN DPI Release, Security Council SC/7143, 4370th Meeting, 12 September 2001: "Security Council Condemns 'in Strongest Terms.' Terrorist Attacks on United States. Unanimously Adopting Resolution 1368 (2001), Council Calls on All States to Bring Perpetrators to Justice."

11 Letter sent to South African officials, 18 March 2003. Full text available at http://nowararchive.greenpeace.org/images/scan1_lg.gif.

12 Ambassador John Negroponte, Georgetown University, 27 February 2002.

13 Helen Duffy, "Responding to September 11: The Framework of International Law," Interights, Lancaster House, London, October 2001.

14 "'UN Must Place People at Centre of Everything It Does,' Secretary-General Says at Opening of High-Level General Assembly Debate," GA/9956, 10 November 2001.

15 Hans Blix, "Comment: The Iraq War Wounded the UN, But It Won't be Fatal," *Guardian*, 29 November 2004.

16 Bush speech to UN General Assembly, 12 September 2002. Available at edition.cnn.com/2002/US/10/22/iraq.bush/.

17 President Says "It is a Moment of Truth" for UN, remarks by the President at the 2003 "Congress of Tomorrow" Republican Retreat, 9 February 2003. Available at www.whitehouse.gov/news/releases/2003/02/20030209-1.html.

18 President George Bush Discusses Iraq in National Press Conference, White House transcript, 6 March 2003. Available at www.whitehouse.gov/news/releases/2003/03/20030306-8.html.

19 "Striking First," Richard Perle debate with Phyllis Bennis, *News Hour with Jim Lehrer*, 1 July 2002. Available at www.pbs.org/newshour/bb/military/jan-june02/strikingfirst_7-01.html.

20 Richard Perle, "Thank God for the Death of the UN," *Guardian*, 21 March 2003. Available at: www.guardian.co.uk/Iraq/Story/0,2763,918812,00.html.

21 David Manning, "The Secret Downing Street Memo," *Sunday Times* (London), 1 May 2005.

22 "UN Secretary-General Kofi Annan Statement to the Security Council," UN Press Release, 26 March 2003. Available at http://www.escwa.org.lb/information/press/un/2003/mar/26.html.

23 Salim Lone, "It Wasn't a Bomb But US Policy That Destroyed the UN Hopes in Iraq," *Guardian*, 20 August 2004.

24 Felicity Barringer, "UN Senses It Must Change, Fast," *New York Times*, 19 September 2003.

25 Barringer.

26 Rajiv Chandrasekaran, "Envoy Bowed to Pressure in Choosing Leaders," *Washington Post*, 3 June 2004.

27 "UN Envoy: Iraqi Government Could Be Set Up Soon," CNN, 28 April 2004.

28 "Kofi Annan's Top Envoy Calls Israel 'The Great Poison'," *The Globe and Mail* (Toronto), 24 April 2004.

29 Patrick Seale, "It's Brahimi vs. Chalabi for the Future of Iraq," *The Daily Star* (Beirut), 3 May 2004.

30 William Safire, "New U.N. Iraq Envoy Making Serious Errors," *New York Times*, 27 April 2004.

31 "Israel Condemns 'Poison' Remarks," BBC, 27 April 2004.

32 Julian Borger, "Row Grows Over Government Powers," *Guardian*, 29 April 2004.

33 David Shelby, "Senators Study Negroponte's Nomination as Ambassador to Iraq," Washington File. Available at japan.us embassy.gov/e/p/tp-20040428-04.html.

34 "Iraq War Illegal, Says Annan," BBC, 16 September 2004.

35 Iraq Index, Brookings Institution, June 2005.

36 Patricia Reaney, "Study: 100,000 Excess Civilian Iraqi Deaths Since War," Reuters, 28 October 2004.

37 "FAO Unveils Global Anti-Hunger Program," FAO Newsroom, 4 June 2002. Available at http://www.fao.org/english/newsroom/news/2002/ 5500-en.html.

38 Dr. Peter Piot, "AIDS: The Need for an Exceptional Response to an Unprecedented Crisis," UNAIDS, 20 November 2003. Available at www.aegis.com/news/unaids/2003/UN031106.html.

39 "Immunize Every Child," UNICEF, February 2000. Available at www.unicef.org/immunization/immunize_every_child.pdf.

40 "Report of the World Panel on Financing Water Infrastructure," World Water Council, March 2003. Available at www.gwpforum.org/gwp/library/FinPanRep.MainRep.pdf.

41 Thom Shanker and Erik Schmitt, "Iraq War Costing About $5 Billion a Month: "Pentagon Weighs Strategy Change to Deter Terrorism," *New York Times*, 5 July 2005.

42 John Bolton, former undersecretary of state for international organizations, speech at Global Structures Convocation, Washington,

DC, February 1994.
43 Eduardo Salgado, "UN Chemical Weapons Chief Sacked by US," *Veja* magazine (Brazil), 1 May 2002. Available at cosmetic democracy.blogspot.com.
44 "White House Week: Foggy Bottom's Case of the Missing Memo," *US News and World Report*, 9 May 2005.

5. INTERSECTIONS

1 Arundhati Roy, "The New American Century," *Nation*, 22 January 2004.
2 www.pww.org/article/articleview/2981/1/139.
3 Naomi Klein, *Toronto Star*, 26 March 1999.
4 Michael Ratner (Center for Constitutional Rights) and Jules Lobel (University of Pittsburgh Law School), "A UN Alternative to War: 'Uniting for Peace'," March 2003. Available at www.ccr-nv.org.
5 See, for example, Jeremy Brecher, "UN General Assembly Provides Crucial Opportunity for Global Peace Movement," *Counterpunch*, 2 April 2003.
6 "Final Document of the XIII Conference of Heads of State or Government of the Non-Aligned Movement, Kuala Lumpur, 24–25 February 2003," BBC Worldwide Monitoring, 26 February 2003.
7 Thalif Deen, "'New Superpower' Seeks 'Better World'," InterPress Service, 3 June 2005.
8 James Riker of the University of Maryland, cited in Deen.

INDEX

A

Abdullah, Crown Prince: 44, 45
ABM: *see* Anti-Ballistic Missile treaty
Abu Ghraib: 18, 74, 77, 78, 79, 267
Afghanistan: 22, 30, 103
    debate over US war: 53–55
    demonstrations against US war in: 34, 37, 52, 61
    Geneva Conventions and: 96
    oil pipelines in: 36, 103
    prisoners in: 74, 77
    US war against: x, xvii, 17, 29, 36, 37, 40, 43, 73, 81, 82, 86, 103, 132, 133, 135, 136, 137, 140, 157, 160, 203, 204
Africa: ix, 10, 22, 167, 186, 207
    anti-war movement in: 1, 36, 102, 258n.
    poverty in: 60, 86
    UN and: 156–158, 198, 234, 235
African Growth and Opportunity Act (AGOA): 143, 158, 176
African National Congress (ANC): 50, 92, 99, 244
Ahmad, Eqbal: 9, 140
al-Assad, Bashar: 153
al-Herfi, Suleiman: 130
al-Jazeera: 4, 85
al-Qaeda: 18, 58, 74, 97
al-Sadr, Moqtada: 94
al-Sistani, Ayatollah Ali: 94
Albright, Madeleine: 24, 77, 191, 197, 206, 257
American Enterprise Institute (AEI): 14, 229
Amnesty International: 74, 131
Amy Goodman: xiv, 54, 80

Angola: 23, 85, 150, 156, 157, 158, 185, 235, 243
Annan, Kofi: 3, 4, 45, 47, 50, 87, 105, 150, 206, 207, 212, 213, 214, 215, 218, 221, 228, 229, 230, 257
ANSWER: 22, 61, 75, 135, 136, 220, 231, 233
Anti-Ballistic Missile treaty: 13, 23, 115, 124, 199
Arab League: 44, 45, 165, 239, 255
Arafat, Yasir: 43, 45
Arar, Maher: 75, 76
Aristide, Jean-Bertrand: 178
Arms inspections: 53, 151, 227
Australia: 1, 101, 112, 126, 130, 131, 172, 195, 198
Azerbaijan: 22
Aznar, José Maria: 2, 91, 151

B

Ba'athists: 93, 98, 108
Bahrain: 42, 43, 47, 165
Barringer, Felicity: 218
Basra: 94, 168
Belafonte, Harry: 3, 4, 5
Belinga-Eboutou, Martin: 146
Berlusconi, Silvio: 2, 169, 170
bin Laden, Osama: 18, 77, 138
Biological Weapons Convention: 122
Black Voices for Peace: 62, 64
Blair, Tony: 2, 26, 82, 85, 91, 174, 175, 209, 232
Blix, Hans: 2, 167, 209, 211, 212
Bolton, John: 24, 123, 224, 225, 226
Borger, Julian: 24
Bosnia: 11, 19, 115

Free Trade Area of the Americas (FTAA): 66, 188

G

Garner, General Jay M.: 73, 266
Gaza: *see also* Palestine 38, 39, 42, 44, 139, 225
Geneva Conventions: 74, 79, 95, 96, 126
Germany: 25, 26, 60, 83, 85, 91, 104, 111, 112, 124, 148, 150, 151, 152, 153, 154, 155, 157, 168, 174, 176, 177, 179, 181, 182, 186, 189, 191, 209, 218, 234, 235, 245
Gillerman, Danny: 220
Global Call Against Poverty: 256
Global compact: 251
global justice movement: 58, 59, 60, 64, 101
Global South: 52, 55, 88, 102, 120, 125, 138, 142, 144, 156, 167, 171, 195, 218, 223, 224, 236, 244, 246
Global Sustainable Development Facility: 249
globalization: xvi, xvii, 9, 36, 37, 52, 64, 66, 83, 102, 142, 159, 246, 250
GlobalSecurity.org: 173
Glover, Danny: ix–xii, 5
Gold Star Families for Peace (GSFP): 82
Great Britain: *see* United Kingdom
Greenstock, Sir Jeremy: 145
Grossman, Marc: 163
Group of 20: 9, 23, 66, 185
Guantánamo Bay: 74, 78
Guardian (London): 24, 116
Guinea: 23, 85, 142, 143, 151, 156, 157, 176, 185, 189
Gulf War: *see* Iraq

H

Haberman, Clyde: 39
Haiti: 11, 178, 238, 239
Halliburton Oil Industries: 118
Halliday, Denis: xiv, 251
Hamas: 41, 225
Hamilton, Alexander: 111
Hammad, Suheir: 32
Hastert, Dennis: 154
Hedley, Stephen: 184
Hezbollah: 41
Hinzman, Jeremy: 80
HIV/AIDS: 206, 222, 231
Ho Chi Minh: 92
Hoon, Geoff: 175
Howard, Jown: 65, 173
Human Rights Commission: 13, 120, 121, 198, 199
Human Rights Watch: 48, 49, 51, 136
Hussein, Saddam: 6, 9, 17, 21, 36, 54, 56, 62, 65, 93, 94, 96, 105, 108, 118, 146, 150, 178, 207, 228, 229

I

Independent (London): 4, 19, 54, 63, 82, 85, 123, 126, 128, 136, 153, 206, 208, 228, 235, 239
Indonesia: 139, 235
Institute for Policy Studies (IPS): xiii, 31, 57, 62, 64, 65
Insulza, Jose Miguel: 187
Inter-Parliamentary Assembly: 179
International Atomic Energy Agency (IAEA): 21, 145, 149, 181, 211, 212
International Court of Justice: 249
International Criminal Court (ICC): 13, 23, 101, 105, 113, 139, 170–171, 199
International Herald Tribune: 107, 124

Khalil, Hany: xiv, 71
King, Jr., Martin Luther: 8, 29, 46
Koh, Harold Hongju: 199, 274
Koonjul, Jagdish: 142, 143
Korean War: 254
Kuala Lumpur: 167, 244
Kuwait: 16, 73, 84, 137, 165, 217,
Kyoto Protocol: 13, 14, 115, 124,
  199
Kyrgyzstan: 22

L

Lagos: 176
Lancet: 107, 221
Lantos, Tom: 128
League of Nations: 108, 193
Lebanon: 16, 44, 194
Lee, Barbara: 34, 53, 58
Lehman, Nicholas: 36
Levitte, Jean-David: 145
Libya: 21, 174
Lone, Salim: 58, 217, 218
Lugar, Richard: 220
Lula, Richard: 186

M

Malaysia: xiv, 25, 189, 243, 244
Malloch Brown, Mark: 250
Mamdani, Mahmood: 130
Mandela, Nelson: 92, 93
Markey, Edward J.: 76
Mauritius: 142–143, 150
McCain, Senator John: 154
McGrory, Mary: 46, 263
Megally, Hanny: 51
mercenaries: 106, 168
Mexico: 23, 66, 85, 141, 142, 144,
  146, 151, 156, 157, 158, 159,
  160, 176, 185, 189, 209, 235,
  241, 242, 243
Middle East Report: 69
militarism: 2, 11, 25, 112, 115,

179, 180, 197, 242
military bases: 22, 76, 152, 155,
  164, 167
Military Families Speak Out
  (MFSO): 72, 82
Millennium Development Goals:
  230, 256
Monbiot, George: 24
Morocco: 16, 46, 47
MoveOn: 67, 68
Mubarak, Hosni: 136, 137
multilateralism: 11, 12, 13, 24,
  112, 113, 114, 117, 146, 177, 222
Musharraf, General Pervez: 157, 160

N

NAFTA: *see* North American Free
  Trade Agreement
National Guard: 81
National Network to End the War
  Against Iraq: 264–266n.
NATO: *see* North Atlantic Treaty
  Organization
Negroponte, John: 204, 220, 224
Neo-conservatism: 8, 12, 14, 15,
  53, 117
Neo-liberalism: 90, 102
Netanyahu, Binyamin: 39
New Delhi: 1
New York: 1, 2, 5, 8, 9, 10, 34, 62,
  65, 66, 67, 71, 83, 89, 100,
  145, 149, 200, 203, 213, 237,
  243, 245, 247, 251, 253
New York Times: x, xv, 4, 6, 7, 14,
  25, 26, 31, 39, 53, 75, 119,
  120, 121, 122, 133, 178, 182,
  183, 218, 220, 228, 229, 246
New Yorker: 36
New Zealand: 1, 164, 173
Niger: 161, 212
Non-Aligned Movement: 167, 244
Non-Proliferation Treaty (NPT):
  13, 21, 23, 105, 181, 182, 183,